TEACHING THE PRIMARY
CURRICULUM FOR
CONSTRUCTIVE LEARNING

Edited by
Michael Littledyke and Laura Huxford

David Fulton Publishers
London

David Fulton Publishers Ltd,
Ormond House, 26–27 Boswell Street, London WC1N 3JD

First published in Great Britain by David Fulton Publishers 1998

Note: The right of Michael Littledyke and Laura Huxford to be identified as the editors of this work has been asserted by them in accordance with the Copyright, Designs and Patents Act 1988.

British Library Cataloguing in Publication Data
A catalogue record for this book is available from the British Library

ISBN 1–85346–515–1

Typeset by Textype Typesetters, Cambridge
Printed in Great Britain by The Cromwell Press Ltd, Trowbridge, Wilts.

Contents

*This book is dedicated to the memory of Sandy Marshall, a valued
colleague and friend who inspired many children, students and
teachers over her career as a talented dance teacher, and who
planned to contribute to this book, though tragic illness prevented her
from doing so.*

Foreword

I welcome the publication of this book which makes a valuable contribution to the debate about constructivist views of children's learning and associated approaches to teaching. Its significance lies in the breadth of its treatment – exploring, as it does, constructivist perspectives within each subject of the National Curriculum. These analyses reveal important similarities and differences which help us understand the holistic nature of learning in the primary school while recognising the particular contribution individual subjects make to that learning. Throughout the text, the authors offer a critique of positivist epistemological assumptions and argue for a view of knowing in which learners actively construct unique understandings of the world around them, often through the support they gain from their teachers.

Within this viewpoint, it is timely to reflect on the authors' recognition that constructivists do not claim to have 'correct' answers, nor to be offering a model which provides a perfect match with reality. They are sharing their current, tentative constructs of the nature of children's learning and the role of teachers. You, as reader, will bring your own experiences and existing understanding to what you read and inevitably construct your own unique interpretation of their ideas. This illustrates important similarities between child and adult learners. All bring to new learning opportunities existing skills, ideas and attitudes. What we already think, know and can do has implications for what and how we learn. This applies to teachers' continuing professional development as well as to the teacher as a learner in the classroom – for example, seeking to understand more about individual children through gathering assessment data.

Another recurring theme highlighted is learning as a social as well as individual activity and it is evident that the writers have, themselves, practised what they preach. The evolution of the book has been a collaborative process that has involved constructive dialogue during which ideas have been shared, explored, challenged and developed. Reading it and, ideally, discussing it with others, should help you engage in a similar process: encouraging you to reflect on and clarify your existing ideas about children's learning and, if you are a teacher, your professional practice; challenging you to reconsider and perhaps modify your understanding; and inviting you to apply new ideas in professional contexts. Improving teachers' understanding of how children learn has the potential to enhance the quality of that learning. I hope this book is successful in achieving this goal.

Dr Ron Ritchie
Bath Spa University College
January 1998

Notes on contributors

The authors are (unless otherwise stated) Senior Lecturers from the Department of Professional Education at Cheltenham and Gloucester College of Higher Education who are presently involved with a range of Initial Primary Teacher Training courses with students (BEd, PGCE) and inservice and postgraduate certificate courses with teachers (GEST funded courses, Certificate of Professional Development, Advanced Diploma, MEd or MPhil/PhD). They all have previous backgrounds as teachers, head teachers or advisory teachers in schools.

Dr Michael Littledyke. *Specialisms*: science, design and technology, with an interest in drama in education. *Research interests*: he has published extensively in the fields of science, science education, environmental education and drama in education. He is the author of *Live Issues: Drama Strategies for Personal, Social and Moral Education* (Questions Publishers, 1998).

Dr Laura Huxford. *Specialisms*: English and special education needs. *Research interests*: she has published widely in the area of acquisition of literacy skills by young children.

Chris Eddershaw. *Specialisms*: English. *Research interests*: teaching literature. He is co-author of *Not-So-Simple Picture Books* (Trentham Books, 1994) and has contributed to *What's in the Picture?* (Paul Chapman, 1998).

David Coles. *Specialisms*: mathematics. *Research interests*: the use of information and communications technology in the teaching and learning of mathematics. In his current research he is exploring the relationship between the development of mathematical subject knowledge and teaching competence.

Alison Price. *Specialisms*: mathematics. Previously at Cheltenham and Gloucester College of Higher Education she is now at Oxford Brookes University. *Research interests*: early numeracy, language in mathematics and use of symbols.

Dr Keith Ross. *Specialisms*: science (primary and secondary) and information and communications technology. *Research interests*: he publishes in the area of language and learning in science and ICT and environmental education. He is co-author of *The Science of Environmental Issues* (Cheltenham and Gloucester College of Higher Education, 1998).

Richard Brice. *Specialisms*: design and technology, information and communication technology. *Research interests*: children's learning in design and technology and strategies for helping children to design. He is also interested in ICT, particularly the use of multimedia to create learning materials.

Les Watson. *Specialisms*: information and communications technology. He is Dean of the Faculty Information Services, is a member of a number of national panels for organisations associated with ICT and is national chairman of Micros and Primary Education. *Research interests*: the use of ICT in schools. He is a regular contributor to the information technology pages of the Times Educational Supplement.

Sally Palmer. *Specialisms*: early years and nursery education, maths, information and communications technology and geography. Course Leader for MEd in early years and CACHE course for nursery nurses. Associate Lecturer for Open University teaching MA courses. *Research interests*: published work includes research into the effects of media on school children in St. Helena.

Kate Thomson. *Specialisms*: geography and history. *Research interests*: exploring literacy skills through the humanities and investigating the needs of more able pupils in these subjects. She has published history teaching materials with Cambridge University Press.

Tim Copeland. *Specialisms*: history. He is the Head of the International Centre for Heritage Education and is a member of the Council of Europe's Cultural Heritage Committee. *Research interests*: published widely in the use of the historic environment in education.

Dr Barbara Brown. *Specialisms*: physical education and special education. She is an OFSTED primary team inspector. *Research interests*: physical education and special education.

Dr Lynne Hoye. *Specialisms*: English, art and personal, social and health education with a specific interest in psychology and the affective domain. *Research interests*: the professional development of teachers and learning and teaching.

Sarah Hennessey. *Specialisms*: She is a lecturer in music education at Exeter University, and has previous experience in primary and secondary schools, further education and as an advisory teacher. *Research interests*: the education and continuing professional development of music teachers and children's musical development. She is author of *Music 7–11: Developing Primary Teaching Skills* (Routledge, 1995) and the editor of a new international journal for Music Education Research (Carfax).

Dr Melissa Raphael. *Specialisms*: religious studies and religious education. *Research interests*: she is the author of numerous articles and several books in the field of religion and gender and twentieth-century concepts of the sacred.

Susan Shorrock. *Specialisms*: English and special needs – previously Head of Unit for children with language disorders. *Research interests*: English and special educational needs. In 1991 she was seconded to Bath University for 2½ years as an ESRC funded Research Officer specialising in English and special needs. She is co-author of *Understanding Teacher Education Case Studies in the Professional Development of Beginning Teachers* (Falmer Press, 1997).

Introduction

Michael Littledyke and Laura Huxford

There is a current preoccupation with educational standards with claims that overall standards of achievement have fallen, or as Von Glasersfeld puts it:

> something is wrong because children come out of school unable to read and write, unable to operate with numbers sufficiently well for their jobs, and with so little knowledge of the contemporary scientific view of the world that a large section still believes that the phases of the moon are caused by the shadow of the earth. (1995, p. 3)

The need for improvement in children's learning has high priority. This has been the intention of the National Curriculum, with its emphasis on learning objectives and assessment, to direct teaching for improved learning, while OFSTED inspections, with primary focus on children's achievements, are designed to monitor the effectiveness of the process. The question of how to improve learning is clearly central in education, but a concentration on *what* should be learnt at the expense of *how* children learn could result in superficial learning without understanding of the underlying processes and with little transferable knowledge to new situations. Such an approach to teaching can prioritise giving the 'right' answers at the expense of the deeper educational issues of how children learn in a way which is meaningful to them. This can be the case if the National Curriculum is interpreted in a narrow, prescriptive manner.

The purpose of this book, therefore, is to address the question of *how* children learn across the primary National Curriculum subjects, with implications for effective teaching approaches. The book emphasises a constructivist view of learning, which acknowledges that children have views and attitudes which are formed as a result of experiences in and out of school and that these must be taken into account if meaningful and transferable learning is to be achieved. This model is well established in science and mathematics education, and has been shown to reflect the extensive research on how children learn in these areas. However, research into constructivist principles of teaching and learning, as applied to other curriculum areas, has been less extensive and the implications are consequently less well developed.

In this book an agenda for constructivist approaches to teaching across the primary curriculum will be presented. This will address learning in each National Curriculum subject and religious education and will encompass effective and affective learning domains. This extends the constructivist view of learning beyond cognitive development to include discussion on how children develop processes, skills and attitudes across the curriculum, as well as moral, aesthetic, spiritual and physical development. For this reason we use the term *constructive learning* which identifies the constructivist background to the approach while signalling a learning process which goes beyond concept formation, which is usually associated with constructivist ideas.

This book, therefore, presents an agenda for teaching and learning across the primary curriculum which is firmly based on what is known about how children learn. The book cannot be comprehensive, because of the wide range of subjects and learning domains covered, but the ideas, strategies and examples of teaching and learning which are presented provide a perspective which will help to inform teachers and students how to achieve constructive, and hence meaningful, learning in children. This is the ultimate goal of raising standards which all who are involved with education should be striving for if children are to develop into critically aware adults who can respond flexibly, humanely and intelligently to the demands of an increasingly complex world. This is the kind of adult population which we need to develop if we are to achieve an acceptable and sustainable standard of social, economic and ecological existence, and it is the role of primary educators to lay the foundations for this.

Before addressing the wider issues of constructive learning across the whole curriculum Littledyke, in chapter one, discusses some of the psychological and philosophical issues concerned with how we understand the world. Positivism and constructivism, as contrasting and opposing views of learning, are compared and the evidence for each is considered. This is important because assumptions about how children learn shape approaches to teaching, and positivist views, in particular, and associated institutional structures are pervasive and very influential. Understanding the implications of positivist and constructivist views of the world lies at the heart of most educational choices. The discussion in this chapter draws particularly on the developments in science and science education as preoccupied with pursuit of knowledge about the world and having undergone major transformation since its early positivist domination. Developing this line of discussion further, in chapter two, he identifies important features of constructive teaching and learning in the various learning domains as drawn from constructivist principles of concept formation. In this chapter the implications of teaching for constructive learning in the context of the National Curriculum are addressed.

Chapters three to fourteen present the implications for teaching for constructive learning in each National Curriculum subject and religious education. The writers address central features of each subject and discuss, using case study examples in some cases, how children learn and what this implies for teaching.

Chapters three and four address different aspects of the English curriculum. Huxford traces the development of children's understanding of written language across a number of different alphabetic languages. She notes that when very young children construct their own form of written language they tend to use features of the language they experience; development in their understanding is manifested in a closer approximation to the conventional written form. Eddershaw demonstrates how, through discussion in which they are encouraged to relate their personal experience, upper primary school children construct their understanding of text. Using a picture book, a novel and a poem, he illustrates teaching within a social constructivist perspective.

In chapter five Coles and Price discuss how constructive teaching should incorporate a variety of strategies to cater for the complex features of learning in mathematics, as well as appropriate structured approaches to skills and knowledge acquisition. Ross, in chapter six, emphasises the importance of language in science education to enable children to make meaningful sense of science concepts. He exemplifies this by showing how understanding of science concepts can support understanding of important environmental issues.

Brice shows how constructive learning is integral to design and technology in chapter seven, and provides examples of how this can be developed, highlighting the constructive features of the 'design and make' process. Watson and Ross, in chapter eight, argue that the ICT in schools can only be justified if it is used as a tool to support learning. They show that the skills gap, often used to support a mechanistic view of computer use, is likely to close as home computer ownership becomes significant.

In chapters nine and ten Copeland (history) and Thompson and Palmer (geography) argue the impossibility of understanding their subjects without a constructivist approach. Copeland has developed a model for the teaching of history which relies upon children's active involvement in engaging with primary or secondary sources. At the heart of the chapter by Thompson and Palmer lies the use of geographical enquiry to deepen understanding and develop a sense of place.

Brown's chapter eleven on physical education emphasises the importance of teachers helping children to construct an understanding of how their own bodies operate in space and how parts of their bodies operate in relation to each other and in relation to the apparatus they use. Hoye discusses constructivism and art education and shows, in chapter twelve, how children's developing visual aesthetic sense can be fostered through a constructive teaching approach and provides examples of resource material to support this. In chapter thirteen, Hennessey draws on the research and thinking on young children's imaginative play and suggests parallels between this play and the process of composing music in schools. She illustrates this with several practical examples. Raphael shows in chapter fourteen that the experiential dimension is central to religious education and that knowledge of religions, while important, should not supplant the need to develop children's spiritual awareness.

The final chapter addresses the needs of children who have difficulty accessing the full curriculum. Brown and Shorrock contend that by definition a constructivist framework for teaching and learning places the learner in a position of power. They describe classroom structures and processes to give all children access to learning.

The book is intended for a wide range of groups involved in primary education, including, primarily, student teachers engaged in initial teacher training courses and higher education tutors involved in running such courses. It would also have relevance to practising teachers engaged in postgraduate degree or inservice courses and their course tutors, as well as other teachers who are keen to keep abreast of developments in teaching and learning. The book provides a perspective on teaching and learning which has implications for research into primary teaching and learning.

REFERENCE

Von Glasersfeld, E. (1995) *Radical Constructivism: A Way of Knowing and Learning*. London: Falmer.

CHAPTER 1

Constructivist ideas about learning

Michael Littledyke

This chapter will address constructivist principles of learning, as these ideas underpin the approaches to teaching for constructive learning across the curriculum which form the basis for the rest of the book. Firstly, however, to understand the significance of constructivist ideas about teaching and learning it is helpful to compare ideas about positivism and constructivism as contrasting models of how we interpret the world.

WAYS OF KNOWING: PRIVATE AND SHARED UNDERSTANDINGS

To understand how we can know about the world we must first ask the questions:

- How do we construe events in the world?
- How may we come to shared understanding?
- What happens when we differ?

A positivist answer to these questions will differ from a constructivist perspective. These two views have different epistemological assumptions and different implications for approaches to teaching and learning.

The positivist's view

A positivist emphasises an independent external world which can be known objectively in a realist or true sense through the mediation of our senses and cognitive processes, acting as a 'mirror to nature' (Rorty 1979). A positivist's view also emphasises a dualist state where 'the existence of an external world (typically a material reality) is set against the existence of a psychological world (cognitive, subjective, symbolic or phenomenological)' (Gergen 1995, p. 18). The positivist considers that the application of reason is necessary to gain an uncontaminated view of the world, tends to refer to 'events out there', and asserts that individuals will tend to come to shared understanding of 'true' events if they have an accurate and reasoned view of them. In this perspective, differences in views will occur when there are what are regarded as distorted perceptions, though people may also share such distorted views (see figure 1.1).

The positivist view of knowledge, therefore, is that truths exist objectively and they can be known through objective reason. Keen observation and dispassionate enquiry is emphasised and emotion or motivation can be seen as obstructions to the neutral and objective approach to truth. Positivism is also a 'common sense' view of the world in that our actual experience of phenomena is that we seem to be able to

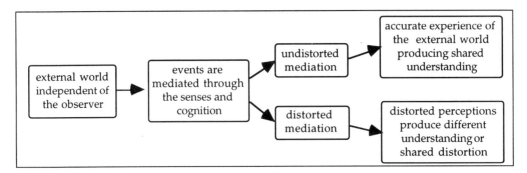

Figure 1.1 A positivist interpretation of shared and different understanding

perceive events occurring independently of us as observers. This pragmatic outlook enables us to identify and name features of the world and to communicate them to each other, based on an assumption that we can hold shared perceptions of an independent external reality. It is not surprising, therefore, that many people hold such positivist views, including many teachers (Clayden *et al.* 1994, Littledyke 1997), and that the positivist view of the world has been greatly influential in shaping our social, economic and ecological relationships, as well as our educational systems.

The constructivist's view

A constructivist has a very different model of reality. When asked the question 'how do we construe events?' a constructivist would assert that events do not exist 'out there' but are created by the person doing the construing. Something exists, but we cannot perceive it completely objectively. Hence, there is no such thing as an independent reality which we can know, describe and communicate in an absolutely true sense. What we experience is a dynamic interaction of our sensations, perceptions, memory of previous experience and cognitive processes which shape our understanding of events. According to this model, individuals actively create experience and meaning which contribute to form a personal construction of the world (Kelly 1955).

Jancowicz refers to the 'phenomenal flow' as the totality of people, places, things which contribute to experience. Within this totality individuals select a part of the flow and call it an 'event' which is characterised by a set of 'assertions-and-contrasts, or constructs' (1997, p. 1). When individuals construe meaning from events they impose previous experiences, or pre-existing patterns, on the phenomenal flow, so that sense can be made of it in the light of their existing construct system. As everyone has unique experiences individuals will therefore have personal and unique construct systems. The extent to which people are similar or different is dependent on how similar or different their construct systems are. Individuals with similar experiences and similar construct systems are likely to hold similar interpretations and views of events, while individuals with different experiences or different constructions of meaning from similar experiences will hold different views (see figure 1.2).

Constructivism which emphasises personal constructs as the essential way in

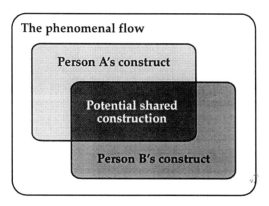

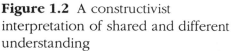

Figure 1.2 A constructivist interpretation of shared and different understanding

which we construe the world has been referred to as *radical constructivism*. In this view:

> radical constructivism . . . starts from the assumption that knowledge, no matter how it be defined, is in the heads of persons, and that the thinking subject has no alternative but to construct what he or she knows on the basis of her/his own experience. What we make of experience constitutes the only world we consciously live in. (Von Glasersfeld 1995, p. 1)

Radical constructivism offers a radical break from the dualism of the positivist view, seeing perception and understanding as being part of a dynamic process. It also refutes the possibility of objective truth in any absolute sense, in that knowledge as a construction cannot be seen as something separate from the construer. However, this view raises the problem of the status of communication and of shared knowledge. If knowledge is constructed by individual minds, how can we come to have shared understanding?

Postmodern writers (e.g. Derrida, Lyotard, Rorty) who are concerned with deconstruction of texts, would argue that communication is possible because we do not individually invent the meaning of words but use them in an agreed way. Thus, communication is possible because words achieve meaning in the way they are used with other words. Texts achieve meaning because they are used in context with other texts. Views are also allied to ideologies which are influenced by cultural and social conditions. All this implies that knowledge, as it is constructed through such social interaction, is a social process.

Social constructivism, therefore, acknowledges and emphasises how personal constructs are formed within a social context involving exchange, accumulation and challenge of individuals' views. In this context there will be social constructs generated which are generally agreed to, though individuals may have their own private perceptions of them. The primary focus for knowledge in this analysis is language and how it is used and shared (Berger and Luckmann 1966).

HOW VALID IS POSITIVISM OR CONSTRUCTIVISM AS A WORLD VIEW?

As the constructivist view of knowledge is incompatible with the positivist model we will therefore consider the evidence for both viewpoints. We will draw extensively on science and science education, as a subject which is preoccupied with pursuit of knowledge about the world, to help us with this.

The commonly held view of scientific knowledge is as proven knowledge and scientific theories as 'derived in some rigorous way from the facts of experience acquired by observation and experiment' (Chalmers 1982, p. 1). Science in this model is conveyed by Harlen (1992, pp. 2–3) as:

- objective;
- capable of yielding ultimate truths;
- proving things;
- having a defined and unique subject matter;
- having unique methods;
- being value free.

This positivist view of science assumes that scientists uncover scientific 'truths' through empirical and objective investigation and science education is designed to teach these 'truths'.

In contrast, an epistemology that sees knowledge as tentative views science as a process of testing ideas to develop provisional theories of natural phenomena. Harlen (p. 3) describes this model of science as:

- human endeavour to understand the physical world;
- producing knowledge which is tentative, always subject to challenge by further evidence;
- building upon, but not accepting uncritically, previous knowledge and understanding;
- a social enterprise whose conclusions are often subject to social acceptability;
- constrained by values.

This model of science is compatible with the constructivist's view and the evidence is overwhelmingly in its favour.

The history and philosophy of science shows that scientific knowledge is constantly changing in the light of new evidence and theories (Loseé 1993). Thus, scientific knowledge, as far as it can be 'known', has a permanent conjectural nature (Popper 1963). Hawking (1988, p. 10) expresses this tentative and provisional nature of science as follows:

> Any physical theory is always provisional, in the sense that it is only a hypothesis: you can never prove it . . . [because] you can disprove a theory by finding even a single observation that disagreed with the predictions of the theory.

Dominant paradigms, as scientific models which are generally accepted at a particular time, can influence the interpretation of new evidence so that a theory may be held even when evidence contradicts it (Kuhn 1970). These paradigms can also shape and restrict the direction of scientific research programmes (Lakatos 1970). Furthermore, the presentation of the so called scientific method as a prescribed set of rules with a step by step linear and objective process has been shown to bear little relation to actual research (Medawar 1979). Philosophers of science now recognise that construction of scientific knowledge takes place in a social context and this influences the nature of that knowledge and the processes by which it was constructed. Thus, positivism has been largely discredited as a philosophical position and 'constructivism is today's generally accepted philosophical stream' (Nussbaum 1989, p. 530).

The discrediting of positivism is also borne out by the most recent evidence from fields of science such as quantum mechanics (Bohm 1983, Capra 1982, Davies, 1983) and complexity (Prigogine and Stengers 1984, Kaufmann 1992, Lewin 1993, Cohen and Stewart 1995, Waldrop 1994), which also includes chaos theory (Gleick 1988). Findings from these developing areas of science indicate that matter and complex systems are inherently unpredictable in a finite sense, and that systems can spontaneously change or new emergent forms may appear. Also any action of an experimenter involves her/him through the process of selection and interaction in what is observed, so that experimental results are influenced by how the experiment is approached. This is particularly marked at the quantum level where results of investigations may be contradictory according to our usual way of explaining the world, which indicates that the universe is a far 'stranger' place than how we actually experience it. Hence, scientific ideas can often confront our common sense view of the world (Wolpert 1992). This also confirms that the goal of attaining absolute scientific truth through detached, objective observation of the world is an unattainable illusion.

Constructivism is also supported by evidence from the fields of neurophysiology and psychology which indicate that consciousness is a manifestation of a dynamic interaction between the observer and what is observed. Dualism, which is the cornerstone of positivism, and which separates the mind of the observer from the 'outside world', confirms what we seem to experience through our senses; that is, that the world appears to exist and function independently of us as observers. Dualism is, however, a manifestation of an illusionary 'Cartesian Theatre' (after Descartes) which has evolved to give a sense of the separateness of self which is essential for biological survival (Dennett 1993).

Sense organs do not passively accept incoming data:

> More neural connections run from the brain to the ear than from the ear to the brain. And about ten percent of fibres in the optic nerve go the 'wrong way' . . . The brain has to tune the organ, so it can detect what is needed. (Cohen and Stewart 1995, p. 348)

There is no such thing as naive or objective sense data. The images which we create with our brains are not like photographs or TV pictures, though they may seem like that to us. The brain selects and interprets information in the light of previous experience. Thus, we are not born with the ability to perceive the world as an adult would. Kittens prevented from seeing early on cannot see at all in later life, and if they are deprived of certain patterns they are unable to respond to them later. We also have to learn to see, hear, make sense of the world, so that feral children who have been brought up in the wild cannot learn language at all if they have not been exposed to it before the age of twelve. Young children's brains are set up in context with the world around them and our view of the world is actively created and is always influenced by what has gone before.

There have been some critics of constructivist ideas, however. For example, Matthews (1993, p. 366) considers that:

> Constructivism is correct in stressing the inventive, humane, culturally, and temporally dependent aspects of creating the theoretical objects of science . . . [but] the fact that knowledge is humanely constructed does not mean that knowledge claims cannot be true, nor should the creations of science be tied to 'sensory inputs' in the way constructivists often do.

Such criticism focuses on the debate about what can be known through science. Scientific theories and mathematical models, which accurately predict events in the world, can be seen to represent verifiable aspects of reality. However, most scientific philosophers would agree that scientific knowledge represents models as metaphors of reality which are *ultimately* bound in human thought processes, even though the models may *attempt* to describe aspects of reality which are independent of us (Barbour 1974). This rules out the possibility of achieving complete objectivity and supports the view that science is an essentially socially constructed process even though its methods aspire or pretend to objectivity.

Critics of constructivism also may argue that constructivist pedagogy (discussed in detail in chapter two) could tend towards relativism in which any view that a child reaches is acceptable as long as it is considered acceptable to him/her. Clearly, such an extreme relativist pedagogy would be inappropriate in that it ignores the socially constructed aspects of scientific knowledge from scientific activity within the scientific community, whilst over-emphasising the place of personal knowledge construction. Such personal constructs can be influenced by a wide range of cultural and experiential factors and can often be contra-scientific. The challenge for education, then, is to strive to achieve an appropriate balance in the learner between the personal construction of meaning and the desirable learning outcomes which constitute the social constructs of curriculum knowledge.

MODERNITY AND POSITIVISM

The influence of positivism on western thinking has been enormous. And we will turn again to developments in science to trace this.

Positivism is associated with the 'project' of modernity which developed in the seventeenth and eighteenth centuries through the intellectual efforts of Enlightenment thinkers to advance objective science as a means of understanding and controlling the world:

> Generally perceived as positivistic, technocentric and rationalistic, universal modernism has been identified with the belief in linear progress, absolute truths, the rational planning of ideal social orders, and the standardisation of knowledge and production (PRECIS 6, in Harvey 1989, p. 9)

Universal law, morality and art were ways of responding to the internal rules of nature, and knowledge could be used to control nature for human benefit, as well as liberating human thought from superstition and myth.

In the latter part of the twentieth century postmodern analysts have challenged the beliefs and assumptions of the modern era which have dominated and shaped western society for some three hundred years. Significantly, according to postmodern analysis, a positivistic view of knowledge associated with the modern era is untenable.

Two strands in postmodernism have been identified; *deconstructive* and *reconstructive* (or *revisionary*) postmodernism (Griffin 1988). *Deconstructive* writers fundamentally challenge the notion of grand theories and universal truth claims. Lyotard, for example, asserts that 'as science spawns disciplines it becomes harder to maintain that they are all part of the same enterprise' (Lyon 1994, p. 12). As the 'traditional sense of knowledge is thus decomposed' we are left with 'local language games' (p. 13). Derrida discusses the 'deconstruction' of texts and proposes that cultural life involves subtle interconnections of texts which influence in 'ways we can never unravel' and which stress the 'indeterminacy of language' (p. 13). Foucault stresses that power and knowledge are linked, so that the important issue is one of discourses of power rather than the universal imperative of any knowledge claims. Thus we can say 'farewell to "knowledge" as once construed; welcome instead to pliable discourses' (p. 12). The deconstructive postmodern position is effectively summarised by Rorty:

> Science does not get progressively closer to truth any more than the humanities or social sciences. What counts as reality is the world under a given description. The 'world' is a name for the objects that inquiry at the moment is leaving alone: those planks in the boat that are at the moment not being moved about. For those who espouse a postmodern perspective, reality is nothing but a temporary text constructed out of other texts. (1982, p. 15)

A *reconstructive* (or *revisionary*) postmodernism, in contrast, seeks to revise the modern view of science to create

> a new unity of scientific, ethical, aesthetic and religious institutions. It rejects not science as such but only that scientism in which the data of the modern sciences are alone allowed to contribute to the construction of our world view. (Griffin 1988, p. x)

This is part of the replacement of the modern scientific paradigm by what some authors refer to as a more ecological (Birch 1988, Ferré 1988) or 'organicist' (Griffin 1988) one. This new paradigm identifies the destructive influences inherent in the pursuit of objective science (which contrast with evident social benefits in improved medicine and other scientific/technological developments). Thus, the modern preoccupation with the pursuit of universal knowledge achieved through objective, positivistic rationalisation has contributed to objectifying human relationships, with a result in the justification of exploitive, dominating and prejudiced views and actions based on assumptions of superiority of dominant groups in matters such as sex, class or racial discrimination. Objectification and anthropocentrism have also contributed to massive exploitation of the natural world and the production of ecologically damaging technologies (Griffin 1988, Orr 1992). In this way positivist approaches to science and technology have contributed significantly to the present environmental crisis (Roszak 1970, Sessions 1974, Drengson 1979, Naess 1989, Fox 1990) in which we are presently involved in what Diamond (1992) refers to as the sixth major extinction period, when over half of existing species are likely to be extinct by the middle of the next century. Reconstructive postmodernism, in response to the destructive elements of modernity, seeks to achieve a view of the natural world which acknowledges our part in it as well as our responsibility for our actions within it.

While the philosophical debate between constructivism and positivism seems to have been decisively won by constructivism, positivism has had a great influence in the past and still dominates institutional structures, including education. Modern, positivist influences in education have the effect of inculcating children with suitable modes of enquiry and knowledge of prescribed truths. The implications of the positivist view of knowledge for curriculum planners, therefore, is to select what children should learn. The mind of a child is a *tabula rasa* on which the function of education is to inscribe the truths of the features of the world. According to these premises, the function of teaching is to devise ways of ensuring that children learn what has been prescribed and assessment procedures will verify the effectiveness of the process. This implies prescribed and narrow objectives for learning, transmission or instrumental modes of teaching, and assessment procedures which are preoccupied with assessing individual knowledge acquisition.

The ideology of education associated with such an approach also tends to emphasise the functional importance of education to society rather than to the individual, which is a view echoed by Robert Lowe, a Victorian school inspector:

> We do not profess to give these children an education that will raise them above their station and business in life: that is not our object, but to give them an education that may fit them for that business. We are bound to take a clear and definite view of the class that is to receive the instruction: and, having obtained that view, we are bound to make our minds up as to how much instruction that class requires, and is capable of receiving, and we are then bound to have evidence that it has received such instruction. (Robert Lowe 1862, in Bergen 1988, p. 41)

CONSTRUCTIVIST MODELS OF LEARNING

The focus of a constructivist, in contrast to the positivist's view, is the way in which people construe understanding, and the priority of curriculum planners in support of constructivist learning is to create an environment where individuals may build up a meaningful understanding of the world through appropriate experience and reflection on its significance.

This approach derives from the work of Piaget (1955, 1959) who advocated a constructivist view of learning with teaching priorities focused on the developmental needs of the individual. Piaget said that conceptual development occurs as schemas, or units of organised information, in which a child draws connections between these and new experiences. All new experiences interact with what the child already knows and when a new situation is met s/he seeks a schema which will explain it. The existing schema is reorganised to accommodate the new knowledge in the light of the conflicts which are created. Piaget also proposed his theory of cognitive development with age related stages which children must pass through in their development. This theory was very influential in approaches to teaching children of different ages and stages. The details of the stage theory have been criticised by some authors, however (e.g. Donaldson 1978), because children can operate at different levels in different areas of learning and can move between stages accordingly. Hence, children's actual learning may be more complex than Piaget postulated.

A number of other authors focus on the starting point of the learner in different ways, as outlined below.

Jerome Bruner's (1966) ideas were, in broad terms, similar to Piaget's in that he claimed that intelligence developed through stages. He contended that the individual represents her/his knowledge by action (Enactive), image (Iconic) and symbol (Symbolic) in a developmental sequence which mirrors Piaget's stages of intellectual growth. From this he goes on to suggest that the pupil probably learns best if the material is presented to her/him by the processes which correspond to her/his stage of development. Thus, a child at the second stage learns by means of her/his own actions and perceptions and represents what s/he has learned through actions and visual images. The use of language, which is symbolic, may only come later.

Bruner emphasised the following:

- sequencing in development;
- predisposition to learning and motivation;
- a spiral curriculum where areas of learning are met at different ages and levels;
- discovery learning;
- intuition and creativity;
- role of language;
- he said you can teach anything to a child if it is adapted to the level of the child;
- the teacher has a role in structuring experiences and 'scaffolding' the child's learning.

Lev Vygotsky (1962) also emphasised the role of language in development and said that thought realises itself through words. He described zones of proximal development in children where learning may occur if they are stimulated by guidance and interaction with a teacher or in collaboration with more able peers. Vygotsky and Bruner stressed the social construction of knowledge and saw the role of a teacher as stimulating learning and helping children to understand socially agreed forms of knowledge. This provides a place for teacher instruction in a way which will be compatible with children's personal construction of meaning.

Robert Gagné (1970) specified the conditions for learning complex tasks, which illustrates further the development of increasing complexity in learning. He stated that what a person can learn depends on what s/he already knows. He identified eight types of learning which he arranged in a hierarchy, including:

1. Signal learning   *Simple*
2. Stimulus – response
3. Chaining: connecting two S – R's
4. Verbal association
5. Discrimination learning
6. Concept learning
7. Rule learning: 'If A, then B'
8. Problem-solving: thinking about a new rule or combining
    previous rules.   *Complex*

Learning at any level depends on having learned all the relevant material at the lower levels. Any task can be arranged in terms of all the steps in the learning process which must precede the current step. The analysis may be complex but it reminds us that the problem can be broken down into its component parts making sure that the basic ideas are understood before proceeding to the more complex.

David Ausubel (1968) proposed that meaningful learning can occur when new ideas can be incorporated into a structure of thought that has already been established by previous learning. He thought of learning in two dimensions; the degree of meaningfulness and the mode of encounter (see figure 1.3).

Ausubel posited three conditions which are necessary for meaningful learning:

1. The material itself must be meaningful; it must make sense or conform to experience. (It does not have to be true.)
2. The learner must have enough relevant knowledge for the meaning in the material to be within her/his grasp.
3. The learner must intend to learn meaningfully, that is s/he must intend to fit the new material into what s/he already knows rather than to memorise it word-for-word.

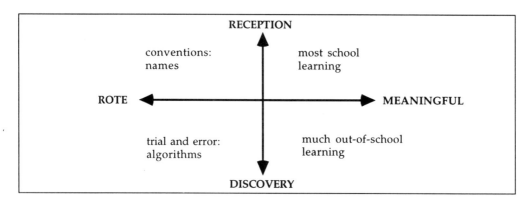

Figure 1.3 Ausubel's dimensions of learning (McClelland 1985, p. 136)

There is also an important issue of the relatedness of the new material to existing knowledge. Learning is affected by:

- How complex the new material is;
- How it relates to what is already known.

Ausubel identified six levels of relatedness:
   The new knowledge:

1. could be derived from what is already known;
2. extends, elaborates or re-codes what is already known;
3. draws together several concepts into one higher level abstraction;
4. is inherently meaningful but cannot be directly nor specifically related to what is already known;
5. is inherently arbitrary and lacking in potential meaningfulness (or the learner approaches it in this way);
6. is inherently meaningful but denies or negates an existing stable, high-level concept.

The characteristics of the learning which takes place in each case are as follows:

1. Learning occurs rapidly and easily; there is relatively rapid loss of specific recall. This is not the same as forgetting, because, although it falls below a threshold of recall, subsequent relearning is even easier than before.
2. Not so easy nor rapid to learn: relatively long-lasting. An example is vocabulary learning in a second language.
3. Provided the initial concepts are clearly held and the new material is successful in drawing them together, learning can be very rapid, with a 'Eureka' effect. The new concept becomes more stable than its predecessors which may become incorporated into it beyond specific recall.
4. Very difficult to learn and liable to rapid forgetting unless links can be forged to create stability.
5. Relatively easy to learn by heart in small amounts but rapidly becomes more difficult as the amount increases.
6. Most difficult of all, even painful, the more so the higher-level and more stable the concept with which the new material conflicts.
   (Summarised from McClelland 1985, pp. 133–41)

McClelland comments that, although children bring to school a great deal of knowledge and experience it is usually not highly elaborated or organised, so much school learning is likely to fall into the fourth category. Some may fall into the sixth.

Ausubel (1968, p. v) summarises his ideas in this way: 'If I had to reduce all psychology to just one principle I would say this "The most important single factor influencing learning is what the learner already knows. Ascertain that and teach him (sic) accordingly" '.

A number of authors have interpreted the above in slightly different ways but all focus on the starting point of the learner (from Osborne and Freyberg 1993):

- find the sub-skills that the learner has, then develop the learner sequence starting from these sub-skills (Gagné and White 1978);

- find the logical structures of thought the child is capable of and match the logical demands of the curriculum to them (Shayer and Adey 1981);
- find the prior concepts of the learner and determine the necessary links between what is to be taught and what the learner already knows (Ausubel 1968);
- find the alternative viewpoints possessed by the child and provide material in such a way as to encourage the child to reconsider and modify these viewpoints (Driver 1986);
- find the meanings and concepts that the learner has generated already from her/his background, attitudes and experiences and determine ways so that the learner will generate new meanings and concepts that will be useful to her/him (Wittrock 1977).

Ros Driver (1985), commenting on Ausubel's ideas, highlighted the need to consider the child's pre-conceptions:

- they are very tenacious and resistant to extinction;
- the unlearning of pre-conceptions might well prove to be the most determinative single factor in the acquisition and retention of subject matter knowledge.

Driver identified four pointers for classroom practice:

- curriculum development needs to pay attention to the structure of thought of the child. There is a need for a shift from logical processes to the content of knowledge;
- teaching programmes need to be structured to be more in keeping with the developmental paths in understanding more important ideas. The logical order of teaching a topic may not correspond to the psychological order of learning;
- we need activities which challenge alternative interpretations as well as confirm accepted ones;
- we must allow children time to think through the implications of their findings in lessons. Teachers' explanations do not always spring clearly from the data. Many children need help to make sense of what they observe. This might be achieved by their talking in groups or talking with the teacher.

IMPLICATIONS FOR TEACHING

From the previous discussion there are a number of implications for teaching:

- Be aware that children come to a subject with a range of life experiences and often some previous school experiences.
- Try, as far as possible, to get to know what knowledge they bring with them.
- Different groups of children may need different experiences to extend, confirm, or challenge their current frameworks of knowledge.
- Each child may need a range of related experiences to help refine and clarify a concept at a particular level.
- Readiness is still a useful concept. (For example, when are children ready to learn quantum mechanics? At what level do you expect eleven year olds to

tackle the concept of the gene?)
- The teacher needs to keep in mind the overall concept or over-arching idea towards which particular learning activities are directed.

The main principles of the constructivist view of learning are summarised by Driver and Bell (1986) as:

- learning is influenced by prior knowledge and attitudes;
- individuals construct meaning through experience;
- construction of meaning is an active process which may involve conceptual change, but which may or may not lead to belief;
- learners are responsible for their own learning; some meanings can be shared socially.

Biddulph and Osborne (1984) and Driver and Oldham (1986) recommended models for the development of approaches to science on constructivist lines. This has been developed into constructivist teaching strategies presented as a series of phases, including:

- orientation to arouse interest and curiosity;
- elicitation to help children clarify what they think;
- intervention or restructuring to encourage children to test their ideas and extend or modify them;
- review to help children to recognise the significance of what they have found out;
- application to help children relate what they have learned to their everyday lives.

This perspective on children's learning has resulted in extensive research programmes in science education, and mathematics education, where features of children's learning have been demonstrated and children's development of concepts has been investigated across a range of topics (e.g. Eggan *et al.* 1979, Driver 1983, 1985, 1986, Driver *et al.* 1985, Osborne and Freyberg 1985, Needham and Hill 1987, Scott *et al.* 1987, Von Glasersfeld 1989, 1995a, 1995b, Davis *et al.* 1990, Jaworski 1994).

The constructivist view of learning in science was endorsed in the National Curriculum Non-statutory Guidance (NCC 1989, p. A7) and research into children's learning in science at secondary (CLIS 1984–91) and primary levels (SPACE 1989–92) has shown the potential of adopting teaching methods which are based on constructivist learning approaches. In recent years constructivist methods have been advocated for science education at all key stages and the constructivist philosophy has been generally accepted by most science education researchers and teacher educators (see, for example, Driver *et al.* 1994; Ollerenshaw and Ritchie 1997).

The implications of constructivist teaching methods are that processes of learning and suitable environments for learning are particularly important:

Rather than identifying the set of skills to be gotten in children's heads, attention shifts to establishing learning environments conducive to children constructing their science in social settings. (Wheatley 1991, p. 12)

This view is supported by numerous writers, for example Carey and Evans (1989), who assert that the science curriculum should reflect a constructivist epistemology, and by others, such as Davis *et al.* (1993), who consider that many assessment techniques are based on a positivist paradigm which discourages a constructivist pedagogy. Given the large research evidence to support constructivist ideas there has been a call for a paradigm shift to constructivism in the spirit of Kuhn (1970) who described how scientific knowledge develops by paradigm shifts through changes in thinking and approaches. The implications are that there is a need for an appropriate paradigm shift in science education.

From this discussion on science education, the purpose of teaching for effective learning is, therefore, to facilitate constructs which are both personally meaningful and also congruent with scientific thinking. The locus of control in constructivist learning is in the learner, the teacher acting as a facilitator of learning, providing experiences which challenge and extend understanding, rather than an instructor. This model of learning has become the principal means of interpreting scientific or mathematical concept development and has been advocated as an approach to teaching and learning concepts across the curriculum (Brooks and Brooks 1993, Steffe and Gale 1995). We will explore the implications of this for teaching in the next chapter.

ACKNOWLEDGEMENT

Some of the content of this chapter is derived from course material for primary science initial teacher education which was initially written by Dennis Sutton and the author.

REFERENCES

Ausubel, D. (1968) *Educational Psychology.* NY: Holt Rinehart and Winston.

Barbour, I. G. (1974) *Myths, Models and Paradigms.* London: SCM Press.

Bergen, B. H. (1988) 'Only a schoolmaster: gender, class and the effort to professionalise elementary education in England, 1870–1910', in Ozga, J. (ed.), *Schoolwork: Approaches to the Labour Process of Teaching.* Milton Keynes: Open University Press.

Berger, P. and Luckmann, T. (1966) *The Social Construction of Reality.* Garden City, NY: Doubleday.

Biddulph, F. and Osborne, R. (1984) *Making Sense of Our World: An Interactive Teaching Approach.* Hamilton, NZ: University of Waikato.

Birch, C. (1988) 'The Postmodern Challenge to Biology', in Griffin, D. R. (ed), *The Reenchantment of Science: Postmodern Proposals.* Albany: State University of New York Press.

Bohm, D. (1983) *Wholeness and the Implicate Order.* London: Ark.

Brooks, J. G. and Brooks, M. G. (1993) *In Search of Understanding: The Case for Constructivist Classrooms.* Alexandria, Virginia: Association for Supervision and Curriculum Development.

Bruner, J. S. (1966) *Studies in Cognitive Growth.* New York: Wiley.

Capra, F. (1982) *The Turning Point.* New York: Bantam Books.

Carey, S. and Evans, R. (1989) 'An experiment is when you try it and see if it works: a study of grade 7 students' understanding of the construction of scientific knowledge', *International Journal of Science Education* **11**, 514–29.

Chalmers, A. (1982) *What is this thing called Science?* 2nd edn. Milton Keynes: Open University Press.

Children's Learning in Science Project (CLIS) (1984–91) *Research Reports.* Leeds: Centre for Studies in Science and Mathematics Education, University of Leeds.

Clayden, E., Desforges, C., Mills, C., Rawson, W. (1994) 'Authentic activity and learning', *British Journal of Educational Studies* **60**, 163–73.

Cohen, J. and Stewart, I. (1995) *The Collapse of Chaos*. New York: Viking.

Davies, P. (1983) *God and the New Physics*. London: J. M. Dent and Sons.

Davis, N. T., McCarty, B. J., Shaw, K. L., Sidani-Tabaa, S. (1993) 'Transitions from objectivism to constructivism in science education', *International Journal of Science Education* **15**, 627–36.

Davis, R., Maher, C. and Noddings, N. (1990) 'Suggestions for the improvement of mathematics education, in Constructivist Views on the Teaching and Learning of Mathematics', *Journal for Research in Mathematics Education*, Monograph, No. 4. Reston Va: National Council of Teachers of Mathematics.

Dennett, D. C. (1993) *Consciousness Explained*. London: Viking.

Diamond, J. (1992) *The Rise and Fall of the Third Chimpanzee: how our animal heritage affects the way we live*. London: Vintage.

Donaldson, M. (1978) *Children's Minds*. London: Fontana.

Drengson, A. R. (1989) *Beyond Environmental Crisis: From Technocratic to Planetary Person*. New York: Peter Lang.

Driver, R. (1983) *The Pupil as a Scientist*. Milton Keynes: Open University Press.

Driver, R. (1985) 'Pupils' alternative frameworks in science', in Hodgson, B. and Scanlon, E. (eds) *Approaching Primary Science*. London: Harper and Row.

Driver, R., Guesne T. and Tiberghien, A. (1985) *Children's Ideas in Science*. Milton Keynes: Open University Press.

Driver, R. (1986) 'Students' thinking and learning in science', *School Science Review* **64**, 157–160.

Driver R. and Bell, B. (1986) 'Students' thinking and the learning of science: a constructivist view', *School Science Review* **67**, 443–56.

Driver, R. and Oldham, V. (1986) 'A constructivist approach to curriculum development in science', *Studies in Science Education* **13**, 105–22.

Driver, R., Squires, A., Rushworth, P. and Wood-Robinson, V. (1994) *Making Sense of Secondary Science*. London: Routledge.

Eggan, P. D., Kauchak, D. P. and Harder, R. J. (1979) *Strategies for Teachers: Information Processing Models in the Classroom*. Englewood Cliffs, N. J.: Prentice Hall.

Ferré, F. (1988) 'Religious World Modelling and Postmodern Science', in Griffin, D. R. (ed.), *The Reenchantment of Science: Postmodern Proposals*. Albany: State University of New York Press.

Fox, W. (1990) *Toward a Transpersonal Ecology*. Massachusetts: Shambala.

Gagné, R. M. (1970) *The Conditions of Learning*. 2nd edn. NY: Rinehart and Winston.

Gagné, R. M. and White, R. T. (1978) 'Memory structures and learning outcomes', *Review of Educational Research* **48**, 187–272.

Gergen, K. J. (1995) 'Social Construction and the Education Process', in Steffe, L. P. and Gale, J. (eds) *Constructivism in Education*. Hove: Lawrence Erlbaum.

Gleick, J (1988) *Chaos*. London: Cardinal.

Griffin, D. R. (ed.) (1988) *The Reenchantment of Science: Postmodern Proposals*. Albany: State University of New York Press.

Harlen, W. (1992) *The Teaching of Science*. London: David Fulton.

Harvey, D. (1989) *The Condition of Postmodernity*. Oxford: Blackwell.

Hawking, S. W. (1988) *A Brief History of Time*. London: Bantam Press.

Jancowicz, A. D. (1997) 'Professions: Public Arbiters of Private Meaning', keynote address at the One-Day Conference 'Constructing Meanings Within Professions' of the Southern PCP Group, University of Reading, 21st June.

Jaworski, B. (1994) *Investigating Mathematics Teaching: A Constructivist Enquiry*. London: Falmer.

Kaufmann, S. (1992) *The Origins of Order*. Oxford: Oxford University Press.

Kelly, G. A. (1955) *A Theory of Personality. The Psychology of Personal Constructs*. New York: W. W. Norton.

Kuhn, T. (1970) *The Structure of Scientific Revolutions*. Chicago: University of Chicago Press.

Lakatos, I. (1970) 'Falsification and the Methodology of Scientific Research Programmes', in Lakatos, I. and Musgrave, A. (eds), *Criticism and the Growth of Knowledge*. Cambridge: Cambridge University Press.

Lewin, R. (1993) *Complexity: Life on the edge of chaos*. London: Phoenix.

Littledyke, M. (1997) 'Science education for environmental education? Primary teacher perspectives and practices', *British Educational Research Journal* **23**(5), 641–59.

Loseé, J. (1993) *Philosophy of Science*, 3rd edn. Oxford: Oxford University Press.

Lyon, D. (1994) *Postmodernity*. Buckingham: Open University Press.

Matthews, M. R. (1993) 'Constructivism and Science Education: Some Epistemological Problems', *Journal of Science Education and Technology* **2**, 359–70.

McClelland, J. A. G. (1985) 'Ausubel's theory and its application to introductory science: Part 1 – Ausubel's theory of learning', in Hodgson, B. and Scanlon, E. (eds) *Approaching Primary Science*. Milton Keynes: Open University Press.

Medawar, P. (1979) 'Is the Scientific Paper a Fraud?', London: BBC Publications, reprinted in Brown, J., Cooper, A., Horton, T., Toates, F. and Zeldin, D. (eds), *Science in Schools*. Milton Keynes: Open University Press.

Naess, A. (1989) *Ecology, Community and Lifestyle: Outline of an Ecosophy*. Translated and revised by Rothenberg, D. Cambridge: Cambridge University Press.

National Curriculum Council (NCC) (1989) *Science: non-statutory guidance*. York: NCC.

Needham, R. and Hill, P. (1987) *Teaching Strategies for Developing Understanding in Science*. Children's Learning in Science Project, Leeds: Centre for Studies in Science and Mathematics.

Nussbaum, J. (1989) 'Classroom conceptual change: philosophical perspectives', *International Journal of Science Education* **11**, 530–40.

Ollerenshaw, C. and Ritchie, R. (1997) *Primary Science: Making it Work*, 2nd edn. London: David Fulton.

Orr, D. W. (1992) *Ecological Literacy: Education and the Transition to a Postmodern World*. Albany, NY: State University of New York Press.

Osborne, R. and Freyberg, P. (1985) *Learning in Science*. Oxford: Heinemann.

Osborne, R. and Freyberg, P. (1993) *Learning in Science: the Implications of Children's Science*. Auckland: Heinemann Education.

Piaget, J. (1955) *The Child's Construction of Reality*. London: Routledge and Kegan Paul.

Piaget, J. (1959) *The Language and Thought of the Child*. 3rd edn. New York: Basic Books.

Popper, K. (1963) *Conjectures and Refutations*. London: Routledge and Kegan Paul.

Prigogine, I. and Stengers, I. (1984) *Order Out of Chaos: Man's new dialogue with nature*. New York: Bantam Books.

Rorty, R. (1979) *Philosophy and the Mirror of Nature*. Princeton, NJ: Princeton University Press.

Rorty, R. (1982) *Consequences of Pragmatism*. Minneapolis: University of Minnesota Press.

Roszak, T. (1970) *The Making of a Counter Culture*. London: Faber and Faber.

Sessions, G. (1974) 'Anthropocentrism and the environmental crisis', *Humboldt Journal of Social Relations* **2**, 71–81.

Science Processes and Concept Exploration Project (SPACE) (1989-92) *Research Reports*. Liverpool: Liverpool University Press.

Scott, P., Dyson, T. and Gater, S. (1987) *A Constructivist View of Learning and Teaching in Science*. Children's Learning in Science Project, Leeds: Centre for Studies in Science and Mathematics Education.

Shayer, M. and Adey, P. (1981) *Towards a Science of Science Teaching*. London: Heinemann.

Steffe, L. P. and Gale, J. (eds) (1995) *Constructivism in Education*. Hove: Lawrence Erlbaum.

Von Glasersfeld, E. (1989) 'Learning as a constructive activity', in Murphy, P. and Moon, B (eds) *Developments in Learning and Assessment*. London: Hodder and Stoughton.

Von Glasersfeld, E. (1995a) 'A Constructivist Approach to Teaching', in Steffe, L. P. and Gale, J. (eds) *Constructivism in Education*. New Jersey: Lawrence Erlbaum.

Von Glasersfeld, E. (1995b) *Radical Constructivism: A Way of Knowing and Learning*. London: Falmer.

Vygotsky, L. S. (1962) *Thought and Language*. Massachusetts: The MIT Press.

Waldrop, M. M. (1994) *Complexity. The Emerging Science at the Edge of Order and Chaos*. London: Penguin.

Wheatley G. H. (1991) 'Constructivist Perspectives on Science and Mathematics Learning', *Science Education* **75**, 9–21.

Wittrock, M. C. (1977) *Learning and Instruction*. Berkeley: McCutcheon.

Wolpert, L. (1992) *The Unnatural Nature of Science*. London: Faber.

CHAPTER 2

Teaching for constructive learning

Michael Littledyke

The principles of constructivism and the rationale for adopting these in approaches to teaching were presented and contrasted with positivism in chapter one. This discussion provides a justification for constructivist pedagogy, though Brooks and Brooks (1993) and Steffe and Gale (1995) offer a more extensive background for interested readers.

Although applied previously most extensively to scientific and mathematical concept formation, constructivist principles also have application to other domains of learning. This chapter will examine the implications for approaches to teaching and learning across the curriculum. However, before we turn to this, it is important to dispel a few misconceptions which some may have about the implications of constructivist principles to teaching.

WHAT CONSTRUCTIVE TEACHING IS NOT

It should be clear from the discussion in chapter one that the constructivist principles of teaching and learning supported here represent a balance between meaningful personal construction of knowledge and a curriculum which is formed from educationally desirable social constructs. However, some may mistakenly see constructivist teaching as being preoccupied with individual views at the expense of established knowledge, as expressed sometimes by cynical remarks such as 'I hope the aeroplane I'm about to fly in was not made by constructivists'. Constructivism is not about individuals learning in a knowledge vacuum. Clearly there are important curricular objectives for learning which are presently embodied in the National Curriculum. The central message of this book is that in teaching to these objectives children's experiences and views must be taken into account if constructive learning is to take place; that is, learning which is meaningful, lasting and transferable to other contexts. It should be emphasised, therefore, that this is not so-called 'discovery learning' where children may be expected to find out principles through their own unaided investigation. The role of the teacher in facilitating constructive learning of identified curricular objectives is centrally important. (However, it is also understood that children will also learn in ways which cannot always be predicted, hence learning will inevitably be wider and more complex than the objectives set.)

In addition, it should be made clear that constructivist teaching does not imply individualised curricula. Teachers cannot practically respond in detail to all possible children's experiences and views in an individualised way. However, knowing the common experiences and views which are likely to influence learning is very important for achieving constructive learning within a group.

Hence strategies for finding out such information and acting on it are a key feature of constructive teaching. Within such a teaching climate, where children's views are actively considered, individuals will be able to test their own understanding against experiences initiated by the teacher (as well from their own investigations) and against the views of others in the group.

Constructivist teaching, then, is not about 'putting the clock back' to what were once described as the days of 'child-centred' or 'progressive' teaching, though constructivist teaching certainly acknowledges the child as the constructor of his or her own learning. The significant difference from 'progressive' education, which focused primarily on the developmental needs of individuals, is that we now recognise more fully the centrally important role of social constructivism in the process of individual learning in a context of social interaction as well as in the actual construction of the curriculum. This gives status to the sharing of individual views and experiences as well as to establishing content to be learned, as identified in the National Curriculum.

So, having established what constructivist teaching is not, we will now turn to what it may mean for the learning domains embodied in the subjects of the National Curriculum.

CONSTRUCTIVE TEACHING ACROSS THE CURRICULUM

Constructivist principles, as established in science and mathematics education, clearly apply to other curricular areas which involve concept formation within the effective learning domain, such as concepts of place in geography, or how evidence is constructed to formulate interpretations of the past in history. However, constructivist principles also apply to affective learning domains. Thought does not take place in a vacuum, and feelings of various kinds are always associated with thinking. This is confirmed by neurological tests which show that the limbic system of the brain and the endocrine system, both associated with emotion, are also activated when the cerebral cortex, associated with reasoning and other cognitive functions, is active. The body, in fact, is an integrated system where effective and affective functions are closely linked, where the physical and physiological are interdependent, where cognition is influenced by moral, spiritual and aesthetic inclinations, as well as by memory and existing concepts (Pinel 1993).

Constructive learning is a term we use here to extend the constructivist analysis to include other forms of learning. The implications are that physical, emotional, aesthetic, moral and spiritual development are also influenced by experience, hence children come to any lesson with an array of resources which they will draw on, and hopefully extend, if learning is to be successful. Programmes of teaching should therefore take these resources into account.

However, in developing appropriate constructive approaches to learning it is also important to be aware of the implications of positivist approaches. Positivist assumptions can prevail in any area of teaching, leading to restricted approaches to teaching and inhibiting meaningful learning in children. For instance:

- Teaching based predominantly on presenting subject-based 'facts' and prescribed procedures may result in a degree of memory-based learning, but it will fail to engage children in meaningful learning which can be applied to understand the world outside the classroom. This is true particularly of subjects such as science, mathematics, geography and history.

- Language teaching which sees children as passive absorbers of 'correct' approaches to English may inculcate a degree of accuracy in language in some respects, but this approach is unlikely to develop literate, imaginative and critical adults who are also motivated to read and to extend their language capacities.
- Approaches to physical education (PE) which prescribe movement in restricted ways will not allow the children to explore and develop their individual physical potential or help them to become aware of their own bodies.
- Art education which does not draw on the children's own aesthetic sense and previous aesthetic experience is unlikely to develop aesthetically sensitive and aware individuals.
- Music education which does not offer opportunities for children to explore their individual responses to music through music appreciation and composition through improvisation will fail to develop creativity or sensitivity and appreciation of music.
- Approaches to design and technology (DT) which present solutions which do not draw on the children's inventive resources and existing experiences of design in their environment will not result in understanding of the 'design and make' process and will inhibit the development of DT capability.
- Information and communications technology (ICT) education which prescribes use of particular software in narrow ways will fail to draw on the great potential of children's home experience with computers, as well as missing the point of ICT education in developing practical understanding of computers as a tool for learning and exchange of ideas.
- Religious education (RE) syllabi which merely present the details of religions may not engage the children's spiritual awareness and experience and hence become sterile and miss the non-rational heart, purpose and object of religion.
- Teaching programmes which only prescribe what is right and wrong may prevent children from testing their own perspectives and fail to help them develop an owned sense of morality which they put into practice in their lives. This applies to interpersonal relations as well as attitudes to self (as in health issues), to other living things, and to wider environmental issues.

Positivist assumptions about education can result in instrumental approaches to teaching and learning which commonly produce rote learning without meaningful understanding. In such educational environments children tend to form two opposing construct models; a *life world* and a *school world*. The *school world* model can involve parroting information transmitted through the classroom and is created to satisfy adult demands in the educational world, including those of teachers and parents, or as a strategy to meet assessment requirements. In contrast, the *life world* model is the one which is believed and used in the everyday world, though this may not match what is educationally desirable. It is the central challenge for teachers to help children form constructs from school experiences which are also incorporated into life world models. Hence, teaching which draws on children's resources and previous experience, in a constructivist sense, and which actively encourages sharing of views and experiences, will help children to develop personal constructs which make sense of the curriculum as they experience it and to use these constructs actively in their lives. This approach is illustrated in chapter six, for example, which shows how meaningful understanding of key scientific concepts is essential for understanding many environmental problems. This understanding provides a strong rationale for environmental action leading to a greater chance of producing environmentally sensitive adults. This link between science and environmental education is evidenced by the enhanced environmental awareness and strong support for environmental education in teachers who have a good scientific background (Littledyke 1997b).

PRINCIPLES OF CONSTRUCTIVE LEARNING AND TEACHING

Constructive learning applies to areas of experience involving the whole person, as well as to cognitive learning. Constructive learning is essentially meaningful learning. Meaningful learning, in this context, applies both to concepts and to experiences which have value when they lead to purposeful engagement in real life or new situations.

The elements of constructive learning across the curriculum follow. These are drawn from constructivist principles and include affective and physical learning domains in addition to the effective domain (adapted from Driver and Bell 1986):

A constructive view of learning

1. Learning outcomes depend not only on the learning environment but also on the prior experiences, knowledge, attitudes and goals of the learner.
   The learner's previous experience matters.
2. Learning involves the development of effective, affective and physical constructs through experience in the physical and social environment.
   Individuals construct their own meaning and response to their environment, which may involve effective, affective or physical processes.
3. Constructing links with prior experience is an active process involving comparison, checking and restructuring of effective, affective and physical constructs.
   The construction of meaning and affective or physical responses to the environment is a continuous and active process.
4. Learning is not simply a matter of adding to or extending constructs, but may involve their radical re-organisation.
   Learning may involve effective, affective or physical change.
5. Meanings, once constructed, can be accepted or rejected.
   The construction of meaning and affective or physical responses to the environment does not always lead to belief or affective or physical change.
6. Learning is not passive. Individuals are purposive beings who set their own goals and control their own learning.
   Learners have the final responsibility for their own learning.

7. Students frequently bring similar experiences to the classroom. This is hardly surprising when one considers the extent of shared experiences: school life, hobbies, clubs, television, magazines, music etc.
   Some constructed meanings are shared through social interaction, including shared views, shared affective experience, or physical change through learning from others' actions.

Following on from this, a series of phases for teaching strategies to foster constructive learning across the curriculum can also be drawn from the recommended approach to constructivist teaching for concept development (adapted from Scott *et al.* 1987):

A teaching approach based on a constructive view of learning

ORIENTATION
Arousing children's interest, curiosity and motivation.
ELICITATION/STRUCTURING
Helping children to find out and clarify what they think, feel or are able to do.
INTERVENTION/RESTRUCTURING
Encouraging children to test their ideas, feelings or physical capabilities: to extend, develop or modify them.
REVIEW
Helping children to recognise the significance of what they have found out or what has been achieved.
APPLICATION
Helping children to relate what they have learned or achieved to their everyday lives or to meaningful activity.

The role of assessment in constructive learning and teaching

Assessment is an essential diagnostic instrument for teaching for constructive learning. This ensures that planned activities are matched to challenge and extend children's experiences and abilities so that appropriate and meaningful learning is achieved. Assessment is an integral part of the National Curriculum in which teacher assessment and Standard Assessment Tasks are used for summative reporting of children's attainments, while ongoing formative assessment is used to inform and modify teaching in the light of children's responses to particular teaching programmes. The principles of constructive learning acknowledge the importance of such formative and summative assessment procedures. In addition, elicitation of children's ideas, attitudes, experiences or values at the beginning of a programme provides essential formative assessment information which the teacher can draw on for planning and responding to children's starting points.

Good teaching practices have always been responsive and modified in the light of children's learning. Also, responsive teachers have always adopted an array of assessment strategies to inform them of how children are responding to their teaching. Constructive learning draws on such good practice. However, it is also characterised by its emphasis on finding out and responding to children's starting points. This forms essential information which a teacher can use to challenge strongly held misconceptions. For example, children who believe that objects sink when they have holes in them can be challenged to test this hypothesis by putting holes in a range of objects, including, say, balsa wood, a floating plasticine boat, among others, to see if this always make objects sink. Children need a wide range of appropriate experiences before they are able to grasp generalised principles, such as the concept of density (or 'how heavy an object is for its size') which is necessary to understand floating and sinking. If the experiences are presented in the context of their own existing views there is a greater possibility of constructive learning than if they are presented out of context.

It should be re-emphasised that it is not practically possible for teachers to respond to all individual starting points, though during teaching interventions teachers will inevitably respond individually to children as well as to the group as a whole. However, it is important to find out what the common starting points may be, so that these can be taken into account in teaching. A range of resources and strategies are available for eliciting such starting points:

1. Records

There is an increasing amount of information kept on children as record keeping is developed. If the information is passed on with the children it can act as a useful source for learning what the children have already experienced and/or learned at the beginning of the school year.

2. Listening carefully to children's responses

This is an important strategy for which one needs to make time. Much can be revealed by the way children talk to each other or to the teacher. The way in which they use words helps the teacher to assess the nature of their understanding. It can, in a teaching sense, help teachers to devise 'the next question' which encourages the child to refine, extend or modify her/his ideas.

'Brainstorming' can give the teacher a general idea of the knowledge within the class. The teacher leads a discussion on a topic to draw out a range of ideas. From this the teacher may be able to judge which children are most or least knowledgeable. However, there may be several children within the class about whom the teacher knows very little even after the brainstorming session. It can be useful, therefore, to find out ideas in a more systematic way. For example, ask children to tell their friend what they think about a question before hearing answers from the class as a whole, then children can identify which views they agree with by raising their hands. This helps the children to engage actively in the questions and not be passive observers of others. It also helps them to clarify their own thinking about the topic. This is an important feature of constructive learning, as new ideas and experiences may actively contradict existing views. When the child can see how initial ideas do not fit later observations s/he is more likely to take on another model to explain them. This process of systematic elicitation also informs the teacher about who thinks what.

In recording such discussions the teacher may merely make mental notes or make written collated notes on a board, overhead projection transparency or large sheets of paper. These written notes can be taken from the brainstorm in the form of a web or as lists of points. 'Floor books' are often used by teachers of young children. In these the children's statements are written down in a large sugar paper book or on paper which is stuck into the book later. These records help the children to see what views are held, helping them to clarify their own understanding. They can also be referred to directly later so that children's views can be challenged and extended during the teaching. Records of activities during the teaching programme and summative views at the end can also be added to provide a map of the children's learning. This helps consolidate the children's own learning as well as providing assessment evidence for reporting purposes.

3. Observing children engaged in elicitation activities

Teachers will gain much information from observing children engaged in activity which can be set up as part of an elicitation exercise to find out the children's starting points in a project. This could include, for example, ball skills activities in physical education if subsequent differentiation for ability is considered to be desirable. Watching children's behaviour and listening to discussion in small group activity over a range of subject areas will also be valuable. Audio-video recording, or use of an extra adult observer, if that is possible, can also be employed to provide further information about the children's responses outside the immediate influence of the teacher.

elicitation of small group work.

4. Children's recording

Children can be asked to represent their own views, experiences or attitudes as individuals or in groups. Children's *writing* is a commonly used assessment tool. Clearly, the important issue for the teacher when assessing it is to have relevant criteria in mind which relate to the knowledge and skills which are revealed through the writing. The teacher will also want to make a judgement each time about the extent of correction of technical writing errors. Diaries as 'learning logs' of the children before, during and at the end of a project can enable children to identify and consolidate key points in their own learning. These logs can be recorded individually, as part of collaborative group activity or as collations of class learning. This process can also provide valuable assessment evidence for the teacher.

Discussions in small groups can be audio recorded and listened to later, though this can be time consuming. It may be best to provide a structure for such discussions. An example of this is in a project on attitudes to fairness, when each child was asked to complete the statement 'I think it is unfair when . . .' and each child took turns until everyone had exhausted their ideas. This formed the basis for designing a drama teaching programme exploring issues of fairness through drawing on the children's common attitudes and experiences. In this programme role plays were developed which used common scenarios created from the elicitation statements. The children explored feelings and attitudes of all the fictitious characters, so getting insight into how different people can experience real social problems (Littledyke 1998).

Where writing may form a barrier to full revelation of the child's understanding *drawings* can provide a good means to communication. They can also be used as a focus for subsequent discussion with the child which might enable the teacher to probe further the child's knowledge and understanding. Drawings are particularly useful to provide a pictorial understanding of concepts when words alone are less suitable, e.g. parts of the body.

Alternatively, *annotated drawings* or *posters* can offer useful ways of allowing older children to demonstrate their knowledge and can help the teacher to find out about a wide range of children's views or experiences. These can also offer a focus for further exploration and can be an appropriate way of representing concepts linked to experiences, e.g. how we hear sounds.

Similarly, *concept maps* showing connections between ideas are effective ways to find out how much children know about a topic (see, for example, Stow 1997). A common approach is to write key words with link statements, e.g.

sun .... makes it grow .... plant

The teacher may provide key words, but, more usefully for assessment purposes, the children can provide their own. More complex connections can be made through connecting words by arrows and words to make a web of ideas. This can be done by individual children, by small groups together, or by a class brainstorm, led by and recorded by the teacher. The teacher can help with recording the ideas for individuals or small groups of children who cannot write quickly, but this is more time consuming, Stimulus picture cards can also be used to find out about children's views, and this is particularly useful for younger children. Concept maps can be created either by the teacher recording the children's ideas, or by the children themselves, from such stimuli.

Attitude scales are sometimes used to assess views and commonly appear in questionnaires for adults. These include statements with up to seven point scales including the range 'strongly agree' to 'strongly disagree'. Scales which show smiling or sad faces for agree or disagree can be used with children, though it is best to talk it through with them as they complete the questions. A three point (younger children) or five point (older children) scale is most appropriate, with a neutral face at the mid point for not sure and a question over another face alongside the scale for don't understand.

5. Reference to research findings

Teachers may also wish to refer to the extensive research into children's learning in addition to finding out about the children in their particular class. This is particularly well established in science where children's common views over a range of topics have been identified (e.g. SPACE 1989–92, Nuffield Primary Science 1995).

All the above strategies for assessment can be applied at any stage of a teaching cycle for formative or summative purposes. Figure 2.1 shows how teaching for constructive learning involves assessment at various stages in a teaching programme and is integral to the process.

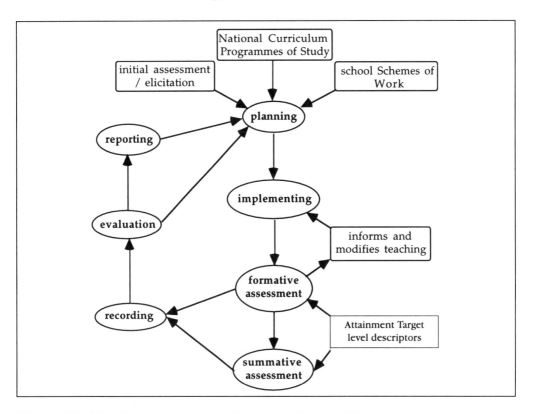

Figure 2.1 Teacher assessment and constructive teaching

TEACHING AND LEARNING: A SHARED EXPERIENCE

The principles of constructive teaching and learning apply particularly to approaches to children's learning, but teachers are also involved in constructing views and strategies for teaching as part of their own professional development. Learning in the classroom can be seen as a collaborative process and a shared experience where children and teachers are learning together, though the primary focus of the learning is different. In this the children engage in developing meaningful constructs from the planned curriculum while teachers form constructs about how to help them learn.

Figure 2.2 shows the factors influencing teachers' professional development, enhancing their abilities to facilitate learning in children. Constructive learning by children is greatly influenced by the professional skill of the teacher in organising the learning environment. This involves developing professional constructs drawn from understanding of curriculum content, how children learn in a generic sense, the developing personal and shared constructs of the children in the class, and developing understanding and skill in effective planning and intervention in teaching. This is an ongoing feature of the reflective teacher (Schon 1987) which involves modification and ongoing improvement of practice influenced by evaluation of children's learning in response to teaching activities. This also includes a synthesis of 'theory and practice' in which knowledge of educational theory about teaching and learning first encountered in initial teacher education

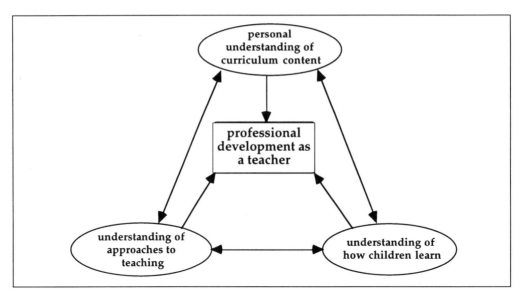

Figure 2.2 The factors influencing teachers' professional development

courses is complemented by developing practical knowledge built up from first hand experience.

Figure 2.3 shows the dynamic relationships of learning in a curriculum orientated towards constructive learning. Children's personal constructs are developed in response to planned activities as they draw on previous experience, attitudes, skills, knowledge and understanding. They are also influenced by other views and experiences initiated by other children or the teacher. Thus, children's

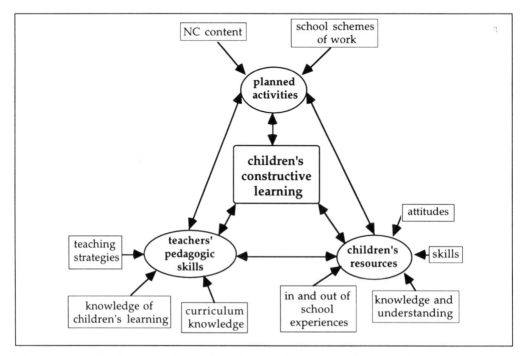

Figure 2.3 The factors influencing children's constructive learning

shared constructs are established through group interaction, which can influence personal construct formation. The teacher also develops a construct system which is orientated to effective teaching. This involves utilising the children's previous experiences to inform the teaching through knowing about the children's learning and achievements as well as the wider social constructs which form educationally worthwhile learning objectives: these, in the present educational context, mainly consist of the National Curriculum Programmes of Study. The school Schemes of Work as derived from the policies for the various curriculum areas provide a structure for planning in this context. The teacher draws on her/his professional constructs to plan, organise, and implement the curriculum in a way which fully engages the children in constructive learning.

While it is clear that too tightly prescribed outcomes may inhibit constructive learning, there is an important place for defined objectives in planning. In constructivist terminology, learning objectives can be viewed as those socially constructed elements which educationalists agree are important for children to learn. A clear understanding of the terrain for learning must be held by the teacher so suitable experiences can be presented to enable children to construct their learning in a way which is valuable to them individually but also inducts them into socially agreed forms of knowledge or experience which form the curriculum.

Constructive teaching and learning in the National Curriculum

Before the National Curriculum, traditions in primary education were centred on 'localised' concerns (Golby 1988) and teacher autonomy in curriculum planning. Integrated approaches to the curriculum were prevalent (though not universal) and this was supported by the curriculum review of Her Majesty's Inspectorate (DES 1985) which identified nine 'areas of experience' as a basis for planning: the aesthetic and creative; the human and social; the linguistic and literary; the mathematical; the moral; the physical; the scientific; the spiritual; and the technological. Processes of learning were emphasised over curriculum content in a so called 'child-centred' or 'progressive' curriculum which stressed the developmental needs of children (Blenkin and Kelly 1987). In the best examples this resulted in high levels of motivation and interest in children with varied and interesting approaches to teaching and learning.

This reflects a *reconstructionist* ideology of education which sees education as a process of social change. In this process education is planned for what society ought to be rather than what it is (Scrimshaw 1983). Teachers become activators of social change through fostering a critical, analytical and active approach to learning and the curriculum is founded on principles of egalitarianism and democracy. Thus the learner is actively involved in the construction of meaning through interaction with the curriculum, which is essentially a constructivist pedagogy.

However, there were increasing criticisms of this approach to education as there was widespread inconsistency in progression and continuity in teaching in many schools. The so-called political 'New Right' had a major influence in the development of the National Curriculum in response to this (Hartnett and Naish,

1990). Greatly increased powers of the Secretary of State were enshrined in the Education Reform Act of 1988 (DES 1988) which enabled the introduction of an educational ideology founded on 'the spirit of consumerism, individual entrepreneurism and competition: the values of the market' (Tomlinson 1989, p. 275). This was part of a strategy to ensure that the 'pervasive collectivist and universalistic welfare ideology of the post-war era is restrained' (Whitty 1989, p. 331) and as an attack on progressive, child centred education. It also reflects a *revisionist* or *adaptive* approach to education in which the main purpose is to fit people into society rather than to change it.

The National Curriculum, as it developed, became predominantly knowledge centred rather than learner centred. And defined objectives for planning and assessment of learning were emphasised above processes of learning. The main features were: a subject based organisation, derived from Hirst's forms of knowledge (Hirst 1974); assessment arrangements based on children's achievement measured against defined learning objectives; reporting arrangements of assessments to parents along with more widely available 'league tables' of results; inspection arrangements to monitor and check the effectiveness of schools. This was designed to highlight the accountability of teachers and schools, so influencing parental choice of school which directly affected school funding via pupil numbers linked to funding formulae. The aim was to drive up standards through applying the principles of economic market competition to education (Littledyke 1996a).

The National Curriculum has put teachers under considerable pressure and it has come under criticism for having too much subject content. It has also reduced teacher autonomy and flexibility to respond to pupils' particular interests, and has made integrated primary planning difficult. Some of the perceived lower status foundation subjects, including the arts, as well as the cross-curricular themes (Health, Environmental education, Citizenship, Economic and Industrial Awareness) have been significantly marginalised in many schools (Littledyke 1996b, 1997b). In contrast, the content led assessment arrangements, particularly the Standard Assessment Tasks, have prioritised knowledge over processes of learning and this has driven many teachers towards instrumental approaches to teaching and learning which is counter to principles of constructive learning.

However, in spite of these problems, the National Curriculum has also produced many benefits. It has provided a structure which has certainly improved some of the previous problems of inconsistent progression and continuity in schools. Teachers have collaborated in producing policies and schemes of work which provide frameworks for planning and teaching. There have also been improvements in school development programmes through focused action plans based on identifying specific needs, implementing action, evaluating effects and monitoring further improvements. Formalised assessment procedures have also made teachers focus closely on children's learning to evaluate the effectiveness of their teaching (Littledyke 1994, 1997a).

There have certainly been some problems in recent years in adjusting to the National Curriculum, but the advantages also offer an opportunity unique in history to take stock of what we have learnt about teaching and learning and to put into practice the best of what we know to be effective. Rather than looking at what has been previously presented as opposing dichotomies of child centred/knowledge centred or reconstructive/revisionist approaches to education, we should now be finding methods of supporting children's learning in ways which will address their developmental needs as well as help them engage in and successfully interpret, and be critical of, the world which they will grow into. We need to address the learning needs of children as well as provide curriculum material which is relevant to the needs of an ever changing society. This involves taking the best from what has been learnt from the responsive and flexible approaches of so-called child-centred teaching and combining it with the systematic planning and identification of important aspects of learning from the objectives model. We should be aware of the dangers of producing 'blind spots' in learning from lack of planned structure which was a feature of the worst of progressive education. We should also be wary of overprescribed teaching approaches which fail to engage children in meaningful, constructive learning.

Teachers are now at a stage where they are familiar with the National Curriculum after initial anxiety about their abilities to implement the changes. They have been through some predictable stages in this process as defined by 'concerns theory' (House 1979). In 'concerns theory' the phases in management of any educational change include early stages of deskilling, confusion, and demoralisation, leading, in time, through degrees of familiarity and competence. Early concerns are characteristically about the details of the reforms while later concerns are about how to manage and monitor them effectively. With regard to National Curriculum response, teachers are generally now moving towards the latter stages of this process and are now more mature and competent about what they have to teach.

Teaching should reflect what we know about how children learn. Constructive teaching takes the best of past experiences in education and research in children's learning. It combines a responsive and flexible approach which recognizes children's previous experiences with acknowledging the need for planned learning objectives. It combines meaningful personal and social construct formation, which is necessary to cater for individual needs within an ever changing society. Constructive teaching and learning requires a critical view and an understanding of the limitations of the positivist assumptions which are inherent in a narrow interpretation of the National Curriculum. It also recognises that the National Curriculum can be interpreted in ways which provide opportunities for breadth of experience which is potentially enriching for children and forms a firm foundation for life.

The rest of this book will attempt to show ways in which this goal can be approached. This is clearly a vast project and we cannot possibly be comprehensive. However, our intention is to present an agenda for constructive approaches to teaching and learning across the whole primary curriculum which teachers may use to reflect on their own work and improve their children's learning. If this approach is widely adopted, as research says it should be, it will match what is known about how children learn and hopefully eventually create more sensitive and critically aware adults within a more truly educated society.

REFERENCES

Blenkin, G. M. and Kelly, A. V. (1987) *The Primary Curriculum: A Process Approach to Curriculum Planning,* 2nd edn. London: PCP.

Brooks, J. G. and Brooks, M. G. (1993) *In Search of Understanding: The Case for Constructivist Classrooms.* Alexandria, Virginia: Association for Supervision and Curriculum Development.

Department of Education and Science (DES) (1985) *Better Schools.* London: HMSO.

DES (1988) *Education Reform Act.* London: HMSO.

Driver R. and Bell, B. (1986) 'Students' thinking and the learning of science: a constructivist view', *School Science Review* **67**, 443–56.

Golby, M. (1988) 'Traditions in Primary Education', in Clarkson, M. (ed.), *Emerging Issues in Primary Education.* Lewes: Falmer.

Hartnett, A. and Naish, M. (1990) 'The sleep of reason breeds monsters: the birth of a statutory curriculum in England and Wales', *Journal of Curriculum Studies* **22**, 1–16.

Hirst, P. (1974) *Knowledge and the Curriculum: A Collection of Philosophical Papers.* London: Routledge and Kegan Paul.

House, F. R. (1979) 'Technology versus craft: a ten year perspective on innovation', *Journal of Curriculum Studies* **11**, 1–15.

Littledyke, M. (1994) 'Primary Teacher Responses to the National Curriculum for Science', *School Science Review* **75**, 106–16.

Littledyke, M. (1996a) 'Ideology, Epistemology, Pedagogy and the National Curriculum for Science: The Influence on Primary Science', *Curriculum Studies* **3**(3), 297–317.

Littledyke, M. (1996b) 'Science Education for Environmental Awareness in a Postmodern World', *Environmental Education Research* **2**(2), 197–214.

Littledyke, M. (1997a) 'Managerial Style, the National Curriculum and Teachers' Culture: Responses to Educational Change in a Primary School', *Education Research* **39**(3), 243–62.

Littledyke, M. (1997b) 'Science education for environmental education? Primary teacher perspectives and practices', *British Educational Research Journal* **23**(5), 641–59.

Littledyke, M. (1998 in press) *Live Issues: Drama Strategies for Personal, Social and Moral Education.* Birmingham: Questions.

Nuffield Primary Science (1995) *Nuffield Primary Science: Science Processes and Concept Exploration (SPACE).* London: Collins Educational.

Pinel, J. P. J. (1993) *Biopsychology.* Needham Heights, MA: Allyn and Bacon, division of Simon and Schuster.

Scott, P., Dyson, T. and Gater, S. (1987) *A Constructivist View of Learning and Teaching in Science: Children's Learning in Science Project.* Leeds: Centre for Studies in Science and Mathematics Education.

Schon, D. A. R. (1987) *The Reflective Practitioner.* London: Temple Smith.

Science Processes and Concept Exploration Project (SPACE) (1989–92) *Research Reports.* Liverpool: Liverpool University Press.

Scrimshaw, P. (1983) 'Educational Ideologies', Unit 2, E204, *Purpose and Planning in the Curriculum.* Milton Keynes: Open University Press.

Steffe, L. P. and Gale, J. (eds) (1995) *Constructivism in Education.* Hove, Lawrence Erlbaum.

Stow, W. (1997) 'Concept mapping. A tool for self-assessment?', *Primary Science Review* **49**, 12–15.

Tomlinson, J (1989) 'The Education Reform Bill – 44 years of progress?', *Journal of Education Policy* **4**, 275–9.

Whitty, G. (1989) 'The New Right and the National Curriculum: state control or market forces?', *Journal of Educational Policy* **4**, 329–41.

CHAPTER 3

Children constructing their understanding of written language

Laura Huxford

That we construct our own understanding is obviously a central tenet of this book and is probably one of the less contentious views held by the broad church of 'constructivists' (Resnick 1987). In this chapter I shall examine the proposition that in order to construct an understanding of written language, children actually need to reconstruct or recreate language for themselves. There is much documented work looking at very young children's writing and recent work on the beneficial effects of early spelling on children's acquisition of phonemic reading skills.

Children's creativity in speech development is well documented (Cruttenden 1979). While there may be a predisposition to acquire language (Chomsky 1972), environment obviously plays a substantial part in language acquisition as children pick up the language of those immediately around them. Children's universal 'babbling' takes on regional features of phoneme and intonation by approximately the age of six months (Nakazima 1975). By the time they go to school children have acquired the majority of the structures of their native language or languages. But *en route* they have communicated through the use of single words or short phrases. The word 'milk' can have a variety of meanings: 'I want some milk', 'the milk is on the floor', 'the cat is drinking milk' etc. At a later stage children pluralise nouns and construct verb endings in accordance with a pattern they have generalised from other words, so they might, for instance, say 'those mans wented'. Gradually, children acquire the phonological and syntactic features of the language of those with whom they live. Oral language learning happens as a result of hours and hours of using language in meaningful situations.

We now accept that children construct spoken language from the 'blooming buzzing confusion' around them (James 1984, p. 21). Not until fairly recently was it suggested that children might be doing something similar during their acquisition of written language. Publications under collective titles such as *Awakening to Literacy* (Goelman, Oberg and Smith 1984), *Emergent Literacy* (Teale and Sulzby 1986) and *How Children Construct Literacy* (Goodman 1986) described children's growing understanding of writing as a form of communication. Though not necessarily acknowledged by each writer, Piaget's 'scheme theory' appears to lie at the heart of the much of this work.

> In order to acquire knowledge about the writing system, children proceed in the same way as in other domains of knowledge; they try to assimilate the information provided by the environment. But when the new information is

impossible to assimilate, they very often are forced to reject it. They experiment with the object to test their hypothesis, they ask for information, and they try to make sense out of the mass of data they have assembled (Ferreiro 1986, p. 13).

COMMON FEATURES OF CHILDREN'S CONSTRUCTION

Forms of writing

The notion of children constructing their understanding of literacy by 'inventing' their own writing system is fundamental to the research. Hildreth (1936) in the USA and Luria (reprinted in Martlew, 1983) in Russia investigated children's early writing and each defined a series of stages through which they considered that children typically progressed. Both researchers claimed that children started to write with aimless, undifferentiated scribbling and moved through a phase in which they used some sort of symbol and finally into the conventional form. Ferreiro and Teberosky (1982) carried out a very detailed analysis of children's writing and their understanding of the form and function of written symbols with Spanish speaking children in South America which has provided a foundation for similar work in other languages: Hebrew (Landsmann 1986), Italian (Pontecorvo and Zucchermaglio 1986), Spanish (Grossi 1986), German (Brügelmann 1986, 1997), Norwegian (Nurss 1988), English (Clay 1975, Harste, Woodward and Burke 1984, Temple, Nathan, Burris and Temple 1988, Dobson 1989, Sulzby, Barnhart and Hieshima 1989, Allen 1989). Taken together these studies support the broad stages defined by early research suggesting a universality of development at least within alphabetic languages.

The place of scribble-writing in the continuum is unclear. Temple *et al.* (1988), Harste *et al.* (1984), Sulzby, Barnhart and Hieshima (1989), Dobson (1989) and Allen (1989) all report children using scribble-writing, but not necessarily as the earliest stage. Where scribble-writing occurs there appear to be two distinct types. At first children scribble in an arbitrary fashion which might be imitative of adult behaviour; no indication is given that they connect these marks with 'something which could be read'. Harste *et al.* (1984), in fact, found that the form of each child's scribble is similar to the writing of their own country's language. At a later stage children connect their scribble with a message and run their fingers along it as they pretend to read, modifying the rate of their fingers to fit with the length of the story, or track the lines of print several times until they complete the story (Dobson 1989, Sulzby, Barnhart and Hieshima 1989).

Ferreiro and Teberosky (1982) considered that the earliest stage in writing is the point at which children differentiate drawing from writing. They pointed out that the physical action of each process was the same, producing straight and curved lines and dots, but that the organisation of the marks was different for writing and drawing in two distinct ways; written symbols did not take on the shape of the object to which they referred (the referent) and they were ordered in a linear fashion. At this earliest stage the defining features of a 'word' were that it should contain no fewer than three letters and that the letters should not be repeated; these rules were consistently held across most of their sample. They also found that the children adopted the letters which they encountered around them when constructing their 'words' rather than devising novel symbols. Other studies tend to show a similar trait particularly with the letters of the child's own name (Landsmann 1986), although they also report the use of numbers (e.g. Brügelmann 1986) and symbols derived from conventional letters (Pontecorvo and Zuccermaglio 1986).

Having established that 'words' can represent objects, Ferreiro and Teberosky (1982) observed children struggling to make a word carry some identifiable feature which would relate it to its referent, i.e. give the 'word' something to indicate its meaning. Children managed this by differentiating the number of letters. Objects which were larger, older or more abundant than others in the text were written with more letters than smaller, younger and fewer objects; however, no word was still able to be fewer than three letters. Other studies have reported children writing words using larger or smaller letters to denote the size of the referent. Landsmann working with children in Israel found that sometimes children tried to 'accommodate the shape of the letters to the shape of the object they were trying to represent' (1986, p. 33). Her example includes a child who used straight letters to write the word 'rope' and round letters in the word 'ball'. She also describes children writing words in colour to depict the colour of the referent.

Speech written down

The next stage which is identified by all researchers in this field, but which is less clearly defined by some, is referred to as the 'syllabic stage'. This stage represents a totally new realisation on the part of the child; for the first time the written word is seen as having a connection (other than semantic) with the spoken or heard word. Children can segment words or the speech stream into syllables and then attempt to accommodate this element of language into their writing by representing each syllable by a letter. Ferreiro and Teberosky (1982) found that some children wrote arbitrary letters for each syllable while others represented each syllable by the initial phoneme of the syllable. It could be argued that the former is an earlier stage. However, there are not many reported examples of this phenomenon. It is possible that recognition of syllables within the speech stream necessarily coincides with an ability to identify the initial phoneme of the syllable and that the children who appear to use arbitrary letters to denote syllables do so because they do not know the correct letter for the initial phoneme of each syllable. At first glance this hypothesis seems to contradict the considerable amount of research into children's phonemic development vis-a-vis 'syllable segmentation' preceding 'phonemic segmentation' (e.g. Fox and Routh 1976, Liberman and Shankweiler 1979, Treiman and Baron 1981). But, in fact, these studies merely differentiate between children who can segment the speech stream into the correct number of syllables and then segment a word into the correct number of phonemes; they do not ask the same children to segment into syllables and identify the initial phoneme of those syllables.

Whether the syllabic stage is triggered by phonemic awareness or not, children who incorporate letters into their writing to denote syllables 'struggle between two parameters' (Landsmann 1986, p. 35). Children are forced to reconcile their own rule of three letters being the minimum requirement for a word with the number of syllables they can hear in the word. This, according to Ferreiro (1986), is more difficult for English than Spanish speakers because English contains a higher proportion of one- and two-syllable words than Spanish. This 'rich conflict' is illustrated by Grossi (1986) who described Esther's writing of her own name. She appeared quite content to write it conventionally until she reached the syllabic writing stage. At this point she began to write her name 'ET', the correct initial phoneme for each syllable of the word. Those who have studied children's writing in this detail have observed that as children become more aware of the connection between the spoken and written form of words they abandon their previously constructed rules of a minimum requirement of three letters per word (Ferreiro and Teberosky 1982, Grossi 1986, Landsmann 1986).

Once children have made that conceptual connection between a word's written and spoken attributes and they learn the specific associations between phonemes (sounds) and letter-shapes, the opportunity for writing words which other people can decipher significantly increases. Read's (1971) research on a cohort of about twenty children provided the foundation for a number of further projects into children's 'invented spelling' (e.g. Clay 1975, Bissex 1980, Henderson and Beers 1980, Gentry 1981). The body of research shows that children's acuity for sound patterns in words and their inventiveness for using their limited knowledge of the orthography to denote the sounds they can hear appears to be considerable. Bissex's five-year-old son, Paul, used his knowledge of letter-names to write the message 'Are you deaf?' as 'RUDF' where the letter names R and U stood for the words 'are' and 'you' and the word 'deaf' is represented by its initial and final phonemes (Bissex 1980).

> HOW R YOU WAN YOU GAD A CHANS SAND IS OL I LEDR.
> AD DOW GT ANE CHRIBLS (age 4)
> (How are you? When you get a chance send us all a letter.
> And don't get any troubles) (Read 1975, p.329).

This message also has examples of different spelling strategies. Certain words are correctly spelled such as 'YOU'. Like the Bissex example, letter names stand for whole words, e.g. R. It would appear that all the remaining words in the message were spelled using a phonemic strategy, that is, by matching the phonemes which the children perceived in words to their current knowledge of graphemes. Like Paul Bissex, the preschool children in this study knew the names of the letters in the alphabet so the phonemes were matched to the most appropriate sound of the letter-name. Read (1971) believed that this might explain some of the choices of vowels. All but one of the vowel-names (E) are diphthongs (A, I, O, U) which, in simple phonetic terms, means that they consist of two phonemes. It is conjectured that children can hear, or feel in the articulation, the different phonemes within the sounds of the vowel-names. (The articulatory relationship between letter-names and phonemes varies with the accent of the speaker. The children in Read's (1971, 1975) study were American.) An examination of the letters used in one of the misspelled words in the above message, GAD (get) illustrates how it is thought that children make choices of letters when spelling words. The child has identified the three phonemes in this word. The choice of vowel letter would probably have been dictated by his limited knowledge of letter-sound correspondence. The letter name A is not dissimilar to the phoneme normally represented by a short 'e'. The choice of a 'd' rather than an 't' to end the word can be explained by an American accent.

It could be argued that Read's (1975) explanations for the choice of letters in these spellings are speculative. In his defence Read (1986) drew attention to the corpus of over 11,000 spellings of individual phonemes which he catalogued, and the consistency with which different children produced the same incorrect letters throughout. From his examination of this corpus he concluded that:

- Children seemed to choose the nearest equivalent vowel name for a wide variety of vowel sounds according to place of articulation, so that 'bait', 'bet', 'bat' and even 'bent' might be spelled 'BAT'.
- Children seemed to be unable to represent pre-consonantal nasals, e.g. 'n' in 'bent', until fairly late in their development as they perceived them to be part of the vowel sound. (This was not the case in the message quoted earlier – 'SAND')
- Consonant blends such as 'tr' and 'dr' were regularly perceived and written as the affricates 'CH' (or as in the example, 'CHR') and 'J'.

Read's work has provoked considerable interest and formed the basis for a number of experimental (Perin 1983, Treiman 1985a, 1985b, 1991, Richgels 1986, Cataldo and Ellis 1988, Clarke 1988), and observational studies (Clay 1989, Tierney, Caplan, Ehri, Healey and Hurdlow 1989, Sulzby, Teale and Kamberelis, 1989). For example, Treiman (1991) replicated the work on the children's confusion between 'tr' and 'chr' with 112 children (age-range 70–93 months) from middle and upper middle-class backgrounds. Further work on initial consonant clusters (e.g. 'sl' or 'pr') was carried out with a class of forty-three first-grade, middle-class children, aged 72–84 months (Treiman 1991). A longitudinal study by Cataldo and Ellis (1988) examined twenty-eight British children, aged 48–60 months. They tracked their developing use of letters in words and found a similar pattern to that described by Read. Gentry's (1981) five-stage model describes the development in children's spelling as it has emerged in the research. It could be summarised by the different spelling versions of, for instance, the word 'stopped'. Children at the earliest stage (precommunicative) are likely to write the words using a random assortment of letters, followed by 'spt' (semiphonetic stage), 'stopt' (phonetic stage) and 'stoped' at the transitional stage, culminating in the correct form.

LITERACY INSTRUCTION

We have here abundant evidence that children can construct their own writing systems. It could be argued that while this is an interesting revelation of children's ability, it has no bearing on literacy instruction as it would be much more efficient to tell children how to write than have them wasting time 'discovering' it for themselves. However, much of this research was carried out with children who were receiving literacy instruction. For instance, Esther had been taught to write her name, but its spelling conflicted with her own understanding of how words came into being (Grossi 1986). A literate environment and direct instruction can furnish a child with the motive and the tools for writing (e.g. form, letters, direction) but it appears that some children need to go through the process of constructing organisational principles in learning to write as they do in other cognitive processes. 'If these organisational principles are strong enough to override orthographic systems, they probably override instructional methodologies as well. Therefore, some strong advice to teachers: If you can't fight them, join them.' (Landsmann 1986, p. 41). The important thing to remember here is that children are not constructing written language from nothing. Usually they have a spoken language and some form of written language environment. Their attention is drawn to the elements of that language not only in the manner in which they are depicted in public print such as enlarged, colourful, interesting fonts on advertisements, labels and packaging, but also in specifically designed television programmes such as 'Sesame Street' which highlight aspects of writing. Spelling phonemically requires an ability to isolate sounds in words and a knowledge of letter-sound correspondence. The ability to isolate sounds is a result of verbal play usually rooted in a tradition of nursery rhymes (Chukovsky 1971). Children without such experience have been shown to be unable to manipulate sounds in words (Maclean *et al.* 1987). Similarly, whether it is learned through exposure to books, street signs or taught explicitly, there is a body of knowledge required in order to match speech sounds to their correct letter shapes. So while there is an element of 'invention', the process is more one of accommodation and assimilation.

It appears, also, that allowing children to construct their understanding of the phonemic system through writing has a beneficial effect on reading. A number of reports have indicated that children acquire the phonemic principle in spelling before reading and have concluded that phonemic spelling is therefore a precursor to phonemic reading. As long ago as 1912, Montessori observed that children at the 'phonetic' stage could spell simple words correctly but were unable to read them. For example, if a child wanted to spell the word 'pot', he or she could figure out the component sounds p-o-t and find the letters which corresponded to those sounds. However, when asked to read the word the child might be able to say the sounds of the letters correctly but would be unable to blend them together to pronounce the word. Chomsky (1979) went so far as to recommend that children be taught to write before they were taught to read because she believed that writing prepared children for the process of reading. Bryant and Bradley (1980) also noticed this trait during informal observations and devised a study to investigate it further. They asked children to read a group of words and then later to spell them. Some of the phonemically regular words such as 'bun' and 'mat' were spelled correctly by some children who could not subsequently read them, indicating that the children could construct the words for spelling purposes using letter-sound correspondence but did not yet have the words in their reading lexicon, and were also unable to use a 'word-building' phonemic strategy to read them. There were examples of other words which the children could both read and spell and others which they could read but not spell. This latter category contained irregular words which could not be spelled accurately using simple letter to sound matching.

In a more recent study with Spanish children, Borzone de Manrique and Signorini (1994) also found that there were words which children could spell but could not read. Huxford, Terrell and Bradley (1992) investigated this phenomenon further in a longitudinal study which traced the development of children's ability to read and spell phonemically. The children were asked to read and spell a list of phonemically regular words. This procedure was repeated at intervals throughout the study. At each test-point almost all the children scored better at spelling than reading, suggesting that the ability to spell phonemically precedes the ability to read phonemically. A study by Cataldo and Ellis (1988) proposed a causal relationship between spelling and reading; by subjecting their data to path analysis they suggested that 'the use of an alphabetic strategy in reading is derived from spelling experience' (p. 105). On the assumption that phonemic spelling necessitated the ability to segment phonemes in words and that phonemic reading necessitated an element of blending phonemes to pronounce words, Huxford, Terrell and Bradley (1992) also asked children to segment and blend a list of words. Results showed that children were able to segment consonant-vowel-consonant words (e.g. 'peg') earlier than they could blend them. In their studies, Byrne and Fielding-Barnsley (1989) and Iversen and Tunmer (1993) found children who could either blend and segment or segment but not blend. They found no children who could blend but not segment. Other studies by Fox and Routh (1976, 1984) and Yopp and Singer (1985) showed that only the children who were already accomplished at segmentation benefited from training in blending. Lewkowitz (1980) considered that children should be taught to blend by teaching segmentation first, 'just as practice in taking apart alarm clocks, for example, might aid in learning to put them together again' (p. 696). This reiterates Chomsky's view:

> Children's minds at four, five, six are far from linguistic empty space into which reading information is to be poured. What I propose is that children be permitted to be active participants in teaching themselves to read. In fact, they ought to direct the process. By reversing the usual order of read first, write later, this can be allowed to happen. (1971, p. 296)

Children construct their understanding of written language using the building blocks they find around them. They see written language and they see people writing and they apply their limited understanding of its purpose and form to their own writing. When they construct a fresh hypothesis about an element of the form, they have to readjust their existing framework of rules. Recognition of a direct relationship between the sounds in words and the marks on the page is a major breakthrough in constructing an understanding of writing and this also appears to have a spin-off into reading. Strickland (1989) writes:

> the new paradigms for learning and teaching suggest that children come to school with a great deal of knowledge about language and literacy, that effective instruction makes use of what children already know about language and supports continued growth of that knowledge, and that all that is known and learned is valued as a significant part of a life-long continuum of reading and writing development (p. 294).

REFERENCES

Allen, J. (1989) 'Reading and writing development in whole language kindergartens', in Mason, J. (ed.) *Reading and Writing Connections.* Needham Heights, MA.: Allyn and Bacon.

Bissex, G. (1980) *GNYS AT WRK: A child learns to write and read.* Cambridge, MA: Harvard University Press.

Borzone de Manrique, A. M. and Signorini, A. (1994) 'Phonological awareness, spelling and reading abilities in Spanish speaking children', *British Journal of Educational Psychology* **64**, 429–39.

Brügelmann, H. (1986) 'Discovering print – a process approach to initial reading and writing in West Germany', *The Reading Teacher* **40**(3), 294–8.

Brügelmann, H. (1997) 'From invention to convention', Paper presented to the International conference 'Integrating research and practice in literacy' at the London Institute of Education, March 1997.

Bryant, P. E. and Bradley, L. L. (1980) 'Why children sometimes write words which they do not read', in Frith, U. (ed.) *Cognitive Processes in Spelling.* London: Academic Press.

Byrne, B. and Fielding-Barnsley, R. (1989) 'Phonemic awareness and letter knowledge in the child's acquisition of the alphabetic principle', *Journal of Educational Psychology* **81**, 313–21.

Cataldo, S. and Ellis, N. (1988) 'Interactions in the development of spelling, reading and phonological skills', *Journal of Research in Reading* **11**(2), 86–109.

Chomsky, C. (1971) 'Write first, read later', *Childhood Education* **476**, 296–9.

Chomsky, C. (1979) 'Approaching reading through invented spelling', in Resnick, L.B. and Weaver, P. A. (eds) *Theory and Practice of Early Reading.* Hillsdale, N.J.: Erlbaum.

Chomsky, N. (1972) *Language and Mind.* New York: Harcourt Brace Jovanovich.

Chukovsky, K. (1971) *From Two to Five.* Berkeley and Los Angeles: University of California Press.

Clarke, L. K. (1988) 'Invented versus traditional spelling in first graders' writings: effects on learning to spell and read', *Research in the Teaching of English* **22**(3), 281–309.

Clay, M. (1975) *What Did I Write?* London: Heinemann.

Clay, M. (1989) *Writing Begins at Home.* Auckland: Heinemann.

Cruttenden, A. (1979) *Language in Infancy and Childhood.* Manchester: Manchester University Press.

Dobson, L. (1989) 'Connections in learning to write and read: a study of children's development through kindergarten and first grade', in Mason, J. (ed.) *Reading and Writing Connections.* Needham Heights, MA: Allyn and Bacon.

Ferreiro, E. (1986) 'Literacy development: psychogenesis', in Goodman, Y. (ed.) *How Children Construct Literacy.* Newark, Delaware: International Reading Association.

Ferreiro, E. and Teberosky, A. (1982) *Literacy before Schooling.* London: Heinemann Educational Books.

Fox, B. and Routh, D. K. (1976) 'Phonemic analysis and synthesis as word-attack skills', *Journal of Educational Psychology* **68**(1), 70–4.

Fox, B. and Routh, D. K. (1984) 'Phonemic analysis and synthesis as word-attack skills: revisited', *Journal of Educational Psychology* **76**(6), 1059–64.

Gentry, J. R. (1981) 'Learning to spell developmentally', *The Reading Teacher* **34**(4), 378–81.

Goelman, H., Oberg, A., Smith, F. (eds) (1984) *Awakening to Literacy.* London: Heinemann Educational.

Goodman, Y. (ed) (1986) *How Children Construct Literacy.* Newark, Delaware: International Reading Association.

Grossi, E. P. (1986) 'Applying psychogenesis principles to the literacy instruction of lower-class children in Brazil', in Goodman, Y. (ed.) *How Children Construct Literacy.* Newark, Delaware: International Reading Association.

Harste, J., Woodward, V. A., Burke, C. L. (1984) *Language Stories and Literacy Lessons.* Portsmouth, N.H.: Heinemann Educational.

Henderson, E. H. and Beers, J. W. (eds) (1980) *Developmental and Cognitive Aspects of Learning to Spell.* Newark, Delaware: International Reading Association.

Hildreth, G. (1936) 'Developmental sequences in name writing', *Child Development* **7**, 291–303.

Huxford, L. M., Terrell, C., Bradley, L. L. (1992) 'Invented spelling and learning to read', in Sterling,

C. and Robson, C. (eds) *Psychology, Spelling and Education.* Clevedon: Multilingual Matters.

Iversen, S. and Tunmer, W. E. (1993) 'Phonological processing skills and the reading recovery programme', *Journal of Educational Psychology* **85**, 112–26.

James, W. (1984) *Psychology.* New York: Harper Row.

Landsmann, L. T. (1986) 'Literacy development and pedagogical implications: evidence from the Hebrew system of writing', in Goodman, Y. (ed.) *How Children Construct Literacy.* Newark, Delaware: International Reading Association.

Lewkowicz, N. K. (1980) 'Phonemic awareness training: what to teach and how to teach it', *Journal of Educational Psychology* **72**(5), 686–700.

Liberman, I. Y. and Shankweiler, D. P. (1979) 'Speech, the alphabet and teaching to read', in Resnick, L. B. and Weaver, P. A. (eds) *Theory and Practice of Early Reading, Vol. 2.* Hillsdale N.J.: Lawrence Erlbaum Ass.

Luria, A. R. (1983) 'The development of writing in the child', in Martlew, M. (ed.) *The Psychology of Written Language: developmental and educational perspectives.* New York: Wiley.

Maclean, M., Bryant, P. E. and Bradley, L. L. (1987) 'Rhymes, nursery rhymes and reading in early childhood', *Merrill-Palmer Quarterly* **33**(3), 255–82.

Montessori, M. (1912) *The Montessori Method* (translated by Anne George). London: William Heinemann.

Nakazima, S. (1975) 'Phonemicisation and symbolisation in language development', in Lenneberg, E. H. and Lenneberg, E. (eds) *Foundations of Language Development: A multidisciplinary approach. Vol. 1.* London: Academic Press.

Nurss, J.R. (1988) 'Development of written communication in Norwegian kindergarten children', *Comparative Education* **24**(1), 33–48.

Perin, D. (1983) 'Phonemic segmentation and spelling', *British Journal of Psychology* **74**, 129–44.

Pontecorvo, C. and Zucchermaglio, C. (1986) 'A passage to literacy in a social context', in Goodman, Y. *How Children Construct Literacy.* Newark, Delaware: International Reading Association.

Read, C. (1971) 'Pre-school children's knowledge of English phonology', *Harvard Educational Review* **41**(1), 1–34.

Read, C. (1975) 'Lessons to be learned from the pre-school orthographer', in Lenneberg, E. H. and Lenneberg, E. *Foundations of Language Development: A multidisciplinary approach, Vol. 2.* N.Y.: Academic Press.

Read, C. (1986) *Children's Creative Spelling.* London: Routledge and Kegan Paul.

Resnick, L. (1987) 'Constructing knowledge in school', in Liben, L. (ed.) *Development and Learning: Conflict or Congruence?* Hillsdale, NJ: Erlbaum.

Richgels, D. J. (1986) 'Beginning first-graders' "invented spelling" ability and their performance in functional classroom writing activities', *Early Childhood Research Quarterly* **1**, 85–97.

Strickland, D. S. (1989) 'Applying a literacy perspective to early childhood curriculum', in Mason, J. M. (ed.) *Reading and Writing Connections.* Needham Heights, MA: Allyn and Bacon.

Sulzby, E., Barnhart, J., Hieshima, J. A. (1989) 'Forms of writing and rereading from writing: a preliminary report', in Mason, J. (ed.) *Reading and Writing Connections.* Needham Heights, MA: Allyn and Bacon.

Sulzby, E., Teale, W. H., Kamberelis, G. (1989) 'Emergent writing in the classroom: home and school connections', in Strickland, D. and Morrow, L. M. *Emerging literacy.* Newark, Delaware: International Reading Association.

Temple, C., Nathan, R, R., Burris, N., Temple, F. (1988) *The Beginnings of Writing.* 2nd edn. Boston: Allyn and Bacon.

Teale, W. H. and Sulzby, E. (1986) *Emergent Literacy.* Hillsdale, N.J.: Erlbaum.

Tierney, R. J., Caplan, R. Ehri, L., Healey, M. K., Hurdlow, M. K. (1989) 'Writing and reading: working together', in Dyson, A. H. (ed.) *Collaboration through Writing and Reading.* Urbana, Ill.: National Council of Teachers.

Treiman, R. (1985a) 'Phonemic analysis, spelling and reading', in Carr, T. H. (ed.) *New Directions for Child Development: No. 23. The Development of Reading Skills.* San Francisco: Jossey-Bass.

Treiman, R. (1985b) 'Phonemic awareness and spelling: children's judgements do not always agree with adults", *Journal of Experimental Child Psychology* **39,** 182–201.

Treiman, R. (1991) 'Children's spelling errors on syllable-initial consonant clusters', *Journal of Educational Psychology* **83**(3), 346–60.

Treiman, R. and Baron, J. (1981) 'Segmental analysis ability: development and relation to reading ability', in Mackinnon, G. C. and Waller, T. G. (eds) *Reading Research: Advances in Theory and Practice, Vol III.* N.Y.: Academic Press.

Yopp, H. K. and Singer, H. (1985) 'Toward an interactive reading instructional model: explanation of activation of linguistic awareness and metalinguistic ability in learning to read', in Singer, H. and Ruddell, R. B. (eds) *Theoretical Models and Processes of Reading.* Newark, Delaware: International Reading Association.

CHAPTER 4

Constructing meaning through literature

Chris Eddershaw

In this chapter I shall consider constructive learning in relation to the teaching of literature in the primary classroom. In the first section I shall take a number of points from an article by Gordon Wells (1992) which refers to social constructivism, and attempt to illustrate them through the work of some nine and ten year old children. I shall then focus on the role of the teacher and comment on that through further examples of children's work. In the hope that the reader might be familiar with them, I have deliberately chosen work relating to well-known books and a poem: *Not Now, Bernard* by David McKee (1980), *The Midnight Fox* by Betsy Byars (1976) and *Keith's Cupboard* by Michael Rosen (Rosen and Blake 1987).

'The Centrality of Talk in Education' is the final article in *Thinking Voices*, edited by Kate Norman, in which Gordon Wells reviews the work of the National Oracy Project. In celebrating the achievement of that work, Wells draws attention to a theory of learning – social constructivism – that not only underpinned the National Oracy Project but appeared to influence the National Curriculum in the emphasis it placed on the importance of talk as a powerful means of learning. Near the beginning of his article, Wells defines social constructivism through three basic principles: knowledge is 'a state of understanding achieved through the constructive mental activity of individual learners'; 'this process of knowledge construction is essentially social and cultural in nature'; this process 'is mediated and facilitated by cultural practices and artefacts' of which 'the most important is discourse' (p. 286).

After I had shown a class of nine and ten year old children the picture book *Not Now, Bernard*, the children were put into small groups so that they could discuss the book. The extracts below are taken from a transcript of the conversation I had with one of the groups when I joined them after they had been discussing among themselves for ten minutes. The conversation had begun to focus on whether Bernard's behaviour towards his parents was deliberate or not. While the children continued to discuss this point, I showed them again the opening pages where Bernard approaches his father from behind to say 'Hello' to him, just as his father is about to hammer a picture hook into the wall.

As part of the first of three basic principles underlying social constructivism, Wells commented:

> Knowledge . . . is a state of understanding achieved through the constructive mental activity of individual learners. Learners progressively construct their own knowledge by bringing what they already know to bear on new

information in order to assimilate or accommodate to the new and to extend or modify their initial understanding. (p. 286)

This point is illustrated in the following extract:

Harry   I reckon he isn't a little monster like they call him, you know they say 'Oh, my kid, he's a little monster' and things, I don't reckon he's that, it's just that he doesn't get any attention and that so he just . . . *they* think he's a little monster because they haven't got any time for him and they don't really care much about him . . .

Teacher   Look at, look at the moment that he's chosen to talk to his Dad.

Harry   Yes, as soon as his Dad's hitting a nail in – yeh, look at his eyes, his eyes are watching (*interruption*) no, I don't reckon now (*interruption*) I think I've changed, I've changed.

Kate   He *didn't* just think 'Oh, I'll make my Dad hit his finger with the hammer,' he just did it by accident.

Harry   No, I don't reckon.

The notion that Bernard may be a little tearaway had been hinted at by Hannah, one of the children in Harry's group, and Harry's initial response captures him in the process of clarifying the distinction between what he senses Bernard's parents feel about their son, a judgement based on Harry's personal experience of the way adults talk about children, and his own judgement of Bernard. However, the extract also captures him at the moment of tentatively changing his opinion in the light of new evidence and beginning to maintain that new stance despite the challenge of Kate's point of view which may be an equally valid interpretation of the evidence. What I was doing was challenging all the children to carefully consider the details of the illustration, as well as the text, so that whatever judgement they might finally make would have to take into account all the available evidence.

In making his second point about social constructivism, Wells goes on to say that, although knowledge is a state of understanding that individuals have to achieve for themselves, the process they go through in doing so is largely a social and cultural one: 'For it is through participation with more mature members of the community in socially significant, purposeful activities that learners encounter the knowledge and skills that are valued in their culture'. (p. 286)

In the above transcript part of that knowledge being made available to the children is the importance of considering all available evidence before making judgements; the other part is that a piece of literature, in this case a seemingly simple picture book, can be open to more than one interpretation. The degree to which any of the children had come to a state of understanding those points – made knowledge for themselves – is difficult to tell, but it is worth noting that I did not ask a question or tell Harry what to think. Consequently it would appear that he was in the process of learning important skills for himself: the need to base judgements on evidence, and the courage to admit publicly that he had altered his interpretation.

Harry and Kate continued a prolonged argument about whether Bernard's parents cared about him or not; however, Harry was prepared to 'see' an aspect of Kate's view of what constitutes appropriate behaviour for a good parent. He embellishes the point she made wonderfully and, I would suggest, finds out exactly what he means in the process of saying it:

Harry   No, but Kate's right when she said that – you're right when you said that – what did you say um (what?) about a good parent would go along with it, I mean now at our age if I said to my Mum that there's a monster in the garden she'd just ignore me because she'd think I was just being stupid, but at that age, five or six, you'd go along with it.

Hannah   (*interrupting*) No, not that, I think four or five.

Harry   Four or five you'd say 'There's a monster in the garden and it's going to eat me up' and you'd say 'Oh no! I'll go and get a gun and blow its head off!'

It would seem that what Harry is doing here is something of what Wells is referring to when he writes:

And by thus engaging with others in collaborative action and in the co-construction of meaning, learners are assisted to take over these cultural resources and make them their own. Moreover, because this process of 'appropriation' involves the active transformation of the information provided by the other participants in the activity, the learner's resulting knowledge is never a straightforward copy, but a new, personal reconstruction. As a result, it may go beyond the 'model' in its potential for finding novel and creative solutions to the original problem. (p. 286)

The latter point made by Wells in that quotation is possibly illustrated by the use Harry made of his 'personal reconstruction' above of the information originally given to him by Kate when she said, in reference to Bernard saying that there was a monster in the garden:

Kate   A proper, a really caring Mum and Dad would go along with it and imagine it was there.

When I came to talk with the group to see what conclusions they had arrived at and was challenging Harry's point of view, Harry, having apparently concurred with part of Kate's argument, used it against her tellingly:

Teacher I'm showing you those pictures because you said that Bernard's parents don't care for him.

Harry   No, I don't reckon they do care because – someone said they do care because they have toys, but that isn't the point because they could just give him the money and tell him to go and buy comics or toys . . . they don't really care.

Kate   They do care but they're too busy at that moment – so if there's a monster in the garden they just play along with it.

Harry   Yeh, yeh they *should* play along with it but *they can't be bothered.*

The third point that Wells makes about social constructivism is to draw attention to the value of discussion as the most important of the 'culturally inherited mediating tools' that facilitate learning in collaborative problem-solving situations:

Discourse is itself a form of action. For in producing and responding to the linked and reciprocally related moves that make up a sequence of discourse, participants are able to act on each other, guiding and influencing each other's understanding of, and involvement in, their joint endeavour. (p. 287)

That point would appear to be borne out by the extracts included so far. The first one and the ones that follow also illustrate Wells' next point about the fact that 'the words and structures of the linguistic code that are used . . . enable the participants to refer, reflexively and reflectively, to the discourse itself'. (p. 287)

Kevin	And you wouldn't have a carpet that looks like that either.
Harry	Look, look we're not meant to get the defects, we're meant to be arguing about it (the issues raised by the book).
Kevin	I am arguing about it, you don't get carpets like that!

At the end of the discussion I suggested that the group listen to the recording of their conversation:

Teacher	. . . it will be interesting for you to hear how you got on as a group, how much you help each other, how good you are as a group.
Harry	We didn't do much helping.
Teacher	What makes you say that, Harry?
Harry	Well a few arguments, not serious ones, just about . . . (*interrupted*) . . .
Teacher	Are you suggesting that an argument isn't helping?
Harry	Yeh, I reckon it does help because (*interrupted*)

It just so happens that one of the 'culturally inherited mediating tools' now is the tape recorder which, of course, gives further opportunity for reflection. After some conversation about the original discussion, Rebecca, one of the group made this comment:

Rebecca	Well, next time we do it (we must) work out one problem at a time because we had too many questions that needed answers all at the same time, and we were getting a bit confused on which to do first.

Because Wells, in his article, was reflecting on the work of the National Oracy Project he obviously focused on the importance of learning through talk, but I would also like to refer briefly to the importance of using writing to aid learning, 'think writing', a kind of written equivalent of what Barnes (1976) called 'exploratory talk'. D'Arcy (1989) defines it well:

using writing itself as part of a learning process – using writing to help them (children) to think, writing to come up with questions, writing to reflect about the work they were doing in science or history or maths or English – writing to map their own progress and to share their thoughts and feelings as learners with their teachers. (p.105)

Perhaps a brief illustration will help make the point. While reading and discussing E. B. White's novel, *Charlotte's Web,* with a class of nine year olds, I had encouraged the children to use a Think Book which monitored what they thought about certain events and issues in the novel at specific moments during the reading of it. I remember when the time came to collect in those Think Books after I finished the novel; one child was reluctant to give me her book because she had changed her mind about some aspects of what she had written. In other words, she had recorded her initial ideas and, of her own volition, through reflection felt the need to refine them, an action akin to what Harry did through talk in the first transcript. The importance of reflection in the learning process is underlined by Barnes (1992):

> It is when we have laid out clearly what we believe to be the case that we can look critically at our assumptions and determine whether we wish to stand by them. Reflection . . . seems to be an essential prerequisite for critical thinking and the modification of what we believe. (p. 127)

If, therefore, taking account of what children already know and think in relation to what the teacher is trying to teach them is so important for the quality of their learning, then how important that is for the teacher of English when teaching literature. Of all subject matter that children meet in the curriculum they surely bring more of their personal experience to bear on the stuff of literature than anything else. While children appear spontaneously to refer to personal experience to make sense of new knowledge the teacher too, especially a teacher of English, will make use of children's experience of life to influence both their cognitive and their affective development. The impact of a good novel can enrich and extend children's experience. Apart from giving children the pleasure of hearing something read well so that they can become involved in the imaginative experience, the teacher should be developing children's ability to engage critically with what they are listening to. In so doing they should be developing, alongside other aspects, the children's awareness of themselves as individuals and their ability to empathise with others:

> Talking well about books is a high-value activity in itself. But talking well about books is also the best rehearsal there is for talking well about other things. So in helping children to talk about their reading, we help them to be articulate about the rest of their lives. (Chambers 1993, p. 10)

The challenge for the teacher is to move the children beyond whatever analogies they happen to make between their personal experiences and what they are listening to so that their initial thoughts might be confirmed or developed in some way.

As an illustration of this it might be helpful to consider aspects of the following approach to the teaching of a novel such as Betsy Byars' *The Midnight Fox*. There is absolutely nothing wrong with the teacher going straight into the reading of that novel without any preparation and allowing the novel to speak for itself, and many teachers would want to argue that is precisely what one should do. However, I decided to involve Year Five children in a task first, before they had any idea that they were going to listen to that novel, in order to get them onto the wavelength of the first chapter in which Betsy Byars shows the parents manipulating the feelings of their son, Tom, as they try to persuade him that he would love to spend the two months of his summer holiday at his Aunt Millie and Uncle Fred's farm while they tour Europe. The challenge for the children was for them to improvise a situation where they tried to get their parents to do them a favour which they know their parents wouldn't be terribly keen on doing. They had not only to think carefully about when and where they would choose to approach their parents (and whether they tackled them together or separately) but also about how they would order their tactics to get their way. They then had to reverse that situation and focus on their parents persuading them to do something.

I had several reasons for approaching the novel in this particular way. The most obvious was so that the children might be more alert to, hence better enjoy, the way Tom's parents tried to get him to do them a favour. Another reason was to encourage the children to empathise with the parents as a way of drawing the children's attention to the fact that the novel is written from Tom's point of view and as a way of deepening their assessment of his character. But I also wanted to involve the children more willingly than they might otherwise have been in a fairly lengthy discussion about the parents, particularly the father, since the kind of man he is so closely parallels the character of Uncle Fred. This was important because Tom, being the kind of boy *he* is (introverted, non-athletic, having a very poor self-image because he felt he did not live up to his father's expectations) finds relating to his uncle even more embarrassingly difficult:

> I still did not feel at ease with Uncle Fred. He was a large man, very powerfully built, and to see us together you would think we would make the perfect cover picture for a story called 'The Boy Who Tried To Be a Man.' There was a tremendous physical difference between us, and there was something else I don't know how to explain. We couldn't talk to each other. One time he took me to the lake and I couldn't think of one single thing to say all the way over or back. It was an awful feeling not to be able to think of one single thing worth saying. (p. 57)

Tom's desperate desire to relate to his uncle is cleverly handled by Betsy Byars in the way she structures the final section of the novel. Tom finds himself in the terrible predicament of having the chance to forge a relationship with his uncle, about which his uncle too is very keen, but only by helping his uncle to kill the midnight fox, the very animal which has come to mean so much to Tom. From my experience of teaching this novel I have found that children do not fully appreciate Tom's predicament, which is powerfully symbolised by the tense atmosphere of the approaching storm; rather their attention, understandably, is riveted on what is about to happen to the fox. The initial discussion about Tom's father triggered by the work on their own experience is, therefore, potentially helpful in focusing the children's attention on his difficulty in developing a relationship with his uncle.

An indication of how the children and I utilised personal experience to help develop insights into what they were listening to may come through samples from the discussions of a group of boys, in this particular case a friendship group. The first section of the transcript refers to the conversation between Tom and his father after Tom has grudgingly agreed to go to the farm but still his father has not left the room. ('My father never knew when to leave me alone' p. 14)

Teacher	What about the way the father handled the situation?
Nathan	He wasn't very good.
Teacher	What makes you say that?
Nathan	He should have left the room when, you know, um he shouldn't have gone on because he was doing *my* dad now!
Teacher	Um . . . um . . . nevertheless he got his son to agree . . . how did he manage that?

The link that Nathan freely made between the behaviour of his own father and that of Tom's presumably helped him empathise with Tom's feelings at that point in the novel. I used that as a starting point to explore how exactly Tom's father had successfully persuaded Tom, against his will, to agree to put on a brave face for his mother's sake and make her feel that he was really keen to go to stay on the farm with his aunt and uncle.

The second section of the transcript refers to that part of the discussion where I had been trying to encourage the children to empathise with the parents' point of view by making them put up a defence for the parents. This they found difficult to do even when I deliberately changed tactics and went on the offensive, jokingly challenging the children to take control of the teaching. However, that approach resulted in a wonderful conversation the likes of which no comprehension exercise is ever likely to promote. Key moments are the teacher's 'Tell me' question and Jonathan's interruption of Roger; the question resulted in Roger beginning to think a bit more from the parents' point of view, and Nathan's question, which also indicated self-awareness, led to Roger's humorous but telling use of personal experience.

Teacher	Don't forget you are supposed to be defending the parents – you are constantly sweeping into the attack.
Nathan	It's hard to defend them because there are so many things you want to accuse them of.
Teacher	Help me, now come on, help me! What I think, I have a feeling that you are being pretty tough on the parents, I feel you've been hard on these parents!
Nathan	(indignantly) Why?!
Mark	(indignantly) Why are we being tough on them?
Teacher	Tell me what I might have done to help you see better the parents' point of view?
Roger	Well, the parents have obviously got other things to think about – they've got hotels to book, they've got travellers cheques to buy, aeroplane tickets and um they've got the basket-ball team to see to (*interrupted*)
Nathan	Which comes first, which comes first, your son – I know I'm accusing them a bit – but which comes first, your son or your holiday?!
Voices	HOLIDAYS! (much laughter)
Nathan	*Your son, your son!*
Roger	Well, when I went to someone's house at the weekend um, um, my aunty said 'I'm sorry your uncle's not home but it comes in this order: work, church, family,' so you know (inaudible) . . .
Teacher	Well, um I mean it depends doesn't it, I mean people have different attitudes and points of view and it depends on your job as well doesn't it as to where you put your priorities, but I'm just going to come back at Jonathan because I remember the year before when Tom's parents were going to go to the Smokies they *did* put their son first because he was ill, so they didn't go on holiday – do you remember? – his dad picked him up on that point (Jonathan defended himself by stating that he was absent when we read that bit!)
Roger	Well I think the parents are trying – I think the parents are *really* giving it all they've got to try to cheer him up but if they didn't have to book all these hotels, travellers cheques and whatever, I think they would have done more for him.

The next section captures a part of the discussion which is concerned with the relationship between Tom and his father. I attempted to prompt the children into articulating what they already knew about that relationship when Roger spontaneously made an analogy between his relationship with his father and that between Tom and his dad.

Teacher	What do we know about Tom's dad?
Roger	He's a basket-ball player, a coach.
Alex	And he tried to persuade Tom to play in the Junior Basket-Ball League.
David	And he was probably using words that he would have used to the team to persuade them.
Teacher	And what do you know about Tom as far as basket-ball is concerned?
Nathan	He doesn't like basket-ball.
Stephen	He's quite good at it but he doesn't (*interrupted*)
Mark	He likes building models.
Teacher	Yes, he likes different things from his father doesn't he.
Roger	I don't particularly like canoeing, rock-climbing and all that sort of stuff but I give my dad the impression that, you know, I'm really enthusiastic about it when really I'm going 'Oh no, I'm not going canoeing am I?!'
Teacher	In order to keep him happy?
Roger	Well, yes, I don't like disappointing him.
Teacher	So we know that he doesn't like basket-ball whereas his dad's a basket-ball coach, and he doesn't appear to do what Roger was saying he does with his dad – to go along and pretend that he enjoys rock climbing and those other things to keep his dad happy – maybe Tom feels his dad is a little bit disappointed in him?

Roger's contributions were particularly helpful to me; they allowed me to use them as further evidence of what the group felt about Tom and to pose an important question about him. It was from that basis that I was then able to encourage the children to speculate about any links there might be between Tom's father and his uncle.

Teacher	I'm just wondering about Tom and his feelings about his uncle and his feelings about his dad . . . what kind of a boy does his dad appear to want Tom to be?
Alex/Mark	Sporty, muscular/Like his uncle.
Roger	He probably thinks that if he – 'I'm not going to have a muscular son so I'm not going to pay much attention to him' . . .
Stephen	I think physically he would like him to look like Uncle Fred.
Teacher	Is there anything else that makes Uncle Fred rather like his dad?
Stephen	Yes, he doesn't seem to care about Tom really, he just seems to, you know, get on with it, partly helping if you know what I mean.
Roger	Not really noticing.
Stephen	Yes, he just says 'would you like to come for a swim?' you know, because he thinks he has to say something.
Nathan	He hasn't found out what Tom likes much, he ought to ask him a few more questions and then go out with him.
Stephen	And not talk about hunting so much because it's pretty obvious that Tom likes foxes.

After extensive discussion on the children's part about Tom's concern that his uncle would shoot the fox I was able to widen their perspective of what else appeared to be concerning Tom.

Teacher	What does Tom want to happen between him and Uncle Fred?
Stephen	Be friends with him.
Teacher	To be friends, yes, so what's he worried (*interrupted*)
Roger	Ah! – so he's worried – he's worried that if he doesn't help him catch the fox then Uncle Fred won't be friends with him.

That final exchange, were it not for Roger's genuinely enthusiastic interruption, was perilously close to that kind of episode where children are forced into a situation of having to guess what is in the teacher's mind which is tantamount to the teacher telling the children what to think. If teachers succumb to the temptation to tell children what to think then the children may not internalise that knowledge unless they appear to be on the verge of grasping it; even then there may be a question-mark over the degree to which they internalise what they are told. Clearly teachers will have an agenda (procedures for approaching the task and an ultimate goal of some sort) but will need to be flexible enough to take on board the fact that children may possibly adopt different procedures and reach different conclusions from theirs. That should not mean, however, that any idea will do: the 'you can make it mean whatever you want' syndrome. Wells makes this point:

> Not all new ideas are valid, of course; often they are incomplete or internally inconsistent. But the best way for learners to discover when their solutions to problems are inadequate is by being taken seriously – by being encouraged to formulate their own ideas in their own terms, and to put them to the test in action or in discussion. (p. 297)

In the following examples the children's ideas were being subjected to the same criteria that applied to the teacher's ideas. In the first example some nine and ten year old children and I were discussing Michael Rosen's poem, *Keith's Cupboard,* which is about a boy who crammed into a cupboard all the toys his parents continued to buy for him even though he never played with any of them. My opening question was generated by the way the children had been talking about Keith.

Teacher	Well, um, um – is Keith happy?
Voices	No, no.
Teacher	Why not?
Oliver	He just wants more stuff – he like plays with it once.
Teacher	Does he?
Oliver	No, he, he probably . . .
Teacher	Does he?
Oliver	No, the new stuff, as soon as he gets it he probably plays with it once.
George	No, he probably treats it like a video – you watch it once and then you leave it.
Philip	You watch it once and then you watch it again and then you suddenly get bored with it.
Teacher	'They keep buying him' – I'm not making this up, I'm not making this up, I'm reading from the poem:

'They keep buying him all this stuff
and he *never* plays with it.' (Teacher's emphasis)

Philip   I know . . . he, he likes – he plays with it – no, he wouldn't, would he. . .

Teacher   'He never plays with it' – that's what it says.

Natalie   So what's the point of them *buying* it then?!

Here the children were using their personal experience to try to make sense of Keith's behaviour and I was challenging the accuracy of their thinking by forcing them to match their ideas with the evidence the poem provides; I might have been more willing to accept their idea had the children begun to discuss the way people sometimes use the word 'never'. The discussion culminated in the exasperated tone of Natalie's question – one of the key questions I wanted to ask about the poem, but it was asked by a child not by me; hence it was a genuine question asked by someone who did not know the answer and who really wanted to know. Again, Wells comments: 'It is when learners have a real desire to understand, and one which comes from a purpose of their own, that they most actively engage in making sense of new information.' (p. 297)

One of the more penetrating responses Natalie received was this comment:

Richard   When parents give kids toys it doesn't mean that they care for them.

She also received what she considered less substantiated comments when the conversation led onto why Keith behaved as he did:

George   Another point of view is where he lives, because if he lives next to a wood, like he might want to go and play in the wood (instead of playing with his toys).

Natalie   But, yeh, but this is the danger in this (these suggestions), we've just got this sheet of paper and what it says on it (the poem).

It would appear that Natalie is beginning to internalise aspects of some of our cultural practices that children need to acquire: the ability to formulate their own questions and the need to base their arguments on sound evidence.

So, through encouraging children to express their ideas by listening to them, and through taking them seriously by allowing them to be put to the test, teachers may overcome the tension that Wells feels to be inherent in the theory of social constructivism:

> To be able to act effectively in the world – and to succeed in school – pupils need to appropriate the ways of acting and thinking that are 'common knowledge' within their culture . . . On the other hand, learning and teaching should not be concerned *only* with cultural reproduction . . . It is equally important that pupils gain confidence in their ability to find their own solutions to problems, since they will not always be able to turn to someone else for the answer. (pp. 296–7)

If children make sense of new knowledge through their existing experience and ideas then it is clearly important for us as teachers to encourage them to talk and to 'think write' in order for us to gain some idea of where they are coming from in relation to whatever it is that we are trying to teach them. As Barnes (1992) argues, 'Young people are more likely to struggle to make sense of new experiences when these are important in their own lives'. (p. 128) Our task is then to help the children to develop their ideas in such a way that they begin to internalise the new knowledge and make it their own. Only when they do so will the learning be really effective.

REFERENCES

Barnes, D. (1976) *From Communication to Curriculum*. Harmondsworth: Penguin.

Barnes, D. (1992) 'The role of talk in learning', in Norman, K. *et al*. *Thinking Voices*. London: Hodder and Stoughton.

Byars, B. (1976) *The Midnight Fox*. Harmondsworth: Puffin.

Chambers, A. (1993) *Tell me: Children, Reading and Talk*. Stroud: Thimble Press.

D'Arcy, P. (1989) *Making Sense, Shaping Meaning*. Portsmouth, NH: Boynton/Cook, Heinemann.

McKee, D. (1980) *Not Now, Bernard*. London/Hutchinson of Australia: Anderson Press.

Rosen, M. and Blake, Q. (1987) *Don't Put Mustard in the Custard*. London: HarperCollins.

Wells, G. (1992) 'The centrality of talk in education', in Norman, K. *et al*. *Thinking Voices*. London: Hodder and Stoughton.

CHAPTER 5

How does a constructivist perspective influence mathematics teaching?

David Coles and Alison Price

In this chapter we will try to draw together a variety of ideas and issues that have been current in debates about mathematics teaching since the 1950s and discuss them in the light of a constructivist view of education. We will also discuss what a constructivist perspective on teaching and learning primary mathematics might lead a teacher to do, using classroom examples to illustrate our points.

WHAT IS MATHEMATICS?

It is important to start by identifying different views of what constitutes mathematical knowledge since this must have a significant influence on how the teaching and learning of mathematics are viewed. The two views of mathematics that we will contrast here can broadly be identified by deciding whether mathematics is viewed as knowledge that is *discovered* or *invented*. The differences can be explored by considering the way in which we decide which of two alternative mathematical ideas is correct; that is, what test of truth or validity is applied to knowledge within mathematics.

If mathematics is thought to be discovered then that implies that some version of the mathematics exists in the real world and the mathematics which we abstract from the real world is, or at least could be, a true representation of that world. This view aligns closely with the positivist view of knowledge in philosophy and science generally. Here mathematics is seen as a body of knowledge which exists outside of the knower and it is to be transmitted to, or discovered by, the learner. Such mathematics is seen as infallible, objective and fixed; mathematical methods are mechanical, formal and logical; mathematics is approached from an objective point of view and the results are right-or-wrong and provable. (Ernest (1991) refers to this as an absolutist view of mathematics.) This view is supported by our everyday experience of the world where, for example, our use of arithmetic to manage and control the world continues to suggest that there is a one-to-one match between mathematics and the world. For the mathematics that is taught in the primary school it is particularly easy to see this view as applicable to the learning of Facts and Skills; number bonds, tables, facts and the skills involved in long multiplication and division or using a set of scales to find the mass of an object are all examples in which this match between mathematical knowledge and some objective view of the real world seem justified.

The view that mathematics is invented, however, is sustained when one considers the way in which *mathematicians* might describe their work. For a mathematician the connection of the subject with the real world is unnecessary. Mathematics is seen as an abstract, logical system which attains its validity by being self-consistent. In this case mathematics is derived from basic assumptions and its truth is demonstrated by *proof* rather than any reference to a match with the real world. This view does not invalidate the previous description of mathematics but it does lead to the inclusion of other characteristics: that mathematics is changing and dynamic as new uses and new ideas are developed; that it can be subjective and as such can be uncertain or even fallible; that informal and intuitive methods of solving mathematical problems may be more efficient than more formal algorithms and proofs; and that it is possible to approach mathematics from an inquiring and creative viewpoint. Above all, mathematics is seen here not as a fixed body of knowledge outside of the knower but as a growing social construct, constructed by people over time and which must be constructed by the individual learner through interaction with other people. These aspects of mathematics can most easily be seen in the development of conceptual structures as one learns mathematics. For example, a pupil's concept of number must expand from its original form in which it encompasses only whole numbers, to include fractions and decimals, scientific notation and perhaps even complex numbers. The five year old does not have an *incorrect* conception of number because they do not understand fractions, but their current understanding may be seen as fallible and incomplete.

These contrasting views of mathematical knowledge have led to different views on what it means to learn mathematics. If teachers see mathematics as a fixed body of knowledge then they will concentrate on ensuring that pupils have the *facts and skills* related to that knowledge. We do acknowledge that as far as the primary mathematics curriculum is concerned, the content base is widely agreed, which can give it the appearance of a fixed body of knowledge, particularly in terms of the facts and skills to be covered. However, if teachers see mathematics as changing and uncertain then they will concentrate more on the underlying understanding and problem solving through which pupils will be able to assimilate and develop new knowledge. This leads to a greater focus on teaching which emphasises the development of conceptual structures and mathematical thinking processes.

From either perspective it is possible to take a constructivist perspective on how children learn mathematics so that it should not be thought that the positivist view of knowledge and constructive approaches to teaching are necessarily in conflict. Within the positivist perspective the teacher will be certain that they know the 'correct' answers and methods and will see teaching as ensuring that children are able to reproduce these 'correct' responses. It is possible to see these understandings as constructed by the pupil from the teacher's explanations and demonstrations and through the practice activities and problems which the teacher sets. Because of the general social agreement about what constitutes good mathematical knowledge, at the level of facts and skills there will be little difference in practice between the positivist and the radical constructivist, though the use of 'ad-hoc' (Haylock and Cockburn 1997) methods in mental arithmetic may be an area which illustrates the potential differences. However, when considering the development of conceptual structures and mathematical thinking processes the differences become more significant, with the positivist focusing more on teaching a 'correct' or 'best' procedure, and the postmodernist led to a *radical* constructivist perspective with more time spent on considering alternative conceptual structures and problem solving strategies.

This distinction in teaching approach has been described in a variety of ways which try to distinguish the type of understanding which the learner will attain. One of the most widely used is Skemp's distinction between *instrumental* and *relational* understanding (1979) or, as he later developed the ideas, between *habit learning* and *intelligent learning* (1989). Broadly speaking Skemp associates habit learning with a focus on the rote learning of mathematical facts and skills and contrasts this with the intelligent learning of the underlying mathematical concepts.

Another way of characterising the distinction between views of mathematical knowledge is to contrast *skill-getting* with *skill-using* (Open University 1982b, DES/WO 1989). During skill-getting activities the pupil is focusing on learning new facts and skills while during skill-using activities the pupil is focused on developing problem solving strategies which guide the selection and use of the appropriate strategies and skills. This latter aspect is the area covered by the Using and Applying Mathematics profile component in the mathematics National Curriculum.

CURRENT APPROACHES TO TEACHING MATHEMATICS

Rote learning

It is sometimes argued that mathematics cannot be discovered through interaction with the environment since it is essentially abstract. The concept of gravity may be 'discovered' through lying under apple trees or explored through experimentation, and appropriate concepts formed to explain events in the physical world. However, since mathematics is abstract and does not seek to explain the physical world it will not be discovered in the same way. It therefore has to be 'taught'. This implies a transmission mode of teaching and learning rather than a constructive one.

Learning by rote has been seen traditionally as an efficient method of learning facts that will then be available in the memory when required. It is an effective way of learning facts for many people, and some adults, who still have access to multiplication tables learnt in school, see this as the answer to poor mathematics

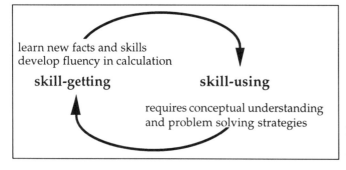

learn new facts and skills
develop fluency in calculation

skill-getting   **skill-using**

requires conceptual understanding
and problem solving strategies

Figure 5.1 The skill-getting/skill-using cycle

skills in some of today's school children. However, it is not sufficient for children to know the facts. The ability to use these facts in new contexts requires a deeper, conceptual understanding. Most mathematical concepts are not simple facts but a complex relationship of facts, skills and conceptual structures. An over-emphasis on teaching facts will often lead to the child forming conceptual structures which emphasise the manipulation of symbols, so that the child has no deeper understanding of the mathematical relationships which the symbol manipulation represents.

For example the concept of addition of positive whole numbers requires an underlying understanding of number, counting, the number system and conservation of number; an understanding of combining two or more sets of numbers to form a bigger set; an understanding of place value to solve addition of numbers greater than ten; and an understanding of associated concepts of recording and symbols; to identify only a few. It would be possible to teach children to recite addition facts, similar to recitation of multiplication facts, but without an underlying concept of addition they would need to learn every possible combination of numbers, as they would not be able to generalise, for example, that 4 and 4 are 8 therefore 14 and 4 would be 18 (requiring place value understanding). Neither would they necessarily know when to use addition if it was not presented to them clearly as a sum. Therefore rote learning, by itself, cannot provide the children with sufficient understanding, though it is a very useful practice to supplement understanding of the concept and underpins fluent computation.

Concept learning: making connections

Whereas with science children start to construct concepts through their ordinary interaction with the world, with mathematics it is necessary artificially to structure their experience to provoke mathematical thinking and the development of concepts. Mathematics education does this by attempting to find activities which will model or represent the abstract in a more tangible or visual form in order to aid learning.

One framework which shows this clearly and is often used for planning mathematical activities is that proposed by Liebeck (1984) and known by the acronym ELPS; the key elements of experience, language, pictures and symbols. Haylock and Cockburn (1997) show how these are interrelated:

The essence of this argument is that in order to construct a mathematical concept for themselves, children are helped by:

- experience with some physical apparatus;
- development of the language that is associated with the concept;
- learning to represent it in pictures and to interpret given pictures that represent the concept; and
- learning to represent and interpret representations written as symbols.

There are clear connections between this model and the cognitive stages proposed by Bruner; Enactive, Iconic, Symbolic (1967), and the Do, Talk, Record model proposed by the Open University Course Team for EM235 (Open University 1982a).

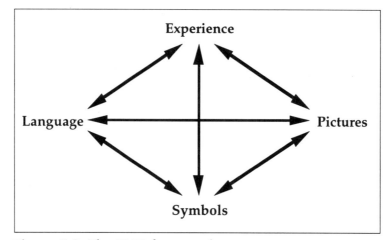

Figure 5.2 The ELPS framework

As the children move from the concrete representation to the more abstract symbols they are constructing their own conceptual structures which will develop deeper understanding than if they had merely learnt by rote. As they gain confidence through the manipulating stage (often through manipulating the physical apparatus) they get a sense of the abstract concept which underlies it and are eventually able to articulate what they understand in words and in symbols (Open University 1982a). The ELPS framework can also be used to explain different levels of mathematical understanding. Understanding of each of the ELPS elements and the relationships between them is necessary for the development of a complete conceptual structure.

However we must not lose sight of the fact that the model is only one representation of the underlying concept and may in itself limit understanding. In this way it is like a metaphor. If it was said that someone was a lion among men we might understand him or her to be brave or scary but are unlikely to imagine that they have a tail and mane. So, when we use Dienes blocks to explain place value, we are not talking about tens and units really being longs and cubes but that the relationships are similar. To this end it is important to use a variety of models (e.g. for place value, money, measures and hundred squares) which emphasise different aspects of the relationships but have very different superficial characteristics. In this situation we must present a variety of specific examples from which the child can construct their own generalisation. So, by using practical apparatus to model areas of mathematics children are enabled to extract the abstract concepts themselves, the mathematics is constructed by them and a constructive rather than a transmission model of learning best describes this process.

We have discussed above, in relation to the ELPS framework, the fact that language is an important factor in the learning of mathematics. The National Curriculum, and most mathematics schemes, note the progression in the use of appropriate language from everyday terms to specifically mathematical terms or a more specifically mathematical use of some words and expressions. Written, as well as spoken, mathematics is a form of communication and requires socially accepted signs and symbols. Consequently it is difficult to envisage mathematics that could be learnt in isolation from the social sphere. Children learn mathematics through what the teacher says and does and need to test their understanding through interaction with the teacher and with their peers (Skemp 1989).

While Piaget believed that children were unable to carry out certain mathematical tasks because they had not yet reached the right stage in their development, Donaldson (1978) and others showed that children are capable of a higher level of understanding when the language was used within a familiar context. When learning language young children rely heavily on actions and context to help them to interpret the words (as do adults learning a new language). The children showed limited understanding of the language of the Piagetian tasks and therefore relied heavily on their social understanding of the actions carried out. When given a task where they could understand what was being done within their own social world, they showed that they could complete the task successfully even when the same language was used. Alternatively the same task could be completed successfully with the same actions but a more child oriented range of language.

These ideas have given considerable impetus to a variety of work on the place of talk in the mathematics classroom (Mathematics Association 1987, Brissenden 1988). Children need opportunities to experience both written and spoken language which expresses their mathematical thinking and it is through language that they test out their own constructions and it is largely through language that their thinking becomes accessible to the teacher. Hoyles (1985) identifies the way in which the immediate feedback and the potential for conflict within discussion may be seen as an important stimulus for learning: '. . . as argued by Balancheff and Laborde (1985) it is the interaction between the construction of meanings by the speaker, their reconstruction by the listener, and the contradictions that can arise, which can generate increased understanding'. (p. 207)

In some cases language may also present significant difficulties for children by obscuring the underlying mathematical conceptual structures rather than clarifying them. For example the English number words between 10 and 20 display many inconsistencies and do not match the *tens* and *ones* pattern of the symbols. For the number words to show a clear match with the symbols, eleven and twelve should be ten-one and ten-two and the subsequent number words like seventeen should be reversed to be ten-seven. Even in numbers above 20 the words for the decades (twenty, thirty etc.) do not show a clear match with their single digit counterparts (two, three, etc.) Fuson and Kwon (1991) have shown how this can make it difficult for children to construct adequate mental representations for multi-digit numbers.

Social interaction: scaffolding

A significant development from the Piagetian ideas about how children construct their understanding involves consideration of the place of social interaction in learning. The ideas of Vygotsky are particularly important here. The *zone of proximal development* identifies the idea that someone may be able to solve a problem with help that they could not solve unaided (Vygotsky 1978). He also suggested that learning may occur first through interaction with others before being internalised as a mental representation. These ideas have led to the use of the metaphor of *scaffolding* to capture some significant features of the teaching process (Wood 1988).

The teacher's role in work with children may be seen as *scaffolding* their development of new concepts. The teacher introduces the activity, models the way in which it is to be used, provides activities and problems which stimulate the children to interact with the apparatus/model and have the appropriate experiences. The teacher uses language and assists the pupil to construct solutions to the problems posed until the pupil is able to complete solutions unaided. The level of support given may be seen as varying from very specific guidance when the activity is initiated to more general guidance when the pupil is being successful in solving the problem. The most specific help will involve the teacher *demonstrating* what to do. Less specific support will involve the teacher using language to guide the pupil, *explaining* the next step in the procedure. When the pupil is nearly able to solve the problem unaided the teacher may need to give prompts which focus attention on problem solving strategies like looking for patterns or working systematically.

The teacher needs to vary the level of support given so that as the pupil is being successful more general support is given, but when the pupil begins to experience difficulties then more specific guidance is given to avoid the pupil experiencing failure. In many cases it is possible to design activities in which the support of peers is sufficient to enable pupils to reach solutions together. This level of interaction and use of language is crucial if pupils are to develop a deep understanding of the mathematical concepts involved (Maclellan 1997, p.33). From a constructive perspective we could argue that the problem solving is initially being controlled using the teacher's conceptual structures and this highlights the need for the teacher to have an extensive knowledge of the subject. During the interaction the pupils are constructing their own version of these conceptual structures.

Individualised maths schemes

Unlike rote learning which has a transmission or positivist basis, individualised mathematics schemes, currently in use in many classrooms, are an attempt to put into practice Piagetian constructivist ideas on learning. Since it was recognised that children construct their own mathematical understanding at different rates, whole class teaching was considered inappropriate and individualised mathematics schemes were designed to enable each child needed to work at his or her own pace without the impracticality of the teacher needing to teach each child on a one-to-one basis. The schemes break mathematics down into small pieces which the children can manage alone. Careful selection of the appropriate stage in the scheme allows the teacher to match the work to the child's needs. However, such schemes have not generally been successful in practice and we identify three main reasons for the difficulties.

Firstly, it is difficult to identify the individual needs of the children and find the appropriate work level for them. In many schools the children work through the workbooks and move on to the next section with little check that they had really understood the mathematics, and little assessment of whether the next section matches their needs. The published scheme normally has a linear structure and sequence of work which very rarely actually matches the learning of an individual pupil. Consequently the required level of match between child and teaching material is rarely achieved.

Secondly, as administered in many schools, individualised schemes do not allow for many of the key elements of learning within a social context. Usually the teachers' handbooks contain practical activities that the children are required to carry out, often within a group of peers, before completing individual written work. The activities give the children the experience and the language elements of ELPS framework (see above) while the picture and symbol stages are often found in the workbook or sheet. However these practical activities are seen by some teachers as difficult to organise, especially when the children are all at different stages in their work, and they require teacher input, especially if the correct use of mathematical language is to be emphasised. They are thus often ignored or treated superficially rather than seen as the core part of the teaching and this leaves the pupils to interact only with the text. The meaning they construct to go with mathematics covered in this way is inevitably impoverished. Though the children may indeed identify patterns and relationships it is likely that these are surface features of the symbols and recording systems rather than the significant relationships between the mathematical concepts involved.

Thirdly, children will often work through text material carrying out the required tasks but with little interaction with text or comprehension. Especially when the books are used by children in the early years of their schooling, the children's reading and writing skills are often insufficient to allow much comprehension. This results in the sort of children we all recognise who, when faced with a sheet of sums will ask 'Are they adds?' and when given an answer can carry out the required operation efficiently. They 'do but they do not understand', to misquote the famous Chinese proverb. The children do not understand the purpose of such activity, often thinking that the aim is to get through as many pages as possible rather than to understand the content. The context of the work is so workbook specific that they do not relate it to wider aspects of life in and out of school. Again the implication is that the children can only construct a very limited meaning for the mathematics covered, based on the surface features of the text rather than on the deeper mathematical structures.

TWO APPROACHES TO CONSTRUCTIVIST TEACHING

There is sometimes an assumption that acceptance of a constructivist view of learning will automatically indicate a better approach to teaching. However, Kilpatrick (1987) states clearly that 'as a theory of knowledge acquisition, constructivism is not a theory of teaching or instruction' (p. 11). We have already seen that individualised mathematics schemes which were based on constructivist principle have not proved successful in the classroom. Here we wish to introduce two very different teaching strategies that have a constructivist basis and discuss their relative merits. We have called them the 'arrow' approach and the 'shotgun' approach since this metaphor indicates key differences, but is of course incomplete. There is no sense in which warfare is a key idea!

The *arrow approach* to teaching starts from the premise that individuals have different experiences which will have shaped their understanding of concepts prior to addressing a particular concept in school. It therefore involves finding out where a child is in his/her understanding of a concept, identifying the experiences needed to move the child on in understanding and scaffolding the learning appropriately (Wood 1988). The teaching is therefore very closely targeted to the needs of the child, hence the arrow analogy.

The advantages of this teaching strategy are that it should result in individual growth of understanding, allowing opportunities to correct 'misconceptions' identified in the child's concept development. However there are also problems inherent within this approach. Firstly, it is not easy to successfully identify a child's understanding; it requires a great deal of time and patience and if misdiagnosis occurs then the resultant teaching may be ineffective. Secondly, if there are 30 or so individual understandings in the classroom then diagnosis is difficult and the children may require very different experiences in order to develop their concepts. This provided the motivation for individualised teaching schemes. Thirdly, if the concept is divided into carefully structured small steps in order to lead the child in the right direction of understanding there is a danger that s/he will not learn to make links between these small steps and begin to see the whole picture. This results in the sort of children who can calculate accurately the problem £6.50 − £3.99 but are unable to calculate, or produce a different solution to, 650 − 399 written in the maths textbook (Nunes *et al*. 1993). The ability to make these links, to see generalisations and to spot patterns is crucial to successful mathematics learning.

It is our understanding that in science children come to topics with commonly held 'misconceptions' which can be addressed in class and there is some evidence of similar situations in mathematics. For example, many children think that 'multiplication always makes bigger', a generalisation/concept which they construct from their experience with whole numbers. This causes problems when children expand their concept of number from whole numbers to real numbers. Now, multiplying by a fraction less than one can lead to smaller answers but pupils unable to accept this have difficulty in answering some real world problems. The pupil in this situation may respond to direct teaching which aims to reconstruct their understanding. However, for many mathematics topics the children do not have common misunderstandings generated by their everyday experience, so that the arrow approach may not be the most useful. Indeed, the multiplication example given above is caused not by prior knowledge derived from everyday life, but by a 'misconception' which arose during teaching. Perhaps we need to be more careful with the examples we give children so that they do not generalise these 'misconceptions' or at least be explicit about them to the children, saying 'you will probably have noticed that the answer is always bigger but this is because we are using whole numbers. Later on you will find something different happens when we start to multiply with fractions'.

The *shotgun approach* starts from the same premise of individual concept formation but attempts a different solution. It says that providing rich and stimulating mathematical experiences and environments for all children will enable them to construct a broader understanding of a concept. The teacher does not expect the child to learn a particular idea in a particular way and so cannot make assumptions that it has been learnt. The child is given the opportunity to construct wider links between elements of mathematical knowledge than if given isolated small chunks to learn. However, the shotgun approach does not allow the teacher to make assumptions about what the children are learning and close observation and discussion are needed to assess their understanding.

We are *not* describing here a 1960s 'child-centred' approach to education which could be seen as an excuse for not teaching and merely providing a rich environment and letting children direct their own learning. The richness of experiences and environment does not just refer to the state of the classroom but also to activities set, the teacher's teaching and the level of interaction between teacher and children and between children and children. Good teaching in this situation will focus on the process of learning mathematics, and the teacher will question pupils about the methods they have used to arrive at answers. Much of the discussion about Using and Applying mathematics is relevant here. If the mathematics curriculum is solely content based – number, algebra, data handling, shape and space – then the children are not learning to use the facts and skills in new situations. Emphasis on the mathematical thinking process skills, (reasoning, generalising, specialising, looking for pattern, explaining etc.), allows children to put into practice what they are learning and to make links between the different areas of mathematics and between mathematics and real world, or at least real classroom, situations.

Very closed teaching tasks (tasks for which there may be only one way to carry them out or only one solution) will still be useful to introduce or practice a new skill or fact, while open ended activities allow children to solve problems, to find their own ways to an answer. The observation of such problem solving shows the teacher the extent of the children's understanding. Children are allowed to invent their own ways of solving problems, with class discussion about the relative merits of different methods allowing them to share and compare ideas. A method that works for me because it fits with my understanding of an underlying concept, even if it takes a little longer to produce an answer, is greatly to be preferred to a rote learned algorithm that may be mis-learned or forgotten. But a method that works for the pupil next to me may also fit with my understanding and be more efficient. At times the teacher may identify a method which appears to work in a particular situation but may want to steer the child away from this as s/he knows that it will cause problems later on. An example of this might be a child who generalises the rule 'you always take the smaller number from the larger' in simple subtraction situations but who may later find problems with column subtraction resulting in errors such as:

$$\begin{array}{r} 22 \\ -17 \\ \hline 15 \end{array}$$

So, we use the word 'rich' to imply a variety of whole class, group and individual tasks, teacher led or child initiated, active and more passive, noisy and quiet, practical, oral, mental, pencil and paper and calculator activities so that children are enabled to construct a wide understanding of the concept. It emphasises the social aspect of learning (Edwards *et al.* 1994). The children must be taught that they have a responsibility to talk to one another, sharing answers and expertise, admitting when they do not understand because so often they are not the only one, having patience with each other's explaining, and expecting and looking for patterns and connections in what they are learning. It is through their conversation that the teacher can assess learning. This is a very different classroom from the poorly focused 1960s child-centred one, from whole class rote learning or from individualised maths schemes.

The role of the teacher is to provide activities at an appropriate level for the children in the class. However, in mathematics we do not have a clear research base for the stages through which children progress in their learning of mathematics. The standard Piagetian tasks show some form of progression but, as discussed before, these are often stages of language and contextual understanding rather than mathematical stages. The fact that it is only in mathematics that a few children regularly pass GCSE at a very young age seems to indicate that for some children it may be lack of opportunity rather than developmental stages that holds them back.

If we think of a model for mathematics learning it is often a tall tower, one concept built upon another, and for many people some of the lower bricks are a bit shaky so the tower cannot grow taller without falling. However, there is evidence to show that mathematics is not learnt in such a linear fashion but as a mass of interconnected ideas and concepts, like neural pathways, a map of the underground or a complicated construct-a-straw model (Denvir and Brown 1986). A wider range of mathematical experiences in the classroom, some of which may be very challenging and require help and encouragement from the teacher, will allow more connections to be made in the children's minds and provide a firmer structure for future learning.

Although we have identified two very different models of teaching mathematics, in reality they can both be used to advantage in the same classroom.

EXAMPLES FROM THE CLASSROOM

Teaching early number: Key Stage 1 classroom

The children, all four to five years old, are in the reception class of county primary school. They are developing an understanding of number, the number system and early stages of arithmetic, mostly addition. The school uses a commercial mathematics scheme with a variety of teacher initiated activities used to supplement it. The classroom is well resourced with easy access to equipment and attractive displays including mathematical ones, and tasks introduced during teaching time are often left out for the children to 'have a go' when they have a few spare minutes, and they are used.

The mathematics scheme has a very structured approach to the development of concepts of numbers to ten. The children spend up to a week concentrating on each number, learning to read and write it in word and numeral, creating sets of objects represented by that number with beads, pegs, unifix and sorting toys. They draw a set of objects and label it. Later on they count out objects to represent that number and divide the set into two showing the different ways that two smaller numbers can be added together to produce the original number.

They work together in groups talking about their tasks with one another and with the teacher or another adult. They do some recording and written work in the scheme worksheets, but much of their work is practical and oral. The children are developing a sound understanding of each of the numbers to ten and are able to carry out the required tasks well.

The children are also given a wider view of number. They work on more abstract tasks with number lines and 100 squares. They play games where the teacher moves the numbers around on the line and they have to find and replace those that are wrong. They look for patterns in the number square and identify how the tens and units increase in different directions. Much of this work is teacher led and carried out as a whole class lesson on the carpet. This enables them to recreate a number square as a group using number tiles, and individually on squared paper. When learning addition they carry out tasks with objects but also play counting on games on the number line and use a wide variety of language to interpret what they are doing. They learn that + can represent and, altogether, count on, add, more, etc., and are encouraged by the teacher to articulate the similarities and differences of these expressions. Throughout, the teacher is listening to and watching the children as they work. She questions them about what they have done and why. This allows her to identify those children who may require additional or alternative experiences more closely targeted at their particular needs.

The more traditional Piagetian approach given in the mathematics scheme breaks up the mathematics into child sized portions. These are more easily assimilated but there is no encouragement to make links between them. The children may have a clear understanding of the three-ness of three but not that it is one more than two or one less than four. The richer, wider 'spread' of activities and the interaction with the teacher allows the children to make clearer links between the items of knowledge and so to construct more effective concepts, while the continued monitoring of the children's understanding allows the occasional 'arrow' when necessary.

This approach to teaching is by no means easy! It requires the teachers to have a clear understanding of the mathematics themselves in order for them to provide for and teach the children. It involves a high level of organisation, planning and assessment. But it can be done and the resultant learning will be richer for it.

Teaching number: Key Stage 2 classroom

The teaching pattern in the Key Stage 2 classroom is very similar. The school uses a commercial mathematics scheme as the core of the teaching programme with a variety of supplementary material. The classrooms are well resourced with equipment which is well organised and easily accessible to the children. There is a variety of mathematical displays; some reinforce current mathematical ideas in words and pictures, some pose new problems and some are pupil reports of solutions to previous problems. There is some whole class teaching as well as work in pairs, groups and individually. There is a balance of activities between skill-using and skill-getting with many problem solving activities leading to the learning of new skills as well as the reinforcement of previously mastered skills.

The commercial mathematics scheme is used to structure much of the work in the classroom. The teacher introduces topics to the whole class giving everyone the opportunity to hear mathematics discussed. The class is divided into four groups based on the results of formative assessment of the pupils' attainment. These groupings are flexible and often differ as the topics change. Two groups are likely to be working on activities (investigations or 'game' activities) which the class teacher has identified as appropriate to the current work and matched to the attainment of that group. These activities are designed to develop conceptual understanding and the pupils' ability to use and apply mathematics. They incorporate work with apparatus, development of mathematical language, the use of pictures and diagrams and recording in symbols. The teacher's attention is focused on these groups. She gives clear instructions and explanations and asks probing questions to help children develop conceptual understanding of the mathematics (Maclellan 1997, p.33). She monitors their oral and practical responses to the tasks as well as their written responses so that she can assess their development more accurately. She encourages the children to talk to each other and to her about their thinking. It is clear that the pupils know they are expected to be able to explain their methods as well as getting 'correct' answers. They also know that problem solving skills are an important part of their learning.

The other two groups will be completing work started on a previous day or working on practice and reinforcement of skills by completing examples from the mathematics scheme. These pupils may refer to an answer book from time to time to check their own work. If they are having difficulty in getting an answer they may talk to another pupil or use some apparatus or diagrams to reconstruct the method. They do not interrupt the teacher in her work with the other groups. Overall this is the *shotgun* approach which is roughly targeted on an aspect of mathematics at an appropriate level for the pupils so that they are challenged but have a reasonable chance of completing the task successfully.

The *arrow* approach is used when individuals or small groups of pupils are identified as having particular problems with topics which have already been covered by the shotgun approach. Similar activities are used with a continuing focus on using apparatus and language to enable methods to be understood, but the teaching is more directed and the scaffolding of the pupils' thinking by the teacher follows a stricter plan. The teacher will consider using alternative demonstrations of the concept if the pupil continues to have difficulty. The aim of this teaching is to enable the pupil to 'catch up' so that they can continue to work as part of the group.

Place value is a key concept in understanding and using our number system and developing that understanding requires that children experience a wide range of activities to enable them to construct a robust and complete conceptual structure during Key Stage 2. The classroom starting point for this development will be the use of a range of concrete apparatus (Dienes apparatus, abacus, number line, hundred square); each of which will assist in the development of different aspects of the conceptual structure. Other work will develop the idea of the mental image based on these concrete experiences so that increasing speed and fluency in calculation can be achieved.

Particular strategies for calculation may be shown with specific pieces of apparatus. The number line, as shown below, may help to show the pattern involved in adding 10. Work with an abacus may enable a pupil to see why subtracting 99 is most easily done by subtracting 100 and adding 1. Patterns on a hundred square like those in figure 5.4 may illustrate what is meant by addition and subtraction being inverses.

Appropriate language needs to be developed alongside these experiences. The language serves to capture and consolidate the conceptual structure. The accurate use of language in explaining methods of calculation is also a key way in which we can assess the development of the pupils' conceptual structures. The typical lesson will close with further whole class work, perhaps in mental arithmetic, perhaps with one group explaining the work they have undertaken during the lesson. This is the opportunity for some of the children to practise using mathematical language and for children to hear about other methods of solving problems.

Assessing mathematical understanding is difficult. Fluent use of symbols as a way of recording calculations can also be seen as a result of the approach described here. Fluent performance of skills and knowledge of number facts is a key to successful progress but they are more helpfully seen as the result of successful concept building than as a way to build concepts. It is possible for pupils to get correct answers to 'paper and pencil' calculations while having weak or incomplete conceptual understanding. A more accurate assessment of conceptual understanding needs to take into account the pupils' ability to explain their working using accurate mathematical language, diagrams and concrete apparatus.

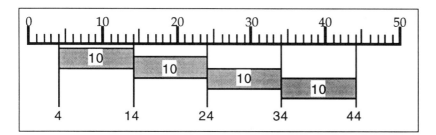

Figure 5.3 Adding 10 on a number line

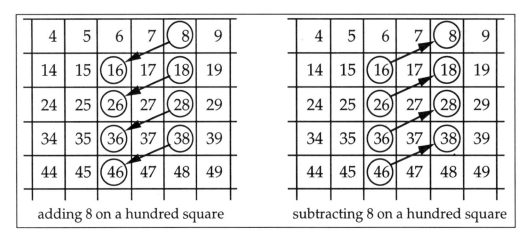

4	5	6	7	(8)	9
14	15	(16)	17	(18)	19
24	25	(26)	27	(28)	29
34	35	(36)	37	(38)	39
44	45	(46)	47	48	49

adding 8 on a hundred square

subtracting 8 on a hundred square

Figure 5.4 Patterns in a hundred square

IMPLICATIONS OF CONSTRUCTIVISM FOR THE MATHEMATICS TEACHER

A constructivist approach to teaching starts from the premise that pupils must construct their own meaning for the concepts and symbols used in mathematics. From this we draw the following points about the way in which a teacher can assist in the process of making mathematical meaning and develop mathematical thinking. Since the exact nature and sequence of learning cannot be specified in advance, understanding will be developed through:

- the active engagement of pupils with their learning;
- the use of a variety of apparatus to model the mathematical structure of a concept;
- a variety of activities which focus on related facts, skills and conceptual structures;
- the use of diagrams and pictures to help pupils develop strong mental images;
- activities which require pupils to use mathematical language correctly;
- opportunities for children to test their understanding through discussion with their peers and their teacher;
- opportunities for the discussion of problem solving strategies within the mathematics lessons;
- acceptance that there is a variety of ways to solve a problem and that the pupils should be aware that their task is to be able to explain their method not just to get the correct answer;
- continuous assessment through observation and discussion, resulting where necessary in more closely focused teaching.

These reflect a more holistic view of teaching, relating to classroom ethos and attitudes as well as provision. Putting a programme of mathematics teaching which follows this pattern into practice is a challenging task for the teacher. Nevertheless it is a challenge worth accepting if your aim is to help children develop a real understanding of mathematics which will enable them to tackle a wide variety of problems in their later learning and adult life with confidence and enthusiasm.

ACKNOWLEDGEMENT

The authors would like to thank Tim Copeland for his comments on earlier drafts of this chapter.

REFERENCES

Brissenden, T. H. F. (1988) *Talking About Mathematics: Mathematical Discussion in Primary Classrooms*. Oxford: Blackwell.

Bruner, J. S. (1967) *Toward a Theory of Instruction*. Cambridge, MA: Harvard University Press.

Denvir, B. and Brown, M. (1986) 'Understanding of Number Concepts in Low Attaining 7–9 year olds: Part 1: Development of Descriptive Framework and Diagnostic Instrument', *Educational Studies In Mathematics* 17, 15–36.

Department of Education and Science and the Welsh Office (DES/WO) (1989) *Mathematics in the National Curriculum. Non-Statutory Guidance*. London: HMSO.

Donaldson, M. (1978) *Children's Minds*. London: Fontana.

Edwards, J., Evans, M., Jones, M., Price, A., Hopley, N., Crook, J., Jaworski, B. (1994) 'Rich Mathematical Activity', *Mathematics Teaching* 149, December, 8–13.

Ernest, P. (1991) *Philosophy of Mathematics Education*. London: Falmer.

Fuson, K. C. and Kwon, Y. (1991) 'Chinese-based regular and European irregular systems of number words: the disadvantages for English-speaking children', in Durkin K. and Shire B. (eds) *Language in Mathematical Education*. Milton Keynes: Open University Press.

Haylock, D. and Cockburn, A. (1997) *Understanding Mathematics in the Lower Primary Years*. London: Paul Chapman Publishing.

Hoyles, C. (1985) 'What is the Point of Group Discussion in Mathematics?' *Educational Studies in Mathematics* 16(2), 204–14.

Kilpatrick, J. (1987) *What Constructivism might be in Mathematics Education*. Montreal: PME-XI.

Liebeck, P. (1984) *How Children Learn Mathematics*. London: Penguin.

Maclellan, E. (1997) 'The role of concrete materials in constructing mathematical meaning', *Education 3 to 13* October, 31–5.

Mathematics Association (1987) *Maths Talk*. Cheltenham: Stanley Thornes.

Nunes, T., Schliemann, A. L., Caraher, D. (1993) *Street Mathematics and School Mathematics*. New York: Cambridge University Press.

Open University (1982a) *EM 235: Developing Mathematical Thinking*. Milton Keynes: The Open University.

Open University (1982b) *PME 233: Mathematics Across the Curriculum*. Milton Keynes: The Open University.

Skemp, R. (1979) *Mathematics in the Primary School*. London: Routledge.

Skemp, R. (1989) 'Goals of Learning and Qualities of Understanding', *Mathematics Teaching* 88, 44–9.

Vygotsky, L. S. (1978) *Mind in Society*. Cambridge, MA: Harvard University Press.

Wood, D. (1988) *How Children Think and Learn*. Oxford: Blackwell .

CHAPTER 6

Science: Brenda grapples with the properties of a mern

Keith Ross

MINIMUM ENTITLEMENT

Brenda and Friends (West 1984) was published several years before the first science National Curriculum. It was an attempt to sketch out a 'minimum entitlement' for pupils who follow a course in science during the compulsory years at school. The discussion paper, part of the Secondary Science Curriculum Review, set out ways that an education in science could increase educational opportunity. It described the content of such a programme, with Brenda, and each of her friends, illustrating how the science they had experienced at school had changed and developed the way they thought about their world. This extract is from the section on energy and gives a flavour for those who are unfamiliar with this marvellous publication:

> Rebecca appreciates that the sun is the ultimate source of nearly all the Earth's energy and when she visited relatives in Israel she saw that by means of solar cells . . . the sun's radiant energy can be converted into electrical energy for domestic needs. By experimenting with different conditions in primary school when growing bean shoots in jam jars, Rebecca knows that sunlight is needed to make plants grow . . . [and] that animals cannot make their own food but have to eat other animals or plants for this purpose.
>
> Rebecca found it very interesting when, in her history studies, the class considered how the energy requirements of the average family home in the Western World in the 1980s compared with 100 years ago, but she was disturbed at the thought that not only has the energy consumption per person in the home increased but that the world population has increased too . . . From Geography lessons Rebecca is aware that not only does energy consumption vary very considerably between nations but that non-renewable energy sources are very varied in their distribution . . . she appreciates that, as a citizen of the world, she must exercise responsibility . . . (pp. 60–2)

How refreshing it would be if our present national entitlement were written in the same embedded and purposeful way. Instead we are encouraged to get pupils to learn their science out of context as a sort of recipe for SATs success: 'Pupils should be taught . . .'. While we can hope that teachers will translate the dry content lists that make up the National Curriculum into this meaningful format, it cannot be guaranteed. It is very hard to test how aware pupils have become of the place scientific ideas play in the world while our formal assessment tools

(SATs and GCSE) shy away from such contextualised and relevant applications, preferring to set questions from a science knowledge base.

This chapter will argue that we need to allow children to build the scientific ideas they meet in school into a meaningful, growing and evolving framework which gives them a coherent picture of their world: an integrated holistic picture.

MARKOBINE GANDO

Science educators have invented sets of new words to impress upon teachers in training the dangers of pupils learning their science recipe fashion: 'I want to draw your attention to a remarkable case described as a Gikky Martible' (Watkins 1981, p. 72). 'When an orbal of quant undual to the markobine bosal passes through a dovern mern it is deranted so as to cosat to a bart on the bosal called the markobine gando' (Ross 1990, p. 2). In these passages the scientific words have been replaced with nonsense words to represent the lack of meaning they convey to young pupils meeting them for the first time.

The remarkable thing is that questions following such passages can be answered 'correctly' by anyone knowing the rules of English grammar. For instance, 'What happens to the deranted orbal when it passes through a dovern mern?' In the same way pupils can get the 'right answer' to science calculations at GCSE when they are given the formula, though they have no idea what it all means, and can answer their SATs questions by learning the 'correct' names for parts of the body or a flower, even though they have no idea what function that part may serve. In contrast those who understand the deeper meaning, but use different words, are marked wrong.

Science is not something that should be learnt by heart. Its product is a set of ideas and models which attempt to explain natural phenomena. These ideas use the known to explain the unknown. For instance we might say 'It is *as if* the food goes into a long tube stretching from our mouth to our anus. It is *as if* it has small holes along it where the useful food can enter the body but the rest, which we don't use, stays in the tube and comes out at the other end,' or 'Think of electrical energy being *like* milk, delivered by electron bottles to the house, with the empty bottles returning to the cell. The flow of current (bottles per day) remains constant round the circuit.' These ideas need to be tested through careful observation of the phenomena either in nature, or in 'fair testing' experiments we have devised. Scientific ideas are constructed and developed from our existing ideas by a creative and imaginative process. If children are to be given a flavour of these scientific ideas and processes, the ideas must relate to things they already know. They begin to create explanations very early in life, through a combination of experience and imagination. Finding out what they do know therefore becomes the first task of a science teacher. Ascertain this, and teach accordingly (Ausubel *et al.* 1978).

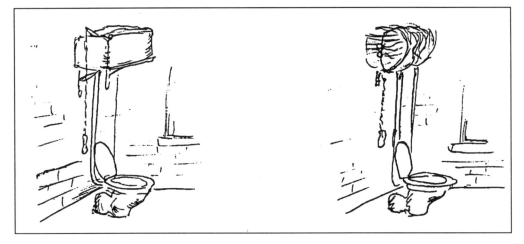

Figure 6.1 Two pictures of a toilet. The second has tank wrapped up in a blanket

INSULATION MEANS MAKING YOU WARM

This is a true story: The water in the tank of the toilet had frozen. Later that day someone had put a blanket round the ice-filled tank. The question is, will that make it easier or harder for the ice to melt? An explanation is also required. (Ross 1990, p. 4)

Most children, and a surprising number of adults, including, presumably, the person who actually put the blanket round the frozen tank, respond to the question by saying the ice would melt more quickly. They say the blanket insulates it and makes it warm. Here the word *insulate* means (to them) *make hot*, rather than *prevent flow of heat energy*. A constructivist approach to science teaching must start from these naive conceptions of learners. Of all subjects on a school curriculum these 'alternative' conceptions are most thoroughly researched in science (SPACE 1989–92, Driver *et al.* 1994). A constructive response to this alternative idea might go something like this (adapted from Driver and Bell 1986, see also chapter one of this book, and Newell and Ross 1996):

- Come into the class carrying two blocks of ice cream and proceed to wrap one of them in a small blanket. This gives the **impact** and **context** for the learning.
- Find out what the pupils think will happen to the blocks of ice cream if they are left unwrapped or wrapped. Finding out individual ideas from each child in a class of 30 may seem an impossible task. Most teachers wait for hands to go up when they ask a question requiring an oral answer. But if you ask the class: 'Whisper to each other which you think will melt first, or if it makes no difference, and explain why you think this way', each child will whisper their idea to their neighbour, allowing them to think it out for themselves and to rehearse a verbal response without making a fool or exhibition of themselves. Those without an answer hear one from their neighbour. You can now collect a few ideas in whole-class mode (with pupils who were not asked thinking to themselves 'Yes – that's what I said', or 'I didn't think that'), and ask if anyone else thought that way, or if there are any other ideas. You can then put it to the vote, thus **eliciting** the ideas of each of your pupils.

You might also **elicit** their ideas about the effect of either wrapping a hot mug of tea in a blanket or leaving it unwrapped. 'Whisper to each other which you think will cool down first . . .'

You will now probably need to **intervene** and challenge their views. Get each group of pupils to set up some ice and hot water wrapped and unwrapped, and ask: 'How quickly does the water cool?' and 'How much water has collected from the melting ice?'

Pupils need time to **reconstruct** their ideas, so use the blanket material to show how it always prevents heat from flowing from a hotter to a cooler place. Begin by asking the children why the blanket material can be used as oven gloves, but also as gloves for making snowballs. Then you can ask why a teddy bear wrapped in the blanket does not get warm, whereas your own body does. The idea of the blanket preventing heat from flowing becomes a better model, a more powerful explanatory idea, than their original idea that blankets are intrinsically warm.

With new ideas moving in alongside the old, or even replacing some of them (but blankets are still warm, surely?) the pupils now need time to **apply** their new ideas. They need to think of cool boxes used to keep things hot, and thermos flasks keeping drinks cool. Fridges lagged to stop the heat energy from the room from getting in, and ovens lagged to stop the energy escaping.

Their ideas can now be used in a project to design and make a cool box (Newell and Ross 1996).

OBSERVATION CAN NEVER BE NAIVE – IT IS ALWAYS THEORY LADEN

Show these two phrases (see figure 6.2) to someone for two seconds and ask them to write down what they saw. People will have no difficulty with the Arabic greeting (as long as they read Arabic) but will make no sense of the 'Good Morning' (unless, like you, they can read English). The same sense data comes into both the English and Arabic brain, but the brain can usually interpret one but not the other. So it is with all our sense experiences; the perception depends on comparisons our brain makes of the incoming sense data with our stored memories. Ask four women: a mother with her child, an architect, a car salesperson and a fashion designer to walk down the High Street observing things as they go. Then ask each of them to describe what she has seen. Four totally different pictures emerge, yet the same sense data, the same sights, smells,

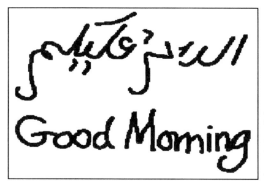

Figure 6.2 Greetings (the Arabic is the greeting 'Saalem Alayakum', and is not very well written, but is recognised by Arabic readers).

sounds, sensations were available to them all. And if it were a father and three other men, the mental pictures would be different again. Our conceptions are a product of existing ideas stored in our brains and the raw data we receive through our senses (see chapter one).

Think again of the blankets. People say 'They keep us warm. So surely they must have heat in them, and so they must be able to melt ice.' This is a logical set of ideas derived from the way we build up mental models. When we experience blankets keeping us warm, we imagine the warmth emanating from the blanket, so we assume that wrapped ice will also melt. When we touch a blanket (at room temperature) our ideas are reinforced. The heat from our hands cannot flow away so the blanket quickly reaches the temperature of our hand, and it feels warm precisely because the place we are touching *is* now warm. A piece of metal, also at room temperature, conducts the heat from our hand away so giving the sensation of being cold. A small metal coin also feels cold, but the heat has only a small volume to fill so the coin quickly warms up in your hand, and soon no longer feels cold.

This is a simple example of a common problem for science teachers. The naive ideas we build up from our everyday experiences tend to work only in very limited situations. The ideas developed by scientists tend to be counter-intuitive, until you are able to see them working in a wider context. In some cases the scientific ideas are too abstract to be of any use to children. One child once said to me, as I was trying to suggest that it was useful to consider that matter is made up of indestructible particles called atoms, 'They are of no interest to me – they are too small to be bothered with'. Yet without this idea the danger of adding lead to petrol, or the reason why combustion must be considered to be a constructive process where new materials are built up (Ross 1991) cannot be fully appreciated.

So the dilemma for the science teacher is that scientific ideas are often counter-intuitive, and, in contrast, pupils' existing ideas clearly work. They provide a simple framework for understanding the world: blankets are warm and burning does destroy. Do we try to substitute the scientific view for their existing view? Research shows that these existing views are firmly held (Driver *et al.* 1994) and traditional forms of teaching which do not take these existing ideas into account simply encourage pupils to learn by rote and recite that the orbal of quant cosats to a bart on the bosal. Full marks, but no understanding.

Solomon (1983) talks of switching between two domains; the everyday and the scientific. We cannot expect, indeed we would not want, pupils to deny their naive perceptions. We would expect them to enter the butcher's shop, despite the notice 'No animals allowed', we would expect them to keep pushing their supermarket trolley, even though 'objects that are travelling at constant speed in a straight line have no net force on them'. And we would not deny them saying 'I need some warmer clothes for Christmas'. The purpose of an education in science must surely be to make learners aware of the conflict, aware of the two domains, and to be able to switch between them. In this way their scientific knowledge is not something that is traded for SATs or GCSE results and promptly forgotten, but something that will provide a useful way of thinking for the whole of their lives. One of my postgraduate teachers in training said 'I haven't done that since A level, so I've forgotten it.' What is important in an education in science is what is left after all the detail has been forgotten: the big ideas – the things that Brenda and her friends have built into their everyday understanding. What use is A level study if some of the fundamental ideas have found no permanent place in the student's head?

TEACHING SCIENCE

Brenda and Friends teaches us that science needs to relate to our real world to help us make sense of the way it works. This has obvious implications for planet care and is discussed later in this chapter. Before that we need to look in more detail at the constructivist approach to teaching science.

Constructivism teaches us that learners need time to restructure their ideas. Existing ideas are often very firmly held. Lessons can be learnt from the history of science where scientists were also not always willing to relinquish their existing ideas. Isaac Newton remained an alchemist despite growing evidence for an elemental view of matter which began around 1661 with the publication by Boyle of the *Sceptical Chymist* (Hellemans and Bunch 1988). Einstein refused to believe in quantum mechanics, and it took the geological world 50 years to adopt plate tectonics as a way of explaining most phenomena related to the restless earth (Le Grand 1988).

We should not necessarily replace pupils' existing ideas, but rather provide a way for them to switch between the two domains. They will gradually see the power of the new ideas, and will be able to apply and use them when they are needed. Below is a final example of how a shift in thinking may occur.

Consider the candle: the bigger it is the longer it lasts. Wax drips down the side. It seems that the wax is retarding the flame, slowing the burning of the wick. One child said 'The wax is fireproof'. How can we, as teachers, challenge this view, and show that burning is a constructive process where oxygen joins with a fuel, producing oxides? How can we persuade children that the wax is the fuel? Figure 6.3 shows the principles of a constructive approach to teaching. If children are to change their viewpoint they first need to become dissatisfied with their existing view. In this case we can ask where the energy comes from in a bigger candle to provide the extra light. After all, more torch batteries would be needed if a torch were used, so what fuels the bigger candle? Children who are not ready for this energetic explanation may respond by reconfirming their existing view: the more wax the slower it burns, so wax must retard the burning. They may choose to ignore or reject the new experience or they may play the game of pleasing the teacher by agreeing to say the wax is a fuel in school, but 'knowing' very well for their everyday purposes that the wax is really a flame retardant. Only when they are ready to take on the new idea can they reconstruct a new explanation. It is only at this point that teaching is beginning to be successful.

Following the discussion of the wax, children can be shown an oil lamp and asked to compare it with a candle. They can see that in the oil lamp the wick holds the fuel allowing it to get hot and evaporate, before it catches fire and burns. In a similar way the molten wax from the solid candle must also be the

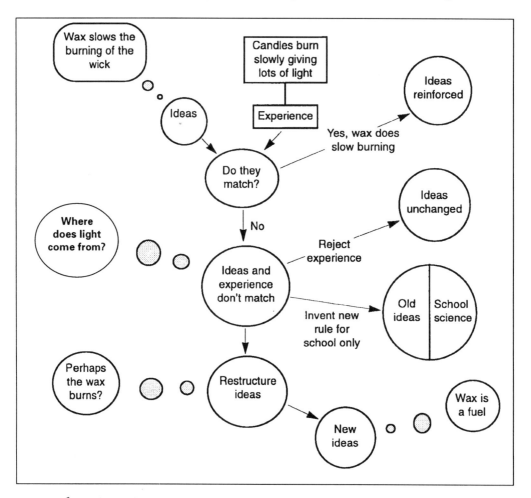

Figure 6.3 Ideas about a burning candle

fuel. Once the fuel is in the form of a gas, it can combine with oxygen from the air and energy is transferred as light and heat energy.

CONSTRUCTIVISM AND PLANET CARE

We are realising that our current way of living in the West is putting undue pressures on the planet. Our use of resources is leading to the double perils of depletion of supplies of raw material and consequent pollution of land, sea and air. But this view of materials is not immediately obvious. Without an elemental view of matter (i.e. matter is made from indestructible elements) resources could come from anywhere, and when finished with could be 'burnt away' or left to decay 'into thin air'.

Many people are unable to understand the scientific ideas that lie behind a particular 'green' action. In this case the idea that 'recycling of materials is at the heart of sustainable development' becomes obvious only when they realise the finite and indestructible nature of the elements that make up the materials we use (if we exclude the radioactive substances). It is not a sound approach to environmental issues to have to tell people what to do to be 'green'. Their education in science should provide them with a sufficient real and active understanding to make them want to be 'green'.

The following scenario suggests a constructive approach to teaching science that has planetary care as its purpose.

Impact: There are some obvious problems that even young children are aware of, where the local issue has global implications (think globally, act locally). Take litter. In fact bring litter into the classroom and throw it around. This provides the focus for discussion and provides the initial impact to capture interest. For safety purposes this would be 'clean' litter.

Elicitation: What do children think happens to litter that is dropped in the streets or in the countryside? If they say somebody picks it up, where does it go? If it rots away, does it disappear completely or does it change into other materials? If it is burnt, is anything left apart from a few ashes? We have been asking new entrants to teacher education such questions, and nearly half, despite a grade C in school science at GCSE, say that when materials rot or get burnt the atoms in them also get destroyed. The idea of unchanging atoms of elements making up the materials in our environment, which survive incineration and the compost heap is not universally held, even by the successful students who go on to train as teachers.

Presentation: Somehow the idea of the conservation of matter has to be shown, even during burning and rotting. One problem is that gases are not perceived as being real matter. In Lavoisier's day gases were classed as 'imponderable' airs (meaning that they were unweighable) and they were put in the same class as light, fire and the aether. It is not surprising that we develop the idea that gases are not of the same 'stuff' as the 'real' tangible objects that we can pick up.

To combat this ethereal view of gases we need to show children that gases are massive. For example if you pump air into a bottle, it gets heavier, suggesting that air is made of the same 'stuff' that solids and liquids are made of. We can show that air is needed for combustion and respiration. A candle goes out when covered by a jar because the air 'is used'. If this jar is placed over a second lighted candle this goes out immediately showing that there is some new 'stuff' in the jar. Children can see water condense onto the sides of the jar, showing water is a product of combustion just as we see condensation from the exhaust pipe of a car, or from our breath.

We can also get children to appreciate 'time lines' for materials. Bread came from flour, came from wheat. Cans came from metal, came from ore. Paper came from wood, came from trees. And when recycled, paper goes to make more paper and cans make new cans. Children also appreciate the water cycle from quite a young age.

We can now extend the consideration of cycles of matter (where things come from, where they go to) by looking at individual elements, rather than fully formed materials themselves. When paper burns or rots, iron rusts, or bread is eaten it seems that the original substance has disappeared and new substances are formed in their place. In what sense can one say that material has not been destroyed in these cases?

We approach this question by introducing the concept of an element, with carbon as the major example. We need to show that the carbon is never destroyed, but is passed in one form to another in the cycle of life. The idea that air contains small amounts of carbon (as carbon dioxide gas) shocked some students graduating from MIT, America's premier Science and Technology Institute (Channel 4 1993). That wood was made essentially from carbon from the air and water is not an easy concept to grasp. When food is respired or candle wax is burnt it is equally hard to imagine that almost all the material, including the carbon, in the food or candle, is converted into volatile materials when they combine with oxygen, and they re-enter the air.

Evidence for this carbon cycle is not easy to provide, but it can be done. For example, by paying attention to products of respiration and combustion (breathed out air and air left after burning are demonstrably different from fresh air; for example, candles covered by a jar of these go out more quickly than candles in a jar of fresh air), and simply by taking note of the importance of air during respiration and combustion (panting after exercise, fanning a fire, quenching a chip-pan fire by excluding air).

Reformulation: Being given a scientific idea that challenges their own beliefs is one thing. However, if learners are to incorporate this new idea into their own framework they need to use the idea, and make it their own. A task that is now worth doing would be to look at all the materials (solid, liquid and gas) that enter our homes and trace their path from source, into the house, through their use, till they are poured/flushed down the drain, thrown into the bin or breathed into the air/sent up the chimney. We can then consider where they all go to *after that*? Those that are recycled, such as those involved with living things, cause no real problems and they go on cycling 'for ever'; but those that are not recycled, either because they are not used by natural systems, or we cannot be bothered to create a cycle for them, may sooner or later cause us two headaches: we will run short of them, and we may be polluted by them.

Evaluation: One of the powerful elements of a constructive approach to learning is when learners reflect on their learning, through learning logs. Once you admit to yourself that you used to think that way, but now think this way, you make a commitment to the new thinking. Not only has a new way of imagining the world been constructed, but you have acknowledged that it has happened. This was from one of our trainee teachers: 'I found the principles of burning very enlightening. The constructive process of oxygen forming oxides and increasing weight now seems very obvious'.

THE NATIONAL CURRICULUM: MAKING SOMETHING OUT OF ZERO

A constructive approach to the teaching of science not only gives purpose to an education in science but also ensures that the scientific ideas 'learnt' are incorporated into the world-view of the learner. It is therefore important to ask if this view of science and learning can be extracted from the National Curriculum. If it can it certainly needs to be made more specific, but if it cannot we need to ensure the message is heard loud and clear by the curriculum reformers working on the revised National Curriculum for the year 2000 following the five year post-Dearing moratorium.

The four Programmes of Study corresponding with Attainment Targets 1 to 4 all state that children 'should be taught . . .'. There then follows a list of statements which could be interpreted very factually as 'this is what science is, and you need to learn it'. There is no sense of the problems that existing ideas may cause to the learner, nor of the provisional nature of scientific knowledge. Much of the non-statutory and other guidance given to teachers does make both of these clear. But not everyone reads such guidance (see, for example, CCW 1991, and NCC 1992). A curriculum that is presented as a description of what might be achieved in a life-world-view would be more acceptable, as, for example, is suggested in *Brenda and Friends*. There is, however, one more part of the science National Curriculum Programmes of Study, the so-called science zero, the part of the programme of study that starts off 'Pupils should be given opportunity to . . .'.

Science zero

It was a victory for many of us to have 'science zero' in the National Curriculum at all. In the 1991 orders this section was hidden in the preamble and few people bothered to read it seriously. Now it has the same format as the rest of the orders. The distinguishing features are that (a) there is no equivalent attainment target, so it is not formally assessed, and (b) it is for pupils to have *opportunities to*, not to be *taught*. It is these two factors that lead to science zero still having a lower status than the remaining four parts of the Programme of Study.

This section had its origins in the old Attainment Target 17 which itself sprang from 'Science in Action', one of the four profile components of the original final report of the science group which drew up the science curriculum in 1988 (Hull 1993, p. 26).

There are 5 sections to science zero. *Systematic study* is covered more or less by science one. *Health and safety* should go alongside all activity work in the other parts of the Programmes of Study. It is the remaining three that deserve mention here: *Science in everyday life* (which becomes *Application of Science* in Key Stages 3 and 4), *The Nature of Scientific Ideas* and *Communication*. In these three parts of science zero are held the key towards incorporating a constructivist approach to science teaching within the National Curriculum.

Science in everyday life

Brenda and Friends showed how a good education in science can lead to a deeper understanding of the world we live in and how it works. It was written in a style similar to the learning logs that are so important to a constructive approach to learning. Not only does it show how abstract scientific ideas are useful in explaining everyday phenomena, but it also shows that this understanding has to be worked at in order to give learners a sense of ownership. 'This is how I now think' is a confident remark of someone who has taken over new, more widely applicable, more useful ways of looking at their world. Not the *right* or *correct* way, for scientific ideas can never be absolutely true, but only our best guess at how things work.

Solomon talks of the need for switching between domains (1983), and

Vygotsky (1962) of allowing scientific and everyday concepts to meet. As teachers we must become increasingly aware of the naive ideas of learners (and of ourselves), so that we can enable them to see the reasons for the failing of their everyday ideas, and the way scientific ideas give a broader (but never complete) picture.

The nature of scientific ideas

Chapter one discussed the provisional nature of scientific ideas in some depth. It is too easy to tell children that this is the truth, that this is how it is, but we must always have at the front of our minds that scientific knowledge is initially a figment of our imagination. It resides in the minds and in the writings of scientists. But it is knowledge that has to be put to the test by the use of sensory data. The more we find we can use an idea the stronger our belief in it becomes and more and more people accept it. The history of the gradual acceptance of the theory of plate tectonics has been wonderfully recorded by Le Grand (1988) in a book aptly named *Drifting Continents and Shifting Theories*. The history of science is punctuated by revolutions in thought as one idea is replaced by another. Thomas Kuhn (1970) used his studies of this history to develop his own philosophy of science, showing that periods of stability, which he called *normal science*, where scientists followed one particular paradigm of belief, were punctuated by *revolutions* where the existing paradigm was clearly no longer adequate to explain the phenomena observed and a new way of imagining the world came to be accepted. Often old protagonists had to die off before the new ideas were fully accepted by the scientific community.

Children's ideas often mirror the changes that have happened over historical time, though clearly there are real and important differences even in those areas where there seem to be the closest parallels. For example most children believe that if you stop pushing something it will stop moving, an idea which can be attributed to Aristotle. It is, of course, an idea that holds up under experimentation, but it is somewhat descriptive, and uses the word force rather loosely. Newton's revolutionary ideas about force and motion suggest that the reason that an object slows down is because there is already a force acting on it. In the supermarket trolley example this would be the frictional forces which oppose motion. If these are removed, we no longer need a force to 'keep it going'. The transition to a Newtonian way of explaining motion seldom occurs in children learning science in school, though some of them can use Newtonian ideas to solve problems in physics books. Chapter 5 in Driver *et al.* (1985) shows that the word *force*, as used by most people, is more like the physicist's concept of *momentum*. If this is so, then saying that moving objects have a force on them (i.e. momentum) in the direction of motion becomes acceptable from an everyday use of the word force.

By helping children through their own revolutions in thought and preparing them for more to come, we can begin to show children the nature of science: not a set of true principles, but our continuing and imaginative attempts to create mental models of our environment which we can use to help us explore ever more deeply, with our senses and sensors.

Communication

Words don't have fixed meanings. Dictionaries do not give the correct meaning of a word. But if, as Humpty Dumpty said, 'when I use a word it means just what I choose it to mean – neither more nor less' (Carroll 1871) then chaos would reign, and communication would cease. There have to be shared meanings, and dictionary definitions help to stabilise these. But each of us uses and understands each word in a slightly different way. It is when words are used differently in science from their use in everyday life that problems really begin. We discussed above the example of *insulation* meaning 'keep warm', *animal* being used in contrast to humans, and *force* being used to mean something more like *momentum*.

It is important to uncover how young children use words. We may accuse them of muddled thinking, when it is simply that they are using words differently. Another example is the use of the words *light* and *heavy*. When a child says a ton of lead is heavier than a ton of feathers, or that heavy objects sink and light ones float, most educationalists throw up their hands in horror (or delight). The children are misconceived!

It could be, however, that the children understand the science well enough and it is their use of the words *light* and *heavy* that we must sort out. To them, weight, the force of gravity on an object, is not an easy quantity to experience. However, they know that certain materials are much 'heavier' than others, meaning (in adult, scientific use of words) that the material is more *dense* than others. The children use the same word heavy for two different ideas: absolutely heavy (this is a heavy book, you are too heavy to lift) and high density (lead is a heavy material, so it sinks). When the same word is used for two different ideas, there is bound to be some degree of confusion.

As teachers, we need to listen carefully to children as they use words, and watch out for understanding conveyed through an underdeveloped and possibly inadequate vocabulary. When children use one word for two separate ideas it is time to teach them a new word. Shadows and reflections are muddled up in the early years. By teaching the word shade, and showing it is the same as shadow, children can associate it with places where light has been blocked out.

Some materials let light through without much distortion – they are transparent. We begin by using the word 'see-through' for such materials. There are other materials which light passes through, but you cannot see through; they are translucent. This is less easy to translate into English; 'lets-light-through-but-you-can't-see-through' is cumbersome. Telling children that the scientific word for see-through is transparent, and the other is translucent, can be like using the words *markobine gando*. They have no meaning, so just have to be learnt. But children know many words with the Latin 'trans' in them; transport, transfer, trans-Atlantic, Ford Transit van. In each case they can see that something is moving, either 'through' or 'across'. Less easy, but worth exploring is the difference between -parent and -lucent (meaning 'see' and 'light'). What other words do they know containing these roots? Apparent, appear, to peer into the gloom are all linked with seeing; and lucid, Lucifer link with clear and light.

Scientific vocabulary should only be introduced when needed, when further delay would cause confusion because the ordinary words become inadequate. It is not always possible to find useful etymologies to help children find meaning in new words, but where their origin can be traced, and it gives meaning, it should be done. For example, think of the origin of the following words: television/telephone/telescope, hydro-electricity/hydrocarbon/hydrogen, microphone/microscope, month, igneous, electricity, mammal, insulate. Which etymology is worth activating to help children come to understand the way the word should be used?

Those derived directly from the Latin or Greek are straightforward and should be translated for the pupils: tele=far, micro=small, vision=see, scope=look at, phone=hear, hydro=water (so hydrogen is the element which generates water when it burns forming hydrogen oxide, or H_2O).

The other words in the list are less obvious, but we can still give powerful clues to their meaning. The moon circles the Earth once in every 'moonth' (this helps with spelling too). Ignite=set fire to, so igneous rocks are from fire. (Greek igni and Sanskrit agni meaning fire.) Electron is the Greek word for amber; the yellow resin that traps mosquitoes that once sucked dinosaur blood. When rubbed it acquires a static electric charge, and so it came to represent the new phenomenon of 'ambericity'. Interesting, but on this occasion of no help to children. Mammals have mammary glands for producing milk. The same Mmm sound used by babies has come to be used as the word for their mother: Mam Mum Mom, hence, mammal and milk. Insular means cut off (a peninsula is half cut off, as penumbra is half a shadow), so insulate means to protect or cut off from.

Children need to know how words got their meaning. It helps them move away from learning markobine gando by rote towards building the word into their real understanding (see Sutton 1992 and 1993).

CONCLUSION: THE MISTY MOUNTAIN

Vygotsky (1962) used the terms 'scientific' and 'spontaneous' (everyday) concepts. Spontaneous concepts are built up subconsciously and everyone needs to use these in the daily course of living, but the abstract 'scientific' concepts have to be learned through education. He realised the need to build links between these two types of concept, otherwise the scientific ideas would be isolated from real life. New ideas need to be retold in terms of existing concepts.

Traditional methods of teaching tend to assume science can be taught by telling children scientific ideas. This is like landing them on a mountain top in the mist, with no idea where they are. We can develop a self consistent picture for that local peak of understanding, but it will be isolated knowledge, and likely to be forgotten in a few years.

So-called 'progressive' methods of teaching assume that children will discover the mountain tops by themselves, inferring that we mustn't tell them. They must find out for themselves. This is like letting them play in the valleys. They never see the mountain tops which are covered in mist.

Constructivist approaches to learning take children's existing ideas into account, by acknowledging their view of their valley of understanding. However, the children can then be led up the mountain, in sight of the valley below, and now are able to see how the whole landscape links up and how limited their existing view was. New ideas give a depth, or, in this analogy, height, and breadth of understanding. Progress is made when we are led up to the mountain top on the shoulders of giant thinkers of the past.

As teachers we need to spend time developing children's ideas and, when necessary, challenging them. We cannot hope that children will spontaneously rediscover these scientific concepts for themselves. But equally we cannot hope that they will come to a real and useful understanding of these concepts simply by hearing them as we, their teachers, recite to them. Instead we need to help learners to construct their own understanding; one that is shared with the scientific community at large, but which is firmly rooted in, and related to, their everyday experiences.

REFERENCES

Ausubel, D. P., Novak J., Hanesian H. (1978) *Educational Psychology: a Cognitive View*, 2nd edn. New York: Holt, Rinehart and Winston.

Curriculum Council for Wales (CCW) (1991) *Starting with Children's Ideas*. Cardiff: CCW.

Carroll, L. (1871) *Through the Looking Glass, and What Alice Found There*. London: Macmillan.

Channel 4 TV (1993) *Simple Minds*. Video.

Driver, R., Guesne T., Tiberghien, A. (1985) *Children's Ideas in Science*. Milton Keynes: Open University.

Driver R. and Bell, B. (1986) 'Students' thinking and the learning of science: a constructivist view', *School Science Review* **67**, pp. 443–56.

Driver, R., Squires, A., Rushworth, P., Wood-Robinson, V. (1994) *Making Sense of Secondary Science*. London: Routledge.

Hellemans, A. and Bunch, B. (1988) *The Timetables of Science*. New York: Simon and Schuster.

Hull, R. (ed.) (1993) *ASE Science Teachers' Handbook*. Cheltenham: Stanley Thornes.

Kuhn, T. S. (1970) *The Structure of Scientific Revolutions*, 2nd edn. Chicago: The University of Chicago Press.

Le Grand H. E. (1988) *Drifting Continents and Shifting Theories*. Cambridge: Cambridge University Press.

National Curriculum Council (NCC) (1992) *Teaching Science at KS1 and KS2*. London: SCAA.

Newell, A. and Ross, K. A. (1996), 'Children's Conception of Thermal Conduction – or the Story of a Woollen Hat', *School Science Review* **78**(282), 33–8.

Ross, K. A. (ed.) (1990) *Can Children Learn Science?* Cheltenham: Cheltenham and Gloucester College of Higher Education (mimeo).

Ross, K. A. (1991) 'Burning: a constructive not a destructive process', *School Science Review* **72** (251) 39–49.

Science Processes and Concept Exploration Project (SPACE) (1989–92) *Research Reports*. Liverpool: Liverpool University Press.

Solomon J. (1983) 'Learning about energy: how pupils think in two domains', *European Journal of Science Education* **5**(1), 49–59.

Sutton, C. R. (1992) *Words, Science and Learning*. Milton Keynes: Open University Press.

Sutton, C. R. (1993) 'Figuring Out a Scientific Understanding', *Journal of Research in Science Teaching* **30**(10), 1215–27.

Vygotsky, L. S. (1962) *Thought and Language*. Massachusetts: The M.I.T. Press.

West, R. (ed.) (1984) *Towards the Specification of Minimum Entitlement: Brenda and Friends*. London: Schools Council Publications.

Watkins, O. (1981) 'Active reading and listening', in Sutton, C. (ed.) Communicating in the Classroom. London: Hodder and Stoughton.

CHAPTER 7

Design and technology: constructive learning in action

Richard Brice

Design and technology (DT) is a subject which embodies constructive learning in that its explicit Programme of Study statements are aimed to draw directly on children's experiences and ideas in the 'design and make' process. It is, however, an area which has been poorly understood and underdeveloped in many classrooms, and OFSTED have reported problems in terms of teachers' knowledge and achieving coverage of the National Curriculum (OFSTED 1995). In the light of this, the aims of this chapter will be:

- to define what actually constitutes DT;
- to illustrate this through examples of children engaged in DT tasks, including realistic strategies for DT work in a primary setting;
- to show how these activities nest within the parameters of the constructivist theory of learning which forms the rationale for this book.

WHAT IS DT AND WHY IS IT RELEVANT TO THE PRIMARY CURRICULUM?

DT might seem, alongside Information and Communications Technology (ICT) (previously called Information Technology), a relative newcomer to the primary curriculum, but its roots stretch back to the earliest period of mass education. Then, craft work for boys and domestic skills for girls were seen as appropriate pre-vocational training. Times have changed with the notion of education for life through the development of flexible skills to adjust to changing work patterns, and the economic need for a work force imbued with contemporary technology (Eggleston 1992). The need for a technologically capable population was identified by Her Majesty's Inspectorate (HMI) as an important priority for education in the debate prior to the National Curriculum (DES 1985) and the associated rapid rise of the status of science and technology was enshrined in the legislated National Curriculum (DES 1988). This was further reflected in the development of the City Technology Colleges of the late 1980s.

At a fundamental level, DT is concerned with the application of knowledge and scientific understanding to the solution of a problem. This problem solving element is intrinsic to all DT activity but clearly requires contextual information. At an adult level this could mean the design of a turntable for cleaning cars at a filling station. For a child, it could mean the design of a house for the three bears using recyclable materials. In each case the four elements of the design cycle are identifiable:

- the identification of a need;
- the generation of a design;
- construction;
- evaluation.

In both instances broad similarities exist, as the adult and child designer follow the same process, although the scale of the tasks and the resources available will differ. The most important difference will be the experience, knowledge and understanding of the designer in handling the materials to be used. Broadly speaking, this means that the range of tasks should reflect and build on the child's experience of the medium to be used. If pupils in a Key Stage 2 class are given the task of designing and making a Ferris wheel or a buggy, they need to be already familiar with the tools and materials they will use. Teachers often overlook this key aspect of DT resulting in children struggling to design and learn material skills at the same time. The adult analogy would be asking someone with no experience of plastics technology to design a child's car seat. Young children, in particular, have little experience of material properties and need to build up a range of skills to be aware of limitations and applications of certain materials, without which informed planning decisions cannot be made (Jarvis 1993).

THE PROBLEM WITH DT

As a consequence of rapid curriculum change in which DT was developed as a new foundation subject within the National Curriculum, DT lacked a clearly defined subject base like maths or science. In comparison to the research interest in primary science, DT attracted considerably less research activity, a fact acknowledged by the Department of Education and Science (DES and WO 1992). More recently, work such as Kimbell *et al.* (1996), drawing on the findings of the Assessment of Performance Unit project in DT 1985-91 (APU 1991), has offered fresh insight. The authors of the 1990 curriculum (DES and WO 1990), by contrast, had little in terms of research into children's learning to guide them.

Not surprisingly teachers, particularly at primary level, lacked understanding of the subject and how to teach it. For example, only 14 per cent of 900 teachers surveyed in 1989, felt confident about teaching DT (Wragg *et al.* 1989). Unfortunately, the National Curriculum orders for DT introduced in 1990 did not provide the guidance teachers were looking for. DT emerged as a subject from Craft, Design and Technology (CDT), Home Economics, some aspects of Business Studies, Information Technology (as it was then known) and Art and Design. At the primary level there were problems with teachers' own technical capabilities in addition to the nature of DT itself which was presented as highly process orientated. Pre-National Curriculum approaches to DT at primary level, such as craft, cooking and textiles, had commonly involved following recipe instructions, with little scope for children's designing. The 1990 document, emphasising the processes of need identification and design generation, left many teachers unclear as to exactly what constituted DT activities in the first place.

The original 1990 National Curriculum publication's adoption of the four elements of the design cycle as its Attainment Targets (AT) led many teachers to believe that all DT tasks had to be tackled from AT1 through to AT4 (Layton 1991). It soon became apparent that teachers were finding the DT curriculum difficult to understand (OFSTED 1993). The newly developed OFSTED teams were quick to note the correlation between teachers' understanding of the Orders, and their ability to provide a challenging curriculum: '. . . overall standards of achievement in primary schools in design and technology are often low. This is often linked to teachers' lack of subject knowledge and practical expertise in the range of design and technology activities.' (OFSTED 1995, p. 3)

Teachers also found the 1990 orders confusing, because the Programmes of Study lacked concrete examples of suitable tasks. This allowed the spectrum of what could be considered DT to become blurred. Many primary schools simply lumped DT into art or science planning. The use of unfamiliar terms such as artefacts, systems and environments was also alienating and ill-conceived. Moreover, the new orders, with the emphasis on process skills, might well have discouraged the teaching of traditional craft skills.

Only in 1995, with the revised orders, were teachers offered a document they could make sense of. The 1995 version (DfE 1995) was both slimmer and clearer. Out went some of the confusing terminology including artefacts, systems and environments and the widely misunderstood AT1. The ATs were now limited to Designing and Making. The notion that context should reflect the child's widening experience was supported by the removal of the need to cover themes from business and industry, allowing teachers to concentrate on the contexts of home, school and community.

CONSTRUCTIVE LEARNING IN DT

At this point it is relevant to bring in the role of the constructivist view of learning as this rightly places great emphasis on the context of the learner. The role of constructivism in developing children's learning in science is well established (see chapters one, two and six). Ollerenshaw and Ritchie (1997), for example, highlight, in particular, the role of the teacher in eliciting children's prior knowledge, and their work is supported by the findings of the earlier SPACE project (SPACE 1989-1992). Ollerenshaw and Ritchie were writing about science, but their findings are equally applicable to DT.

The complex interaction between thinking and action within the 'design and make' process is well detailed by the APU. The APU model shows how internal images in the mind's eye can be examined and refined through concrete expressions such as discussion, drawings, models, prototypes and the construction process to enable clearer and more detailed thinking leading to practical solutions to the problem at hand (APU 1991, p. 2). This model is a particularly clear analysis of constructive learning in DT, in that it shows how the 'design and make' process is actively constructed through interaction of the mind and hands of the child (see figure 7.1).

The stages of the constructivist's view of learning as described for science in chapter one are also very similar to the manner in which children develop technological and problem solving skills. This similarity will be explored in the following discussion.

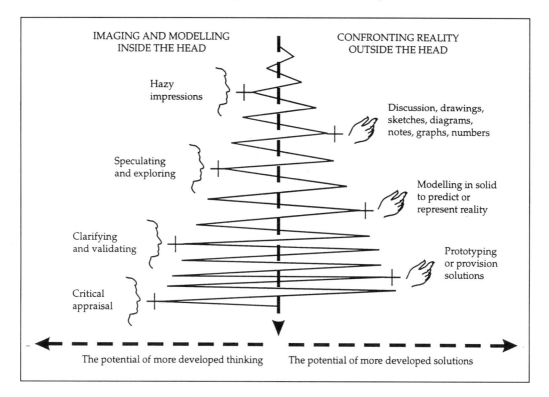

IMAGING AND MODELLING
INSIDE THE HEAD

CONFRONTING REALITY
OUTSIDE THE HEAD

Hazy
impressions

Discussion, drawings,
sketches, diagrams,
notes, graphs, numbers

Speculating
and exploring

Modelling in solid
to predict or
represent reality

Clarifying
and validating

Prototyping
or provision
solutions

Critical
appraisal

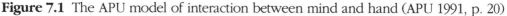

The potential of more developed thinking   The potential of more developed solutions

Figure 7.1 The APU model of interaction between mind and hand (APU 1991, p. 20)

Starting points and the role of eliciting children's ideas

That starting points must be relevant to children, i.e. home, school and community
in Key Stages 1 and 2, leading on to recreation and industry in Key Stages 3 and 4,
is accepted by teachers. What perhaps is less commonly considered or appreciated
is what the learner can bring to the learning situation. This knowledge can be
overlooked and a conscious effort is needed to elicit the understanding (or
misunderstanding) that children have. The extensive research into children's ideas
in science has been particularly useful in showing teachers the common alternative
views children can have. When tackling DT activities, teachers need to pro-actively
seek out children's ideas as a means of later restructuring.

Looking at the current orders for DT, the Programmes of Study propose
children carrying out three types of activity, namely:

- assignments in which they design and make products (DMAs);
- focused practical tasks (FPTs);
- activities in which they investigate, disassemble and evaluate simple products
  (IDEAs).
  (DfE 1995, pp. 58, 60)

These three sorts of activities support each other and are vitally important to the
development of Design and Technology capability (DATA 1995, OFSTED 1995).
Only through the structured development of a programme of IDEAs and FPTs can
children successfully progress onto more open ended and challenging DMAs.

The introduction of IDEAs was an innovation which recognised the role of two complementary processes to develop learning: exploration and evaluation. These are important enough to warrant separate discussion, although they share common themes.

Taking things apart

In order to understand how a thing works we invariably take it apart. In much the same way that adults will start to unscrew the bodywork panels of the broken down vacuum cleaner to see what's wrong with it, children need to explore materials and mechanisms to aid understanding and promote curiosity. A range of inexpensive toys which feature mechanisms can be acquired from car boot sales for the children to take apart. These can range from the simple wooden pull along toys to the more complex wind up variety. Toy manufacturers have even launched a range of simple mechanised toys with see through panels to show the mechanism as a feature. The point is that by exploring the toys children will begin to understand how they work. Technical vocabulary such as axles, springs and cogs are introduced in a concrete way. That children need concrete experiences before moving on to more abstract ones is well documented (e.g. Piaget 1929). That children need to tinker and take things apart to find out how they work is not new; the *Design It, Use It, Build It* groups advocated this sort of activity in the mid to late 1980s (Browne 1991). The novelty was the inclusion of this sort of activity in the 1995 Orders, recognising the potential for learning it offers and making teachers include it in their learning strategies.

Construction kits, e.g. Lego, allow the teacher to develop these themes in a more systematic manner. The Technic/Dacta systems are very useful to develop understanding of mechanisms and all children have experience in using some sort of Lego to explore solutions to teacher led or play problem solving. Any observer in a Key Stage 1 classroom will see children using construction kits in the afternoons as part of choosing time. This might lead one to consider that young children are using these resources to develop their understanding as the curriculum designers hoped. Unfortunately, these sessions are often loosely supervised as the teacher hears children read. Researchers such as Browne (1991) and Browne and Ross (1993) have asserted, with supporting evidence, that a link exists between the use of these resources and the development of spatial awareness and confidence in three dimensional construction. They also point out, again with observational evidence, that the different ways in which the two genders use these resources is very marked. When considering children's prior experience, this could be a key area that is currently underdeveloped.

Teachers have long noticed the reluctance of girls to play with mechanical toys in preschool and nursery situations. In later life this translates into a poor take up of physical sciences and technology. The latest figures for GCSE DT uptake point to a continuing gender divide (though not in terms of results, where girls out-perform boys) with girls generally opting out of DT at the first opportunity (OFSTED 1995).

Gender differences in science and technology have received much attention (e.g. Kelly 1987) and early gender differences can have long lasting effects. Browne, for example, asserts, and my observations and discussions with Early

Years practitioners confirm this, that as early as play group, gender differences are striking, with children having clear perceptions regarding gender domains: 'boys' stuff and girls' stuff' (Browne 1991, p. 3). Browne noted when children were allowed to choose activities, boys were four times more likely to choose and remain with the construction resources. The children clearly felt that Lego, Mobilo etc. were boys' toys, and the boys in the observation tended to monopolise this area of the classroom. The researcher noted resistance tactics being used by girls, when teachers tried to get them to play with the resources, including making a very simple model and then showing it to the teacher. A high level of praise was received for such a limited piece of work, sending the message that not much was expected of her. The Key Stage 1 Standard Assessment Tasks confirmed this and girls were found to have outperformed boys in all areas except AT3: Making (Kimbell *et al.* 1996).

The findings of the APU also highlight gender differences which could stem from lost opportunities in the Early Years. The researchers (Kimbell *et al.* 1996) noted that, while girls outperformed boys in the more reflective areas, e.g. empathising with users, boys were more confident in generating ideas and modelling them. Of real relevance to the teacher was the finding that these differences could be minimised with proactive planning. The APU concluded that offering tasks with a 'people rich' context would encourage the girls to engage, i.e. working from their strengths (Kimbell *et al.* 1996).

Research such as this heightens the relevance and necessity for a constructive approach to DT. Girls may have different experiences and interests, they may lack familiarity with construction kits and need time to catch up and become confident. This requires elicitation on the part of the teacher to assess the extent of the problem and also the conscious planning of intervention strategies to develop girls' learning and confidence. Browne and Ross, for example, found that appropriate role models provided the stimulus to encourage 'cross domain play' (1993, p. 44). Their research also highlighted the different attitudes of the children towards construction kits, and how the role play associated with these resources varies; boys tended to make models which move (cars etc.), and girls created more static models for social role play.

Careful elicitation at Key Stage 1 could allow teachers to plan effective intervention strategies to lessen these differences. A related point is the lack of structured use of construction kits as children progress through Key Stage 2. Resources such as Lego Dacta are expensive, but they can aid the modelling process that the National Curriculum demands at Key Stage 2. The real advantage of these types of resources is that they allow the child to model fairly sophisticated solutions in a manner that would not be practical using recyclable materials. Construction kits are also efficient in terms of time; the bits always fit and relatively sophisticated themes such as gearing systems can be tackled in short sessions.

Another area in which elicitation is important in DT covers another strand of the Programmes of Study, namely FPTs. OFSTED, in particular, have been quick to notice the connection between skills taught and evidence of high attainment in DT (OFSTED 1995). That children need to be taught skills in order to handle tools and materials safely is a factor which good teachers are well aware of.

Effective elicitation to find out about previous experiences would sharpen up the process and allow the teacher to plan short focused tasks to put skills into a practical context, e.g. making a picture frame to learn how to join wood. Those children who have useful previous experience will also provide a valuable resource. And careful organisation, including experienced and less experienced children working together or alongside each other, will help the children to learn from one another. Once the skills have been learned children can design using newly acquired knowledge which fits into the other side of the constructivist cycle (application of new knowledge and understanding) as children apply learning in a new situation, in this case a DMA. The DMA is a large scale project which will represent the culmination of work based around the chosen medium, e.g. paper/card, textiles, following exploration through IDEAs and FPTs.

The relationship between IDEAs, FPTs, DMAs and evaluation in the DT cycle is compared to the constructive learning cycle of orientation, elicitation, intervention, restructuring, application and review in Table 7.1.

EXAMPLES OF SUITABLE THEMES

One factor which has continually worried teachers when planning DT activities is that the Orders do not prescribe a range of tasks. By its very nature DT is not a body of skills or knowledge, rather a process by which the creative and problem solving powers of the learner are drawn towards the development of a solution. The role of the teacher is central in planning the sorts of tasks which will build on the strengths of the learner and guide them through structured interventions towards the development of DT capability, i.e. the ability to devise and implement a solution to a problem.

The following section includes examples of tasks which will lead to the development of capability through the three types of activities, namely: IDEAs; FPTs and DMAs. Through these tasks, moreover, it is hoped to demonstrate the role of the constructive learning.

An important strand of the DT curriculum, where children's prior knowledge is easily overlooked, is the theme of food. In the same way that adults will happily imagine the sort of wine they would serve with a particular dish, children have plenty of ideas as to the sorts of foods that would grace a party table. The gender issue discussed previously also comes to the fore as children may consider aspects of food preparation to be women's work. Clearly it is important to emphasise that food preparation (and eating) is an activity which is available to girls and boys and to men and women.

The following section will focus around the Programmes of Study and the possibilities of using food in a DT framework. There will be opportunities to design, make and consume the results. The starting point could be: is it possible to design with food? The answer has to be an unequivocal yes. Food is particularly easy to model in a cognitive sense. Children have years of experience to call upon, and the modelling has a tangible and concrete aspect. Initially, foods could be modelled using modelling material such as new clay or dough, though the final DMA would feature real food.

These ideas are based on the imaginary theme of a Teddy Bears' picnic. The

Table 7.1 Constructive learning in design and technology

Features of design and technology	Features of constructive learning
IDEAs (Investigation, disassembly and evaluation activities)	**Orientation / Elicitation** Through IDEAs the teacher can find out about children's prior knowledge and understanding.
FPTs (Focused practical tasks)	**Intervention / Restructuring** The teacher takes information from the elicitation stage and plans appropriate interventions to restructure the learner's understanding.
DMAs (Designing and making activities)	**Application** Learners apply new understanding through a 'design and make' activity.
Evaluation Learners compare outcomes of DMA to design criteria. Evaluation helps the learner to recognise the significance of new understanding.	**Review** Learners compare outcomes of DMA to design criteria. Evaluation helps the learner to recognise the significance of new understanding.

School policy and the National Curriculum inform the teacher of the range of ideas, skills and resources to be used. The constructive teacher achieves a closer match through the conscious effort to start from the learner's initial level of understanding.

work would fit in with a Key Stage 1 class project stretching over a half term. In common with much DT at Primary level, a theme has been chosen from a well known story, which identifies a need and context for the work to take place in. The final DMA would involve the class designing and preparing a picnic for parents and classmates. At Key Stage 1 it would include a range of sandwiches and cakes. At Key Stage 2 the theme could be modified to suit the starting point of *The Lighthouse Keeper's Lunch* (Armitage and Armitage 1989) and the task would involve construction of a box in addition to the lunch itself.

Both of these DMAs take starting points from stories, upholding the maxim of starting from the child's interest and viewpoint. Both stories are well known and establish a genuine need for the tasks. There is no perceptible gender preference in the tasks which should have appeal to all members of the class, as they are 'people heavy', draw on children's strengths and have appropriate scope for individual choice (Kimbell *et al.* 1996).

Factors to consider during the planning stage include the experience of the class in work involving food. Research would suggest that a real gender issue exists in this kind of work and we need to ensure our role model is appropriate and that we offer the opportunity for boys to develop skills in these areas

(Browne 1991). The main cross curricular link we need to make is with science in terms of a healthy and balanced diet. Regarding DT at Key Stage 1 the work would cover a range of food related themes such as safety and hygiene, cutting and washing food, to name a few.

Working towards a design

Children's ideas plus promotional literature from supermarkets and sandwich bars etc. could be pooled to develop lots of ideas (Ritchie 1995). Children will have plenty of experience of sandwiches and will be keen to share ideas as to what makes a good sandwich or cake for a picnic. They may also have ideas on what might make a healthy sandwich and why. It is important to encourage wide discussion at this stage so that children hear a range of views and experiences which they can draw on in their own designing.

Because children have such a wealth of prior experience they are quite able to design without the ice-cream melting in front of them. Cognitive modelling or imaging is essential, leading to the children colouring or drawing onto a proforma the filling they want for their sandwich. Some discussion of the need for savoury filling would be appropriate at this stage too. A related activity would be the production of menu designs. IT could be useful in this area allowing rapid re-drafting and editing of ideas. Cost implications need to be considered also. Children need to get used to the limitations placed on designers, of which cost is probably the heaviest.

FPTs and IDEAs

The second theme which could be tackled under the overall umbrella of *The Lighthouse Keeper's Lunch* would be the construction of the lunch box itself. This involves a different material, card, and a different set of skills would be needed to 'design and make' a box sturdy enough to be winched over the water. As with the food work, exploratory work would be needed to assess the children's skills in handling card. The result of such elicitation would inform the teacher whether a short FPT was required to develop the children's knowledge and understanding of the materials prior to starting the design work.

The exploratory stage would also involve some evaluation of other people's design, such as the sorts of bag used by fast food outlets. Investigation of the construction and disassembly will show different designs. A short net-making task would certainly highlight the key skills in turning card from two to three dimensions: accurate measuring, scoring to achieve clean edges and the understanding of the effects of folding card to increase rigidity. Such an input would certainly add value to children's design work as their perceptions of possibilities would be sharpened. Mention would also need to be made of the features unique to this design, for example the need for a string fixing and glue flaps.

The design brief might actually quantify the dimensions required for the healthy lunch not to mention the weight of a typical offering. A pulley system could be set up to test the designs as they were nearing completion. A simple DTP (Desk Top Publishing) package such as Microsoft *Publisher* could also be used to design simple packaging.

Research into DT (Cross 1994, Ritchie 1995, Kimbell *et al.* 1996) has stressed the active, reflective and creative capabilities the subject develops. The following checklist derived from the Programme of Study highlights the common features of a DT activity (see Table 7.2).

In summary, DT is an exciting area of the curriculum that has undergone huge development over the last two decades. At its best the subject offers pupils the chance to problem solve and be 'active, reflective and creative learners' (Cross 1994, p. 8) of the sorts of skills considered highly relevant to a modern world and enshrined in the City Technology Colleges.

At present, however, standards of achievement in DT in schools vary considerably, with particular problems in the primary sector. Centrally funded GEST courses have helped teachers develop their own skills, as have advisory teachers where they still exist, though there is still much need for extending and supporting teachers' skills and knowledge in DT.

For teachers at the chalk face, the bright light in this firmament must be the attitude of children who have given the subject a big thumbs up. OFSTED noted that at all levels children enjoyed the challenges of a problem explored and resolved in concrete terms (OFSTED 1995). As a literature develops for the subject so teachers can use the findings of recent research to support their planning. For the constructive teacher, the subject should pose few problems, because the basic ideas underpinning DT activities fit so neatly into the constructivist framework. The decision regarding materials is covered in Programmes of Study, the level of the children determined by elicitation and exploratory tasks. Structured interventions will ensure that relevant skills and knowledge of materials and techniques are taught allowing the pupils to develop their design capability.

Table 7.2 A checklist to judge children's involvement in design and technology in the food 'design and make' activity (derived from Ritchie, 1995 and DfE 1995)

Does the task reveal children:	**Actual response plus evidence:**
• actively involved in a practical task?	• making sandwiches, handling and combining materials;
• meeting needs, either their own or generated by their teachers?	• teacher has identified the need for the activity, story provides an appropriate starting point;
• generating ideas, leading to plans, designs and construction?	• deciding on the sandwich fillings, drawing simple pictures with some labelling, then making them;
• evaluating their designs and products?	• this would take place on the picnic or perhaps the next day in the classroom.

REFERENCES

APU (1991) *The Assessment of Performance in Design and Technology.* London : SEAC.

Armitage, D and Armitage, R. (1989) *The Lighthouse Keeper's Lunch.* Edinburgh: Oliver & Boyd.

Browne, N. (ed.) (1991) *Science and Technology in the Early Years.* Milton Keynes: Open University Press.

Browne, N. and Ross, C. (1993) *Girls as Constructors in the Early Years: promoting equal opportunities in maths, science and technology.* Stoke on Trent: Trentham.

Cross, A. (1994) *Design and Technology 5–11.* London: Hodder & Stoughton.

Design and Technology Association (DATA) (1995) *Guidance Material for Design and Technology.* London: DATA.

Department of Education and Science (DES) (1985) *Better Schools.* London: HMSO.

DES (1988) *Education Reform Act.* London: HMSO.

DES and the Welsh Office (WO) (1990) *Technology in the National Curriculum.* London: HMSO

DES and WO (1992) *Technology, Key Stages 1, 2 and 3. A Report by HMI on the First Year, 1990–1.* London: HMSO.

Department for Education (DfE) (1995) *Key Stages 1 and 2 of the National Curriculum.* London: HMSO.

Eggleston, J. (1992) *Teaching Design and Technology.* Milton Keynes: Open University Press.

Jarvis, T. (1993) *Teaching Design and Technology in the Primary School.* London: Routledge.

Kelly, A. (ed.) (1987) *Science for Girls?* Milton Keynes: Open University Press.

Kimbell, R., Stables, K., Green, R. (1996) *Understanding Practice in Design and Technology.* Milton Keynes: Open University Press.

Layton, D. (1991) *Aspects of National Curriculum Design and Technology.* York: NCC.

National Curriculum Council (NCC) (1990) *Technology in the National Curriculum.* London: DES and WO/HMSO.

Office for Standards in Education (OFSTED) (1993) *Technology: Key Stages 1, 2 and 3: A Report from the Office of Her Majesty's Chief Inspector of Schools, 1991–2.* London: HMSO.

OFSTED (1995) *Design and Technology: A review of inspection findings, 1993/4.* London: HMSO.

Ollerenshaw, C. and Ritchie, R. (1997) *Primary Science: Making it Work,* 2nd edn. London: David Fulton.

Piaget, J. (1929) *The Child's Conception of the World.* London: Harcourt Brace.

Ritchie, R. (1995) *Primary Design and Technology: A Process for Learning.* London: David Fulton.

Science Processes and Concept Exploration Project (SPACE) (1989–92) *Research Reports.* Liverpool: Liverpool University Press.

Wragg, E. C., Bennett, S. N., Carré, C. G. (1989) 'Primary teachers and the National Curriculum', *Research Papers in Education* 4(1), 17–45.

CHAPTER 8

The use of information and communications technology (ICT) in education: a constructivist perspective

Les Watson and Keith Ross

INTRODUCTION

This chapter focuses on 'learning with ICT' rather than 'learning about ICT'. The aim is to encourage readers to reflect firstly on education and secondly on the use of ICT in learning. We shall do this by presenting, in outline, two apparently extreme philosophies behind the use of ICT from which the reader can choose to define his/her own position. They are those in which knowledge is acquired by conditioning and where knowledge is seen simply as a process.

There is much scope for confusion about the use of ICT in schools as it covers a vast range of possibilities, extending from learning keyboard skills to exploring distant planets. ICT also has its own obscure terminology which serves to further mystify its use. A simple framework for describing the software in the context of education is suggested. The aim of this framework is to relate software to educational philosophy and not merely describe classroom applications of ICT. In fact those aspects of ICT in schools which concern learning about the technology (whether soft or hardware) will be largely excluded from our considerations. Without them ICT cannot be used, but they are only the means to an educational end, not an end in themselves.

Factors surrounding the extension of the use of ICT into the home and other environments provides an opportunity for the development of ICT as a medium for pervasive lifelong learning and will be considered towards the end of the chapter, together with a consideration of the effect of ICT on learning as a social undertaking. Our final conclusions re-emphasise the over-riding need to see ICT as a support for learning, but acknowledging that there will be a transition period during which the number of computer have-nots will inevitably decrease.

ICT WITH AN EDUCATIONAL PURPOSE

Introduction

Information Technology has been used in education for at least the last 20 years. However it is well documented that the use of ICT has been of somewhat intangible benefit. Indeed the Stevenson (1997) and McKinsey (1997) reports both identify a lack of purpose and understanding in the use of ICT in schools. The McKinsey report in particular cites 'lack of educational purpose' as the key factor which has determined the limited success that ICT has had in supporting learning. As McKinsey points out, IT is capable of supporting a range of educational philosophies. What is important is that the teacher has one: 'Whatever [educational] philosophy is followed links have to be made between those educational objectives and objectives for IT' (p. 3).

This lack of purpose is evident in the application of ICT throughout education from school to university.

Learning about ICT

It must be acknowledged that one of the barriers to effective use is that computer systems are generally inaccessible, despite the evolution of the mouse, windows, and pointer systems. Children need familiarity with computer systems in order to make effective use of them for whatever purpose. This basic skilling is analogous to learning to form letters in early writing experiences and provides the gateway to higher use of the technology for composition and editing, just as letter formation provides the gateway to written composition. The danger, and often the reality, is that basic skilling becomes the end rather than the means. Oppeneheim (1997) notes that:

> In a poll taken early last year US teachers ranked computer skills and media technology as more 'essential' than the study of European history, biology, chemistry, and physics; than dealing with social problems such as drugs and family breakdown; than learning practical job skills; and than reading modern American writers such as Steinbeck and Hemingway or classic ones such as Plato and Shakespeare.

It is the inaccessibility of computer systems that enables basic skilling to become an excuse for computer use. The hope is that new methods of computer access, from desk top wizards to speech input, and wider access to computers by individuals will dismantle the usability barrier, as outlined in the case study below. Removing the distraction of the technology itself will encourage teachers to address the pedagogy of ICT use.

Case study one: a class set of pocketbooks

Scene: a Y6 class in an urban school in Gloucestershire. An NCET bid supplied the school with a class set of Acorn Pocket-books and an A5000 portable (called A4) and A link. The immediate aim was to take the Pocket-books to Ironbridge on a field week. During the day pupils made notes using *Write,* the word processor, and in the evening they downloaded the files onto the A4 using the A link. Back in school they imported pictures which were developed as a CD rom into a *Magpie* presentation, with each child creating their own page and linking it to a location map (created using *Draw)* and to other children's pages.

That was three years ago. Towards the end of each year the outgoing Y6 hand over their pocket-books to the Y5 pupils, showing them the ICT skills needed to use them fluently. These skills are consolidated during the early weeks of the Autumn term. Now when you enter the class they may be using pens and pencils, but they may equally be drafting their work directly into *Write,* or redrafting work they began earlier, perhaps with a printout with teacher's comments/suggestions, or they may be in the final stages of spell-checking and editing the work ready to import into a publishing pack on one of the class computers or to print it directly from the pocket book.

Here the basic ICT skills are no longer a barrier. Instead they enable pupils to learn and understand, creating worthwhile, high quality, non-fiction writing which is very much their own.

Two extremes of pedagogical stereotypes

The two stereotypes outlined here mark the extremes of a continuum which informs the ways in which ICT systems may be deployed in educational settings. This continuum is identified by Somekh (1994) as ranging from

> those following Skinner, who see learning as 'conditioning' by means of a carefully planned sequence of 'stimuli' designed to elicit a set of desired 'responses'; [to] those following the ideas of Vygotsky and Bruner, who see knowledge as process rather than a product. (p. 3)

Somekh notes that it is much more difficult to devise software which supports constructive learning and promotes the internalisation of concepts. The pedagogical approach adopted is clearly a key issue in the design and use of ICT to support education as discussed below.

Early educational experiences, largely based on play, form part of initial schooling. These approaches often take a constructivist view of learning. That is, children, through their activities, develop 'personal' constructs relating to the world about them, including the information in that world as well as the physical entities. This constructivist view of education has its early roots in Piagetian thinking (Boden 1979) and has been developed by the work of Vygotsky (Wertsch 1985), as a new social constructivism which takes account of children's current understanding in developing their conceptual frameworks. (See also chapter one of this book.) The constructivist approach allows the learner to build, or rebuild, their own framework of understanding, often with considerable support from their tutors.

The alternative prescriptive 'content based' view provides a clear contrast to the constructivist view. The acquisition of a body of knowledge is the major objective of prescriptivism. Approaches which concentrate on effective communication are used to deliver 'knowledge content' as effectively as possible to learners. This content is accompanied by a structural framework of understanding which the learner needs to acquire, but often doesn't. Price (1989) describes an extreme of this prescriptive approach as taking a Skinnerian, behaviourist stance presenting computer based, or computer assisted, learning (CBL, CAL) as programmed instruction. Price concludes that the application of Skinnerian principles to the design of instruction could produce effective teaching programs. However, he adds that efficiency is not enough to guarantee success in an educational setting. As argued by Brown *et al.* (1989) context independent knowledge may be less than useful, as knowledge acquired from a content driven factual approach is more easily misused by the student, and does not, in general, promote the understanding required for the knowledge to be applied successfully.

THE POTENTIAL OF ICT SOFTWARE AS A TOOL FOR LEARNING

Playing with ideas

Fraundhorf (1996) working with multimedia ICT, identifies this as a key technology for the support of constructivist educational approaches. It is her opinion that appropriately designed multimedia ICT can provide variety to children's experiences and a basis for personal construct development beyond current classroom experiences. In particular, simulation and scenario based software with, for example, adventure content, gives children opportunities to explore worlds beyond those usually available in the classroom. If these are explored 'playfully' then they will support children's development of a range of personal constructs. There are implications for both teachers and children in the adoption of such constructivist approaches to learning. In 'Playing with computers, playing with ideas' Clements (1995) identifies the link between playful approaches to learning, typical of much of the work which has taken place with the computer language logo (Papert 1980, 1993) for example, and the development of creativity. It is clear that if creativity is to be part of the curriculum then playfulness and constructivism must be important components of the educational philosophy underpinning the design and use of multimedia systems. The implication here is, as outlined by Clements (1995), that software will inhibit creativity if it imposes restrictions on pupil activity and choice of actions. Much current computer assisted learning material does just this. Thus an important factor in the design and application of multimedia ICT systems is the degree of 'freedom' the pupil and teacher have. As Clements (1995) recognises:

> Children see play as activity that they choose voluntarily, directed by themselves, and constructed in an uninterrupted time span. Curriculum – computer based or not – that includes mostly practice and assigned tasks will not engender a playful approach in students. (p. 206)

The work of Papert (1980) mentioned above, which focuses on the idea of microworlds, represents a clear attempt to provide the freedom and opportunities for playfulness essential for children to develop their own personal constructs and develop deep understanding of the world in which they live. Further, such microworlds (Clements 1995) facilitate both positive social interactions and positive cognitive interactions and hence link social and cognitive development providing a holistic approach to the education of the child. In parallel with the development of the child, teachers also need to 'play' with ideas about how they might use computers and emerging multimedia systems in particular, in order to promote deep, meaningful and creative learning. This constructivist approach to the use of ICT focuses on the process of learning and the active involvement of the individual pupil. A recent example of a multimedia package based on a constructivist view of learning is described below in case study two.

The Science of Environmental Issues – A multimedia CD-ROM

This multimedia CD-ROM, which has been developed to support student learning in science (Ross and Lakin 1998), is based on two principles. Firstly it uses research on alternative frameworks from the constructivist approach to science teaching to identify the main hurdles preventing conceptual understanding in science. Secondly it focuses on the concern for the environment, felt by many in the population, to provide the context for learning. The CD-ROM was written originally for use with Primary Teachers in Training, but during the evaluation phase it was considered suitable for those trying to understand scientific ideas from pre- and post-16+ pupils in school and for foundation courses in science at further and higher education.

The multimedia pack is designed to challenge people's naïve ideas of science and allow them to construct a good working knowledge of many of the scientific concepts relating to environmental issues. There are six sections each with a series of branches. Most major branches begin with elicitation questions which are responsive to the different answers students may give. Using animation, simulation, video sequences etc. students' alternative ideas are contrasted with currently accepted scientific ideas. Students are able to pace themselves and explore items of interest in some depth. The resource attempts to allow users to examine their own preconceptions about the science of their environment, and to reconstruct a better, more useful, understanding.

In contrast to this much early computer software was of a drill and practice type. Chandler (1983) described this as 'teacher centred'. Such software was overtly prescriptive in its approach. The modern equivalent is the Integrated Learning System which provides individual computer based schemes of work for children to follow. Collins *et al.* (1997) label such systems as 'back to the future'. The jury is still out on the effectiveness of these systems in promoting learning. However an ILS is a good example of a prescriptive approach which through individual tailoring and feedback, for the pupil and the teacher, may well prove to be effective at least in basic skill development. However, as we have been at pains to point out, effective, useful learning begins once the basic skills have been acquired. Our aim is to remove barriers imposed by the need for skills so ICT can be used as a tool for learning.

The ICT tools for learning

A browsing of supplier catalogues of educational software reveals an emphasis on content rich applications with prescriptive tendencies which may not, on first reading, appear to support constructivist approaches to ICT. The following table is provided as a framework of types of software and their modes of use.

Figure 8.1 attempts to classify software in relation to the role of the computer in the learning process by briefly describing the part that the computer plays in the communication of information during use.

The prescriptive – constructive continuum

The prescriptive approach, mentioned earlier, is supported by the Instructional Systems Technologist (IST) school. While prescription and constructivism are at the opposite ends of a continuum they are not necessarily mutually exclusive. Merrill (1991) distinguishes between 'moderate constructivism' and 'extreme constructivism', claiming that the former has much to offer instructional design. Merrill concludes that extreme constructivism makes assumptions about the learning process which may actually prevent the more effective instruction that its proponents claim. In particular Merrill believes that at least some minimal task guidance is required for learners if learning is to be effective: 'There are in fact agreed-upon concepts, principles, facts, procedures and activities that learners must learn' (p. 51); an unfettered 'discovery' approach favoured by 'extreme

	Typical software
Computer as learner	Logo Music software Control software
Computer as tool	Wordprocessor Spreadsheet Database
Computer as teacher	ILS Drill & Practice

Figure 8.1 Software type and learning processes

constructivism' is so lacking in structure that it is unlikely to provide a sound basis for software construction. However, Merrill is misinterpreting the meaning of a constructivist approach to learning, which develops meaning by exposure of existing ideas to new ideas as explained below. Task guidance is at the heart of constructivism.

Kemmis *et al.* (1977) identified four categories of educational software each of which can be placed on the prescriptive-constructive continuum. 'Instructional' software is clearly at the prescriptive extreme. Guided discovery is possible using 'revelatory' software such as a simulation. Increased pupil control is offered by 'conjectural' software such as that used for on screen modelling. Finally 'emancipatory' software includes open ended tools such as multimedia virtual experiments and authoring software which provide opportunities for an element of investigation and 'play' enabling consequent construct development.

Relating software to educational objectives

This book, in exemplifying a constructivist approach, shows the value of examining children's current understanding, or alternative constructs, as a way of understanding the range of commonly held existing ideas and explanations of phenomena. By understanding the child's current constructs the constructivist approach attempts to develop children's understanding starting from where they are and intervening appropriately, rather than imposing a conceptual framework which is unconnected to the learner's current understanding. There is considerable potential in the development of multimedia software to support both constructivist and prescriptive educational approaches, the former being based on knowledge of the common constructs and their alternatives in a subject domain with appropriate interventions for the development of understanding, and the latter being based on a content based approach. This 'versatility' of multimedia systems is recognised in the recent McKinsey report (1997) which articulates a clear need to relate the use of ICT in schools to educational objectives while acknowledging that ICT can support any educational philosophy. Case study two above exemplified an attempt, in a multimedia resource, to use a constructivist approach to learning while retaining, or revealing, a firm content base.

Figure 8.2 links software type to educational approach. Those software types, such as case study two, which provide support for a constructivist approach have a revelatory and emancipatory nature.

THE PERSPECTIVE OF THE TEACHER

Impact of learning approach on the use of multimedia ICT

Clearly the underlying philosophy in the design of a multimedia educational system will affect how and where it is deployed. The philosophy of the deploying teacher and his/her expectations of ICT will also be key factors. As Scrimshaw points out (1997, p. 100):

> To ask how teachers need to use computers is in large part to ask how the computer might be used to support and explore the theoretical and practical implications of their own philosophy of education, with a view to its improvement.

Kay (1995, p. 24) notes that 'Teachers' work with IT is still hamstrung by the perception of the computer as a glorified clerk'. Many multimedia systems are aimed at doing what was done previously in the classroom, but simply doing it by computer because computers exist. Kay argues that the adoption of a new perspective by teachers is an important factor in the effective use of multimedia systems in schools. The new perspective Kay identifies is for teachers to start asking questions rather than trying to answer them. They need to examine their underlying beliefs about learning in conjunction with understanding the computer

	Typical software	
emancipatory		constructivist
Computer as learner	Logo Music software Control software	
conjectural		
Computer as tool	Wordprocessor Spreadsheet Database	
revelatory		
Computer as teacher	ILS Drill & Practice	
instructional		prescriptive

Figure 8.2 Software type and educational approach

as a curriculum resource. Kay's requirement of teachers to 'ask' questions is congruent with a task-based approach to constructivism mentioned earlier.

Progression – acknowledging the capabilities of young children

As also mentioned earlier, basic capability with technology is an essential prerequisite to its successful use. McKinsey (1997) suggests that ICT training of teachers is the most important critical success factor in improving the use of ICT in schools. Clearly both teacher and pupil basic skilling are needed to provide the foundation to successful classroom use of ICT.

Consider this question put by Heppell (1994) in the Ultralab survey of secondary school pupils: 'Do you think your secondary school builds on the computing you did at primary school or ignores it?' The results of the survey revealed 'a very large number of respondees who felt *very strongly* (i.e. they ticked the extreme of the scale) that their primary work had been ignored' (http://www.ultralab.ac.uk).

The fact that secondary school computer experiences do not always build on primary school work is worrying. It is only when there is continuity at the basic skills level that we can hope for a deeper constructivism in the way ICT is used to support learning.

Can ICT change teaching?

As suggested above it is also clear that the potential for ICT to promote systematic change in the classroom is not being met. This is characterised by the Ultralab team (1994) below:

> Generally of course, the rate of change in education has always been slow. A cinema newsreel, filmed in the 1920s, of transport, hospitals, cafeteria, sport, indeed almost any aspect of our daily lives, will remind us of the great technological changes that have characterised the 20th century. However, show a short film of a group of children in a classroom anywhere in Europe and it is extremely difficult to attribute its date accurately to any particular time between the 1920s and today without resorting to the 'non educational' clue of fashion. Our learning environments have not yet been transformed by technology in the way that much of the rest our everyday life has been. (http://www.ultralab.ac.uk).

This may, at least in part, be to do with the 'isolated' nature of the school. As Scrimshaw (1997, p. 107) identifies: 'Historically schools have been partly sheltered from these [change] processes, because in their location, staffing, and to some extent the knowledge they were expected to transmit they were physically and organisationally separate from the society around them.' As initiatives such as the proposed National Grid for Learning become a reality this isolation will be removed and gaps between schools, society, and the home will be narrowed, providing increased opportunity for ICT to change what takes place in schools.

EXTENDING ICT INTO THE HOME

Computers in the home

> Until now, the main thrust of policy on IT in education has been directed at the traditional place of learning – the school. Yet the rapid growth of computers in the home opens up possibilities to extend learning beyond the classroom. (McKinsey and Company 1997, p. 18)

McKinsey reports that the number of post-1989 machines in UK homes is around 5 million. This currently represents some 22 per cent of UK households; more importantly, the growth in home ownership of computers is likely to accelerate. The BIS Strategic Decisions Survey (1994) market survey predicts that around 45 per cent of UK homes will own computers by 2000–2001, and also suggests that ownership may become as high as 55 per cent if sales follow the previous patterns of consumer items such as VCRs. Analysis of numbers of computers in the home, the primary school, and the secondary school clearly shows that availability and quality in the home already exceeds that in many schools in the UK (McKinsey and Company 1997, exhibit 36, p. 33).

The picture from the perspective of the child (age 11 to 14 years) in the UK (Heppell 1994), shows even higher levels of computer ownership, for example 82 per cent of respondents claimed to have a computer at home. However, Heppell acknowledges that there is some margin for error here as there may be 'some confusion about what a computer actually is'. A more revealing statistic is that 48 per cent of all children questioned claimed that they could print at home. This statistic suggests that there is potential for confusion when gathering data on ownership of ICT equipment, though it may be that the exclusion of pre-1989 computers from the McKinsey survey accounts for this considerable difference to the figures.

The McKinsey survey (BIS 1994) also considered the number of machines per home with the surprising result that 'overall the average number of computers held at home was more than 1, but under 2'. Indeed 'the maximum reported number of computers in one child's home was 6 and more than one child reported this number'. Raw numbers of machines may not be the most helpful statistic. The Ultralab team believe that access to a machine is the real issue, and that access can be interpreted in a number of ways. However, it is clear that access to computers in the home in the UK is currently somewhere between 22 per cent (McKinsey), and 63 per cent (Ultralab). It is also likely that the quantity of multimedia ICT systems in UK homes by the turn of the century will be sufficiently large to represent an educational resource which cannot be ignored by education professionals.

The home computer: friend or foe?

Computer games have been regarded as generally undesirable in the educational context. This is a judgement mostly based on intuition rather than fact. Many children have access to multimedia games machines in the home. These have the potential to deliver practice in machine operation, development of eye–hand co-ordination and, depending on the game being used, the development of problem solving skills. Features of modern computer games noted by Heppell (1994) include complexity, interactivity, and the presentation of challenging problem solving environments. They also provide a vehicle for collaborative endeavour and have changed the climate of expectation that surrounds children's computing experiences. Heppell identifies children's 'emergent capability' developed through the use of such games and regrets that educational software developers do not, through a sound educational understanding, build on this capability.

Where multimedia computer systems are available in the home, undoubtedly ICT basic skills will be developed, but appropriate educational use is less certain. The issue with computer systems is that they can do nothing, without appropriate software, and at the same time can do everything. This, therefore, means firstly that 'educational' quality of software is paramount, and secondly that parental knowledge of educational software, and its potential, will be a key developmental factor in the effective use of multimedia systems in the home. For many children, the home offers a greater opportunity for work with multimedia ICT systems than the school. A home with one multimedia system and two, or even three, children, offers a far superior computer to child ratio than most schools. Schools need to acknowledge the extent of multimedia systems in the home and develop ways to exploit it.

The school-home link

The Ultralab team (1993) have identified a clear lack of engagement between school and home in the use of multimedia systems by children:

> The problem for schools is simply how to acknowledge and take advantage of the sophisticated skills that children are developing through computer games if teachers and parents undervalue or are unaware of them. What we seem to be observing is the Andy Pandy generation leading the Sonic generation into the information age, and the Andy Pandy generation have some homework to do. (http://www,ultralab.ac.uk)

This 'homework' teachers have to do is concerned with the identification of the skills themselves and interpreting them in the context of the global information society, with a watchful eye on the future. Information skills are relatively well known and currently cover identification of information, selection of information, use of information, and presentation of information, but each year brings new horizons into view. Children of the information age are developing an Information Capability which encompasses the use of multiple information sources simultaneously, synthesis of sources and types, critical evaluation of information, and avoidance of information anxiety. Their teachers need to keep ahead of them.

While there is a considerable amount of software available for home educational use, some of which may support skill development, McKinsey (1997) identifies that parents have little information on which to make software decisions. Many parents lack understanding of the educational ICT systems beyond the obvious drill and practice applications. If multimedia systems in the home are to be used for anything other than basic numeracy and literacy development parents need guidance. McKinsey recommends a web site with software evaluation and others have suggested that annual multimedia software awards may be appropriate as a means of conveying the educational value of particular software products to parents. Clearly both of these could be useful indicators to parents of the educational worth of particular software. However, more important than the worth of individual packages is the need to ensure an aspect of progression in skills and knowledge development as children make use of ICT systems in the home. It is possible that integrated learning systems (ILS) could provide such progression. Indeed it is not inconceivable that the local school server might deliver appropriate ILS tasks to pupils' homes across the network out of school hours. Such a system would enable tailored tuition for the individual child, with careful mapping of progress, to be delivered direct to the home learning environment.

Beyond such highly structured, indeed prescriptive, approaches most parents lack the cognitive and pedagogical frameworks to make effective use of educational ICT. There is a strong case, in parallel with the case for continuous professional development for teachers, for providing information and support for parents on the use of ICT systems to support learning. Such support might well be integrated with that suggested for teachers through a combined web site and joint Easter and Summer schools.

A constructivist approach to learning will acknowledge home computers as an important resource which can extend learning into the home, including the use of games, especially those which put users in problem solving situations. A survey by Watson *et al.* (1997) confirmed a lack of educational understanding among software producers as mentioned earlier. If home computing is to provide a significant input into overall educational development then there is much work to do in developing partnerships between educators, parents and software suppliers.

The impact of multimedia technologies on social learning processes

This book identifies the importance of constructive development of conceptual frameworks if children are to learn effectively. Human interaction, with peers, parents and teachers has a part to play in the learning process. Many classrooms, especially in the primary sector, put such human interaction at the centre of their learning paradigm. While learning in isolation is possible it is clear that some exposure to group and team work is essential for children to develop the skills of sharing and communicating which enable them to become active members of society. It is important therefore that the use of ICT systems in the home should be seen by the child as an activity shared with parents and siblings. In the Ultralab survey (Heppell 1994) children were asked 'Where do you work on the computer?' The survey found that of the children who owned computers about 75 per cent worked on them in their own bedroom; next most popular, but well behind was the study, followed by other (converted cupboards etc.) and just 4 per cent in the living room. The discovery that most home computer use was of a solitary nature is a concern. The researchers highlight the importance of 'getting the computer out of the bedroom and into the 'social' areas of the house' and believe that there are good reasons for 'helping parents to bring the computer back into family life'.

While the above recommendation can bring ICT into the social hub of the household, communications technologies have the potential to bring society into the home. Collaborative work with peers across networks presents an opportunity for children to work with peers and experts. Dispersed team working across networks presents children with a range of problem solving, data gathering, analysis, synthesis, and creative opportunities which have a broader range of participants and collaborators than current home (and school) environments can offer. The effective development of a network centric learning environment which links school to school, home to school, and home to home, requires positive action by teachers to develop an understanding by parents of the aim and purpose of such computer use. Such collaboration will be crucial to the success of the proposed National Grid for Learning.

Television to computer?

The permeation of technology into the home (and school) is not a new phenomenon. During this century western society has moved from the position of no home having a television to virtually every home having a TV set today. The McKinsey report (1997) states that children spend, on average, 28 hours per week watching television. This compares with 25 hours per week in school if averaged over the year. As ICT systems become consumer items TV time may well switch to become computer time. If only a small part of the 28 hours per week can be captured in the use of educationally valid computer software immense learning gains are possible. In the Ultralab survey (Heppell 1994) 92 per cent of children questioned said that they watched some television daily. The challenge for educationalists is to transfer this daily use of TV to daily use of educational software.

The use of ICT in other non-school environments

In the community many organisations which formerly used passive systems to present information have introduced a more active environment. Museums, for example, used to be passive places which contained artefacts and documents which had text only explanations for the visitor. During their lives children will encounter an increasing range of multimedia systems, kiosks in public places, networked kiosks of cross-county services, and all the information one could ever need to inform purchasing decisions from point of sale kiosks. The citizen of the future may not be able to obtain any information at all without a familiarity and capability with information and communication technology systems.

CONCLUSION

The days of one computer per class are over. It must be recognised that perhaps half the children in any class will have a computer at home. If 'have-nots' are to gain access to the learning potential of the computer, firstly teachers must own computers. They must also be thoroughly conversant with software and hardware that can enhance learning, and know the ICT capability of their pupils. Schools will need ICT policies which provide opportunity for skills training for those without ICT at home. The educational goal for experienced pupils, and for pupils as they become skilled, must be to provide a healthy learning environment in which ICT plays a central part. This 'centrality' must encompass a clearly articulated educational philosophy which justifies the use of ICT in educational terms. Pupils need the freedom to seek answers, learn from the task, and present and publish their findings through the constructive and creative use of ICT, for example as illustrated in case study one. Pupils should be encouraged to make use of the wizards lurking in authoring packages and other software, so they can make full use of the guides and overviews available in multimedia packages. Software needs to have a responsive structure built into it, based, for example, on a constructivist learning philosophy, as in case study two. Pupils then need time and a free rein to access it – not just for a few minutes when it is 'their turn on the computer' but so that they are able to go on line at any time of the day (or night) and the home becomes an extension of the school. ICT must, as Stevenson (1997) states, become as commonplace as electricity. The use of ICT will then be so embedded in educational practice that deliberation and comment will be unnecessary, and 'My pencil needs sharpening' becomes 'My pocket-book battery needs replacing'.

We end where we began. This chapter has focused on 'learning *with* ICT' rather than 'learning *about* ICT'. The aim was to encourage readers to reflect firstly on education – the process of constructing or re-constructing understanding – and then to consider the way ICT can be used do this. The quality and accessibility of hardware and software has reached a mature stage where it should be making a real impact on learning – but it requires the injection of a learning philosophy into the packages, and an ICT literate teaching profession, to enable the journalists of the next century to be able to report a qualitative change in our use of ICT to support learning in school and at home as we move from the 20th to the 21st century.

REFERENCES

BIS Strategic Decisions Survey (1994) in McKinsey and Company *The Future of Information Technology in UK Schools*. UK: McKinsey and Co.

Boden, M. A. (1979) *Piaget*. London: Fontana Paperbacks.

Brown, J. S., Collins, A., Duguid, P. (1989) 'Situated Cognition and the Culture of Learning', *Educational Researcher* **18**(1), 32–42.

Chandler, D. (1983) *Young Learners and the Microcomputer*. Milton Keynes: Open University.

Clements, D. H. (1995) 'Playing with computers, playing with ideas', *Educational Psychology Review*, **7**(2), 203–6.

Collins, J., Hammond, M., Wellington, J. (1997) *Teaching and Learning with Multimedia*. London: Routledge.

Fraundhorf, M. C. (1996) 'Multimedia in the Classroom', http://www.coe.uh.edu/~mcf/m1whyimp.html.

Heppell, S. (1994) 'National Study of Emergent Capability: preliminary observations from the pilot study', http://www.ultralab.ac.uk/pages/ULTRALAB/kids-Capabilities

Kay, A. (1995) 'Unleash the wolf from woolly thinking', *Times Educational Supplement*, 23/6/95, p. 24.

Kemmis, S. with Atkin, R. and Wright, E. (1977) 'How do Students Learn?', working papers on computer assisted learning. Norwich: Centre for Applied Research in Education, University of East Anglia.

McKinsey and Company (1997) *The Future of Information Technology in UK Schools.* UK: McKinsey and Co.

Merrill, M. D. (1991) 'Constructivism and Instructional Design', Educational Technology **31**(5), 45–54.

Oppeneheim, T. (1997) 'The Computer Delusion in The Atlantic Monthly', http://www2.TheAtlantic.com/atlantic/issues/97jul/index.htm.

Papert, S. (1980) *Mindstorms: Children, Computers, and Powerful Ideas.* Basic Books: New York.

Papert, S. (1993) *The Children's Machine. Rethinking School in the Age of the Computer.* Basic Books: New York.

Price, R. (1989) 'An Historical Perspective on the Design of Computer-Assisted Instruction: Lessons from the past', *Computers in Schools* **6**(1–2), 145–57.

Ross, K. A. and Lakin, E. (1998) *The Science of Environmental Issues.* http://www.chelt.ac.uk/env-sci/

Scrimshaw, P. (1997) 'Computers and the teacher's role', in Somekh, B. and Davis N. (eds) *Using Information Technology effectively in Teaching and Learning.* London: Routledge.

Somekh, B. (1994) 'Designing software to maximise learning: what can we learn from the literature?', Proceedings of the Association for Learning Technology, University of Hull, September 1994.

Stevenson, D. (1997) *Information and Communications Technology in UK Schools. An Independent Inquiry.* Labour Party, UK.

Ultralab (1993) 'Children, games and gains', *Times Educational Supplement*, http://www.ultralab.ac.uk.

Ultralab (1994) 'Children of the Information Age and the Death of Text', *The Author*, Summer edition, http://www.ultralab.ac.uk.

Watson, L. with Aston M., de Vries P., Hinder A., Selinger M. (1997) 'Multimedia in Education. The transition from primary school to secondary school', a report by P. J. B. Associates produced for the Scientific and Technological Options Assessment Office (STOA) of the Directorate General for Research – European Parliament.

Wertsch, J. V. (ed.) (1985) *Culture, Communication and Cognition: Vygotskyian Perspectives.* Cambridge: Cambridge University Press.

CHAPTER 9

Developing a sense of place: a constructivist approach to geographical enquiry

Sally Palmer and Kate Thomson

To be human is to live in a world that is filled with significant places: to be human is to have and to know your place (Relph 1976, p. 1).

WHAT IS GEOGRAPHY?

Geography is an area of the curriculum that is difficult to define. While the study of place has always been seen as an essential element of geographical study, debate continues as to the status of geographical knowledge. Geography has been seen both as a subject in its own right characterised by distinctive domain knowledge and as 'a science of synthesis . . . where subject matter is shared with other disciplines but is treated in a different way for geographical purposes' (Holt-Jensen 1988, pp. 4–5). However, what perhaps distinguishes geography from other subjects in the curriculum is its conceptual basis. Geographers are not simply concerned with developing an encyclopaedic knowledge of the world, but with the systematic observation and analysis of places. They aim 'to provide accurate, orderly, and rational description and interpretation of the variable character of the earth's surface' (Hartshorne 1959, in Holt-Jensen 1988, p. 21). In particular, geographers are interested in studying the interaction between people and places, identifying patterns and investigating the spatial distribution of human and physical phenomena. Indeed, Holt-Jensen (1988) sees this concern with 'the earth's surface and its spatial parts in their totality' (p. 7) as a significant characteristic which distinguishes geography as an independent science. It is through studying geography therefore, that individuals can develop an ability to describe places, interpret what is happening there and in doing so develop a wider understanding of the world.

THE DEVELOPMENT OF GEOGRAPHICAL KNOWLEDGE AND UNDERSTANDING

At the heart of learning in geography then is the development of a 'sense of place'. Having a 'sense of place' appears to be characterised by the acquisition of certain place knowledge, the development of geographical skills and concepts and the formation of attitudes and values towards place. There is however considerable debate about how this understanding develops and the significance of an individual's interaction with place in shaping their understanding. While some see 'knowledge of place as a simple fact of experience' (Lukermann 1964, in Relph 1976, p. 43), others see the development of a sense of place as a function of an individual's affective response to localities (Relph 1976). Relph recognises the importance of individuals' perceptions of place in shaping their understanding and believes that 'the foundations of geographical knowledge lie in the direct experiences and consciousness we have of the world we live in' (p. 4). Despite these differences of opinion there appears to be some consensus about key aspects of the development of a 'sense of place'. Place understanding seems to develop over time, is influenced by experience and is unique to the individual. Constructivism appears to offer an explanation for the development of such geographical understanding.

In this paradigm, learning is seen as an active construction of meaning (see chapters one and two). It is in many ways a reaction to positivistic interpretations of learning. Positivists see 'objective' science as universal, and knowledge of the world as value free; reality is fixed and exists independent of human thought. From a positivist perspective, developing an understanding of place means coming to a shared understanding about a set of objective truths. Teaching children about place is often seen simply as a process of transmitting a set body of immutable facts about the world. Teachers taking this approach tend to emphasise the importance of developing children's knowledge base and their ability to locate places and sometimes fail to appreciate the need to develop deeper conceptual understanding. In turn, such teachers also often measure children's learning by assessing the extent to which they are able to memorise locational facts and repeat newly presented information.

In contrast, constructivists see geographical knowledge and place understanding not as a set of objective truths, but as a personal construct which is shaped by experience. They believe that a 'sense of place' results from the complex relationship between individuals and localities and that it is this interaction that results in the development and maintenance of place identity in individuals (Relph 1976). Constructivists maintain that objective analysis and interpretation of places is impossible, since any individual's interpretation will be modulated by their existing knowledge, beliefs and previous experiences. 'Within one person the mixing of experience, emotion, memory, imagination, present situation and intention can be so variable that (they) can see a particular place in several quite distinct ways' (Relph 1976, p. 59).

It is these influences that act as a mental filtering system which enables new thoughts and perceptions to be organised. Some writers have even argued that 'when one learns to see things geographically it is not reality itself one learns, but a perspective on reality' (Holt-Jensen 1988, p. 91). This has important implications for the development of an individual's sense of place, in that it suggests that place understanding is idiosyncratic. While two individuals might follow identical procedures in studying a place, their interpretations or experience of that place will be different. They are each likely to make unconscious comparisons with other places they have experienced, to see different aspects of that place as significant and to make unique mental connections. The cognitive image of the place that results from this experience will inevitably be influenced by subjective perceptions. The development of geographical understanding is therefore complex, since it results from the integration of affective and reasoned responses to place. At the heart of this paradigm is the acknowledgement that individuals do more than simply observe places; they interpret what they see. 'Images (of place) are not just selective abstractions of an objective reality, but are intentional interpretations of what is, or what is believed to be' (Boulding 1961, in Relph 1976, p. 56).

Constructivists are therefore interested in the processes involved in the development of understanding. In this model there is an emphasis on the learning process; here, learning is not seen as a 'mimetic' activity, involving the repetition of a set body of geographical facts, but as a process of transformation. Individuals construct their own understanding of place by internalising and reshaping new information.

The process appears to start with both direct and indirect experiences of place (figure 9.1). An individual's perception of the environment is influenced by the sensory information which is received. An individual cannot possibly internalise every piece of new knowledge about these places, but appears to select information that is relevant. Relevance is determined by an individual's previous place experiences, and his/her personality. He/she is likely to internalise information which either confirms or refutes existing knowledge of place and which is of interest. Not only are individuals selective in the information that they absorb, but through the processes of assimilation and accommodation they transform it in unique ways. Relph (1976) suggests that the construction of place identity appears to consist of the 'complex and progressive ordering and balancing of observations with expectations, (and) *a priori* ideas with direct experiences' (p. 59). He contends that this process continues until a stable image is developed.

The way in which this new information is transformed therefore appears to be determined by a number of influences which are unique to the individual. It is this transformation and organisation of new information that ultimately results in conceptual development. Learning about place involves more than memorising pieces of place information; individuals make sense of the world by looking for order, by identifying links between new ideas, and developing new organisational frameworks. Conceptual understanding in geography appears to be related to an individual's ability to synthesise new ideas and to generalise from the specific, that is, to draw conclusions about place from a limited number of experiences. Since the cognitive structures which result from such learning in turn determine how individuals construe reality, the development of an understanding of place can be seen as a cyclic process. More sophisticated geographical understanding can therefore appear to be a function of maturation and a broad and varied place experience.

While this model provides a rational explanation for the development of a sense of place in young children, it is flawed in that it is rather oversimplified. The construction of new conceptual understanding rarely happens in isolation but is clearly also influenced by a number of external factors, most notably interaction with 'more knowledgeable others'.

Social constructivists have recognised the impact of social interaction upon the construction of new understandings. Vygotsky (1978) recognised the importance of talk in learning, and identified the role it plays in helping children to sort,

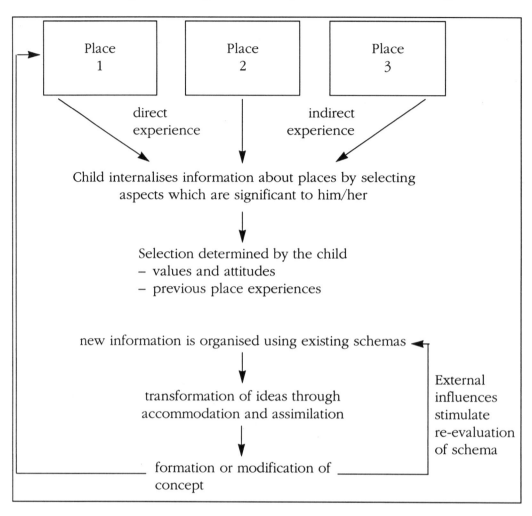

Figure 9.1 Models showing the development of a child's sense of place

organise and assess their thoughts. Interaction with both peers and 'more knowledgeable others' can therefore be seen as an important catalyst in the development of an individual's sense of place. Teachers in particular would seem to play a vital role in helping children to look at places in new ways, and to study place as a geographer would. By guiding children to look for connections, relationships and patterns which determine the nature of individual places, teachers can encourage their pupils to develop conceptual understanding. Indeed such positive interventions have a significant role to play in shaping children's cognitive structures, and encouraging more sophisticated understanding.

BECOMING A CONSTRUCTIVIST GEOGRAPHY TEACHER

Constructivism not only provides a model of learning in geography, but an alternative perspective on teaching. Teaching according to constructivist principles means establishing learning situations that encourage the active construction of meaning. Children should be supported in exploring the concepts that underpin geography, so that they are able to develop deep rather than surface learning. This means encouraging children to look for connections, to reformulate ideas and draw unique conclusions and, most significantly, to take responsibility for their own learning (Brooks and Brooks 1993).

These intended learning outcomes are consistent with the demands of the National Curriculum for geography. Not only do the orders promote the construction of a sense of place by encouraging teachers to introduce children to a range of places and geographical themes, but they provide guidance for the teacher about how this learning might be structured. Teachers are encouraged to show children how to employ a range of geographical skills in order to investigate named places, and to provide numerous opportunities for children to gain both direct and indirect experience of place. Implicit within such investigations is the need to provide children with opportunities to develop affective responses to place and to 'express views on . . . the environment' (DfE 1995, p. 87). The enquiry framework which underpins the geography National Curriculum orders, seems particularly conducive to the development of individualised constructions of place. By carrying out structured investigations children can be encouraged to organise new place information in ways which will foster the development of conceptual understanding.

Teachers who wish to adopt a constructivist approach to the teaching of geography need to think carefully about the most effective ways of implementing the National Curriculum and in doing so explore a range of ways in which they can support children in the construction of their 'sense of place'.

There appears to be a number of things that teachers can do in order to promote more sophisticated geographical understanding.

Introduce children to a wide range of varied places

Children undoubtedly start to develop an understanding of place from the moment they are able to explore their immediate environment. It is through playing, exploring, and travelling in a variety of places that young children start to develop what Bale (1987) describes as their 'private geographies'. Place understanding is therefore a product of these direct experiences, but is also influenced by children's indirect experiences (Goodey 1971). Goodey recognises the importance of the child's location within 'information space', and acknowledges the impact of a wide range of influences such as the media, travel, books etc. upon children's understanding of place. During these early years children's 'environmental cognition' is not only influenced by their place experiences but by their ability to imagine unfamiliar places.

By the time children begin school they have developed very different experiences of the world. While some children will have had broad and varied place experiences, others will have had only a very limited exposure to a range of localities. Place understanding appears to be a product of these experiences. As children are exposed to new places they accommodate and assimilate place information and in doing so develop more sophisticated mental structures. It therefore follows that the more numerous and varied these experiences are, the more complex will be the organisational structures that result.

Teachers would therefore appear to have an important role to play in exposing children to a wide and varied range of places, since every new encounter with a place will encourage children to review their existing cognitive structures. This is consistent with the demands of the National Curriculum. Not only is there a requirement to introduce pupils to a number of place studies both 'local' and 'contrasting' but there is also a clear acknowledgement of the importance of extending children's place knowledge when doing work with a thematic focus. When teaching thematic studies such as Rivers, Weather, Settlement, and Environmental Change at Key Stage 2, teachers can aid the development of children's 'sense of place' by introducing them to examples in named places. By making a careful selection of case studies from the United Kingdom, the European Union and the wider world, teachers can challenge children's existing conceptions of place and can promote the development of more sophisticated place understanding.

Teachers can also promote conceptual understanding by drawing children's attention to similarity and difference in place. By both encouraging children to identify the features which make a place distinctive and helping them to appreciate common characteristics of apparently contrasting places, teachers can promote the development of more sophisticated place understanding. Such an approach is likely to encourage the synthesis of ideas, and stimulate children to make generalisations. It is this ability to make links and connections between new pieces of knowledge that is at the heart of conceptual understanding.

Structure learning in a way that promotes the development of conceptual understanding

While pupils' understanding of place can be extended by introducing them to a varied range of localities, this strategy alone is clearly insufficient. Much more significant is the way in which pupils are taught to study such places. Teachers can have a considerable impact on the development of a child's sense of place if they structure learning in a way that promotes the development of conceptual understanding. It is important that children are encouraged to go beyond simply describing places and are helped to hypothesise about the environment.

The challenge in promoting geographical understanding in young children is to find ways to develop their ability to investigate places in a systematic and orderly manner. Children need to be given structured opportunities to test and review their existing knowledge of place and apply new understandings in a problem solving context. Within the Geography National Curriculum orders there is a clear requirement for teachers to develop an investigative approach to the study of place. By asking pupils to 'undertake studies that focus on geographical questions' (DfE 1995, pp. 86, 88) teachers can promote the development of children's enquiry skills and extend their knowledge and understanding of place.

At its simplest, (enquiry) involves encouraging children to ask questions and search for answers, based on what they might already know and from data sources. As their skills develop, children can move to a more rigorous form of enquiry involving the development and testing of hypotheses. (NCC 1993, p. 27)

In practice this means planning lessons so that every task is led by a key question and finding one or two opportunities during a geography focused project to carry out a more in depth enquiry. Questions should be shared with pupils so that they are clear about the focus of the study and are able to review their learning. Geographical enquiry can be seen therefore not only as a way of integrating the teaching of geographical skills, places and themes, that is as a planning tool, but as a way of structuring children's learning in a meaningful way.

Several authors (e.g. May and Cook 1993, Foley and Janikoun 1996) have recognised the value of such an approach in engaging pupils and fostering the construction of new understandings. 'The enquiry approach gives direction, focus and purpose to the study and encourages active involvement in the learning process' (May and Cook 1993, p. 1). In following a procedure which encourages pupils to pose questions, suggest hypotheses and draw conclusions about available data, teachers can actively encourage children to reflect upon their existing understanding, and review their thinking in the light of new knowledge. This approach to learning about place appears to be successful because it encourages discrepancy resolution, that is, it enables pupils to evaluate existing knowledge in the light of new information.

Although this approach to the teaching of place is clearly useful in promoting the development of a 'sense of place' in young children, the way in which such enquiries are presented is crucial. Teachers need to think very carefully about how the enquiry is going to be structured, and make decisions which are likely to promote maximum conceptual development.

Finding a starting point

When planning a geographical enquiry teachers need to decide on the set of learning outcomes they wish to address. This means targeting particular aspects of the Programmes of Study, and making decisions about lesson objectives in terms of skills, knowledge and concepts. This selection process is in itself quite complex, since it is vital that learning objectives are matched to the needs of individual children.

Constructivist principles suggest that young children will come to school having had very different experiences of the world. In selecting a starting point or focus for a geographical enquiry teachers need not only to assess the extent of each child's experience and knowledge, but also to determine the level of conceptual understanding exhibited by each individual. Meaningful learning will only occur if teaching is matched to the needs of individual children. This in itself can present problems, particularly as an individual's 'sense of place' is difficult to assess.

The challenge for the teacher is to find manageable ways to assess and respond to individual children's existing levels of understanding. Perhaps the most effective way of eliciting such information is to carry out a small number of targeted assessments. Information generated from these elicitation activities can be used to plan a range of core tasks or enquiries for groups of children with similar conceptions of place. For example, a teacher wishing to introduce children to an enquiry into life in Kaptalamwa might assess the children's understanding of life in a Kenyan village by asking them to individually brainstorm words connected with Kenya. The resulting information that this task elicits can then be used to give a focus to the enquiries which follow. The same teacher might for example discover that some children have stereotypical views on life in this distant place and so decide to present them with an enquiry which will challenge their existing understanding and will encourage them to reassess their conceptual frameworks.

Elicitation tasks therefore enable teachers to start to select appropriate learning outcomes for geographical enquiries which are matched to the needs of individuals and to the requirements of the National Curriculum. Indeed Hewson and Thorley (1989) suggest that conceptual development will only occur in situations where teaching is matched to children's 'conceptual ecology'. This means being aware of the conceptual structures that already exist within the child's memory and knowing about the ways in which an individual child organises, assimilates and accommodates new information. They suggest that teachers need to introduce children to concepts which are 'intelligible', 'plausible', and 'fruitful'. This means that when planning tasks teachers might ask questions such as:

- Will the child understand what this means?
- Will the child believe that this is true?
- Will the child gain in any way from this new idea?

It is therefore important that teachers select an enquiry focus which is relevant to the children within a given class. Indeed, Brooks and Brooks (1993) suggest that 'if the conceptions presently held by students are not explicitly addressed, new information is filtered through a lens that may cloud, rather than clarify, that information' (p. 40).

Choosing a question

Geographical enquiries are usually led by a key question. Such questions are an effective way of giving a shared focus to an investigation, and encouraging pupil autonomy (May and Cook 1993, p. 4). However, the success of an enquiry is often determined by the quality of this initial question.

Foley and Janikoun (1996) suggest that there are seven key questions which are fundamental to children's learning in geography:

- Where is this place?
- What is this place like?
- Why is this place as it is?
- How is this place connected to other places?
- How is this place changing?
- What is it like to be in this place?
- How is this place the same as, or different from, another?

These are useful questions in defining the nature of geography and in developing a sense of place. However to develop deep rather than superficial learning a set of more focused, place specific questions need to be devised. These will arise from the elicitation tasks undertaken prior to planning.

Key questions should be relevant, interesting and appropriate in their range and scope, if they are going to promote learning and trigger conceptual change. Good questions are those that are manageable; that can be answered by the child within a relatively short time scale, using available resources. Good questions are also challenging; they stimulate cognitive conflict and encourage children to review their existing mental structures.

Although posing such questions is clearly difficult, it is possible to argue that it is the children themselves that are best placed to do this. It seems logical to suggest that they will devise questions which are not only tailor made to the level of their conceptual understanding, but which they find personally motivating. Furthermore, Brooks and Brooks (1989) suggest that children who pose questions and identify issues, and then analyse and find answers, learn to take responsibility for their own learning and become more effective problem solvers.

However, children who are inexperienced in problem solving and enquiry based work find posing such questions very difficult. They often select either questions that are too complicated to answer, or questions which present them with little intellectual challenge. Teachers can therefore play an important mediation role in helping children to select appropriate questions, which are feasible and well matched to individual children's existing levels of understanding. Children who are presented with carefully structured models of the enquiry process are then often able to work more independently in future investigations.

Task setting

The tasks which are set within an enquiry framework should be effective in extending children's conceptual development and promoting subject specific styles of thinking. Foley and Janikoun (1996) suggest that there are five concepts that are central to the study of geography: locality, spatial pattern, process, systems, similarity and difference. By making these concepts a focus for lesson planning, teachers can encourage children to look for new links and connections in their existing knowledge, and thereby promote the processes of assimilation and accommodation.

Although these concepts underpin the Programmes of Study for Geography, they are easily missed by the non-specialist teacher. Teachers need to make these concepts explicit in their planning and provide opportunities for children to make progress in their understanding of place. For example, tasks which encourage children to make comparisons between places will develop the concept of similarity and difference. This might mean comparing different places within the school grounds; imaginary/real places represented in stories; places with similar features or places with contrasting features.

By adopting an enquiry approach which focuses upon these concepts, children can be helped to go beyond simply describing places and to learn the higher order skills of hypothesising, generalising and explaining patterns in the environment. Framing tasks around these types of higher order thinking fosters the construction of new understandings.

Teachers should also encourage children to be self critical, i.e. to regularly review their thinking, as this assists in the development of metacognitive strategies. For example, a teacher might ask the children 'What do we know about shopping habits now that we have done this survey?', or 'Were we right when we said that rivers get wider as they flow towards the sea?' By reviewing old understandings in the light of new knowledge children can reflect upon how and why their ideas have changed and developed. Analysing the evidence by asking 'Why?' or 'Is that true?' develops the children's skills in questioning factual information and encourages children to look for alternative explanations or interpretations.

Managing the learning environment

The degree of conceptual development that results from a single lesson is in part related to the nature of the learning environment. Hewson and Thorley (1989) suggest that 'the organisation of the classroom interactions is paramount in facilitating conceptual integration, differentiation, exchange and bridging' (p. 544). Since most learning appears to happen within a social context it is vital that teachers think carefully about group management within their classes and establish social groupings which facilitate the meaning making process.

Social constructivists believe that social discourse is an important catalyst in the process of conceptual modifications. By discussing their ideas with each other children are able to share knowledge and understanding. Social discourse enables children to clarify their thinking and reach a new equilibrium in their understanding. 'A personal resolution of different understandings is a critical feature of conceptual change and needs to be allowed for in learning situations' (Murphy *et al.* 1995a, p. 80). Furthermore, discussion encourages children to ask questions in order to challenge each other's thinking.

It therefore follows that teachers need to plan tasks within a geographical enquiry that encourages discussion and collaborative work. Groups settings should vary from pairs to small groups and include some whole class discussion. Howe (1992, in Murphy *et al.* 1995b) concludes that group based tasks are particularly important in creating cognitive conflict and promoting conceptual modifications. She also suggests that the composition of each group is significant. She noted that more effective learning occurs when the group consists of children who have varied conceptions because the degree of cognitive conflict is increased. Children in such groups find it more difficult to reach a shared understanding and as a result talk more; this in turn promotes learning.

Howe and her colleagues (Tolmie *et al.* 1993) later found that the structure of the activity had an influence on how successful the children were at engaging in group talk. She found that activities such as brainstorming were more productive than ones asking for systematic observation because all the children could contribute to the discussion. Howe's work seems to suggest that teachers should pay careful attention to the way they structure enquiries and classroom groupings.

Supporting children's learning

Geographical enquiry promotes higher order thinking and a systematic approach to the study of place. While this approach is clearly beneficial, children find this investigative way of working difficult. If enquiry is to be successful the teacher needs to model the enquiry process. In introducing this approach to children the teacher may need to show children explicitly how to pose relevant questions, collect data, record results and draw conclusions. As children become more confident in operating this type of approach, the teacher can withdraw his/her support in order to allow the children to develop greater autonomy. The teacher's role now becomes one of 'scaffolding' the process in order to help children enquire for themselves. Scaffolding means offering support and making appropriate interventions in the learning process. Interventions might take many forms including asking questions, providing new resources, encouraging collaborative work and helping children to review their learning and synthesise their ideas. Children need to be given 'space' to construct their ideas. It is important that teachers respect this by making considered judgements about the type and frequency of the interventions they might make.

CONCLUSION

Fostering the development of a child's sense of place according to constructivist principles means structuring learning experiences so that children are encouraged to think for themselves, to identify patterns and relationships in the real world, and to review their ideas in the light of new experiences. It is only when these types of learning are encouraged that more sophisticated conceptual understanding will result.

Promoting the development of a sense of place means adopting teaching methods which encourage children to develop more sophisticated constructions of place. Geographical enquiry provides an ideal context in which to extend such conceptual understanding, but in order to be an effective learning tool it must be carefully structured. Teachers need to think carefully about which enquiries are most relevant to the children in their class, select tasks which will encourage cognitive conflict and establish learning contexts which promote independent and reflective thinking.

REFERENCES

Bale, J. (1987) *Geography in the Primary School.* London: Routledge and Kegan Paul.

Brooks, J. G. and Brooks, M. G. (1993) *In Search of Understanding the Case for Constructivist Classrooms.* Alexandria: ASCD.

Department for Education (DfE) (1995) *Geography in the National Curriculum.* London: HMSO.

Foley, M. and Janikoun, J. (1996) *The Really Practical Guide to Primary Geography.* Cheltenham: Stanley Thornes.

Goodey, B. (1971) *Perception of the Environment,* Occasional Paper 17. Birmingham: Centre for Urban and Regional Studies, University of Birmingham.

Hewson, P. W. and Thorley, N. R. (1989) 'The conditions of conceptual change in the classroom', *International Journal of Science Education.* **11**, 541–53.

Holt-Jensen, A. (1988) *Geography: History and Concepts,* 2nd edn. London: Paul Chapman Ltd.

May. S. and Cook, J. (1993) *Fieldwork in Action 2: An Enquiry Approach.* Sheffield: The Geographical Association.

Murphy, P., Bourne, J., Briggs, M., Sellinger, M. (1995a) *E832 Primary Education: the Basic Curriculum.* Milton Keynes: Open University.

Murphy, P., Sellinger, M., Bourne, J., Briggs, M. (1995b) *Subject Learning in the Primary Curriculum*. London: Routledge.

National Curriculum Council (NCC) (1993) *An Introduction to Teaching Geography at Key Stages 1 and 2*. London: HMSO.

Relph, E. (1976) *Place and Placelessness*. London: Pion.

Tolmie, A., Howe C., Mackenzie, M., Greer, K. (1993) 'Task design as an influence on dialogue and learning: primary group work with flotation', *Social Development* **2**, 183–201.

Vygotsky, L. S. (1978) *Mind in Society*. Cambridge: Harvard University Press.

CHAPTER 10

Constructing history: all *our* yesterdays

Tim Copeland

THE PAST AND HISTORY

History is probably the most overtly constructivist subject in the primary curriculum, and the reason for this lies in the subject's relationship with 'the past'.

> The past is over, completed and so much of it is lost in the distance. There are still traces with us, the problem is how to use them to enable us to see the past and to visit the distant past. (Shanks and Tilley 1992, p. 9)

Milan Kundera makes the link between the absent 'past' and the present 'history':

> You think that just because it's already happened, the past is finished and unchangeable. Oh No! The past is cloaked in multi-coloured taffeta and every time we look at it we can see a different hue. (Kundera 1982, p. 42)

The 'cloaks of multi-coloured taffeta' are in fact historical constructions, 'imaginative creations of earlier worlds' (Stanford 1986, p. 76) undertaken by historians who look at the evidence from uniquely different standpoints resulting from their different experiences, interests and assumptions (Husbands 1996).

> Then, although it has happened, and cannot change itself, far from being dead it is dynamic, for essentially it is a construct of our minds. In a very real sense it is our past (wherever we may be born or live), for, to a degree, we fashion it as we will rather than just accepting it as it is, never mind what it was. (Fowler 1992, p. 5)

The past has no existence at all outside its constructions by the historian, 'it appears only when creatively disinterred and its appearance can never be the same as that which the dead experienced themselves' (Rock 1976, p. 355).

What we have from the past are its present remnants, the evidence, which has survived decay, destruction and selective loss. This evidence is dumb; it says nothing for itself. In fact such remnants only become evidence when they are recognised as being significant for a historian trying to make sense of the past. The evidence only 'speaks' when we ask questions of it. The solutions we give these questions from examining the evidence result in Stanford's 'imaginative creations'. An important implication of 'creations' is that the term implies construction rather than re-construction (re-creation). We cannot 're-construct' or 're-create the past', because we do not have enough evidence for any one period or event. 'Even if a reconstruction were successfully accomplished, there are no recognised practices which allow the historian to demonstrate that his is a faithful rather than a spurious explanation' (Rock 1976, p. 358).

Imagination might make history possible, but it also makes it difficult. 'We are material beings living in a material world. But much of the most important and interesting parts of our lives is non-material. Unfortunately, almost all of the evidence of the past that remains for us is material' (Stanford, 1994, p. 12). Imagination also implies some disciplined use of evidence, otherwise the picture of the past that is given might be only random musings. 'Creation' can take place without using any recognised historical procedures, but for the result to be valid historically, it needs to be based on the evidence and there need to be some accepted ways to interpret the evidence: looking for change and continuity; cause and effect; similarity and difference.

In the natural sciences, a large part is played by mathematics and by empirical observation and a smaller part by the balancing of conflicting judgements and what may be inspired guesses. In history it is the opposite. Mathematics and empirical observation play a small, but still significant, role in history. Therefore problems of interpretation, influence, meaning and the weighing of incalculable probabilities are greatly increased. This results in a larger place for personal judgement and a wider scope for disagreement. The imaginative constructions of the historians are likely to be tentative and constructed by historians working under all kinds of pressures which did not, of course, operate on people in the past (Jenkins 1991, p. 10).

But what about historical 'facts'? There are facts in history, but these are statements 'which accord with a judgement about the past with which historians agree' (Stanford 1994, p. 124). These are dates and events which, 'though important, are true but trite within the larger issues historians consider' (Jenkins 1991, p. 32) and are a part of the 'chronicle' aspect of historical discourse, for example:

1620 The Voyage of the Mayflower
1649 Execution of Charles I.

The important aspects of facts are the position, weight, combination and significance they carry in relation to each other in the construction of explanations about the past. It is the pattern of meaning of events in the past that is significant to the historian rather than mere and meaningless dates. The pattern of meaning is arrived at by using historical skills and concepts to place the facts in a 'mesh' in which they are related by explanations of cause, consequence, sequence etc.

A further meaning of 'history' also needs to be examined. 'History' is not just what people think happened in the past, it is also about a process, how historical understanding (construction) is attained, its relationship to evidence, and the ways historians arbitrate between their imaginative creations (Lee 1994, p. 45). To undertake the study of history is also to examine the procedures that are used to make sense of the past and to compare different interpretations. This can also be considered historical understanding. This focus on processes of history is the distinction between history and 'heritage'. Heritage is a very vague concept (Brett 1996, p. 1), but is largely concerned with presentation and dissemination of aspects of the past. It tends to be 'product', manufactured, packaged and promoted with little opportunity to understand how the construction was made or alternatives offered.

APPROACHES TO THE TEACHING AND LEARNING OF HISTORY

Positivistic approaches

> In effect the positivist asserts that he can see things as they really are (or were) and that what cannot be seen is in any case not worth seeing, being metaphysical: the dominant image is that of a photograph of reality. (Lewthwaite 1988, p. 86)

Sylvester (1994) has catalogued the characteristics of a positivistic approach to teaching history, as evidenced in the 'Great Tradition'. It comprised mainly political history as one of the important aims was: 'all boys and girls in Great Britain have, by the mere fact of birth, certain rights and duties which some day or other they will exercise, and it is the province of history to trace how these rights and duties arose' (Board of Education 1905, p. 61).

It was a received subject with passive pupils and the teacher didactically active. The subject matter was fixed and dominated by the knowledge of dates and events that had taken place (the 'chronicle' aspect of history) and the approach was seen as the most effective and efficient way of learning the subject. It followed that assessment was in the form of these facts being tested through memorisation of lists of dates and events. It is clear that history was not taught to promote an understanding of the past, but rather to support another set of values:

> A further and most important reason for teaching history is that it is, to a certain extent, a record of the influence for good or evil exercised by great personalities. No one would dispute that our scholars should have examples put before them, whether for imitation or the reverse, of the great men and women that have lived in the past. (Board of Education 1905, p. 61)

This has reverberations in the History Orders at Key Stage 1: 'Pupils should be taught about the lives of famous men and women . . .' DfE (1995). But the list contains only those who have been deemed to have acted for the common good, including saints.

Positivistic approaches to history still survive in text books used in primary schools and primary teaching (see, for example, Metcalf 1993). Children may work in groups and undertake discussion, but using a text that is didactically active and which replaces the teacher. Illustrations in the books may be pleasantly presented, but demands on the pupils are low level, and are mainly concerned to deliver such a fixed view of the past.

Constructivist approaches

> A more appropriate metaphor for this mode would be of a painter attempting to construct the likeness of a subject faithful to the original, capturing the

'character' or 'personality' rather than merely the profile, despite the singular inconvenience of the sitter's being hidden behind a screen and assisting the artist in his interpretation only by answering such specific questions that are put to him (and in an unfamiliar tongue, to boot). (Lewthwaite 1988, p. 87)

The important factor in a constructivist approach to teaching history is the ability to inquire of the evidence. The approach implies that wherever possible children will have access to real sources of evidence, either primary or secondary sources which use primary sources as illustrative material, and this will be the 'real stuff' that any enquiry is based on. Historical enquiry lies at the heart of the constructivist approach and comprises asking questions about the evidence. Initial questions (often known as Key Questions) frame the enquiry and subsequent questions, which, as they proceed from each other, constitute the enquiry and the answers to the Key Questions. The direction of the enquiry and the context of the narrative depend on the kind of framing questions being asked. In primary school classrooms this often takes the form of an overarching key question, framing the whole enquiry, and 'mini-enquiries' sequentially building up understanding through smaller constructions of the past on the part of the pupils (see, for example, Copeland 1997a).

Equally, because history is being 'constructed', there will be different 'likenesses' produced by the learners, and these will be based on what the learner brings to the enquiry in terms of previous experiences and knowledge. Just because children do not appear to have the salient facts about a particular period or event does not mean that they do not have ideas, which may be simplistic or mistaken. Pupils, through their continuous attempts to make sense of the world, develop assumptions and tacit understandings which, even if misguided, are positive attempts to understand the world around them. The discovery of these ideas is an important task for the teacher, so that they can be strengthened and developed (Lee 1994, p. 44). An essential aspect of the constructivist approach will be to gain an understanding of previous constructions that the learner may have and to ascertain how well these match the evidence and the level of thinking of the pupil.

A further aspect of the constructivist approach will be to share with the pupils how history is 'made'. If there is no one 'correct solution' to the past, then it is essential that pupils understand the process of construction and how meanings can differ and why. 'The ability to recall accounts without any understanding of the problems involved in constructing them or the criteria involved in evaluating them has nothing historical about it' (Lee 1994, p. 45).

HISTORY IN THE NATIONAL CURRICULUM

There is certainly a measure of continuity with the 'Great Tradition' in terms of the aims of the teaching of history in the National Curriculum which structures the teaching of the subject in both primary and secondary schools in England and Wales (DES and WO 1990). The History Orders (DfE 1995) contain both positivistic and constructivist approaches embedded in the Key Elements. The need to acquire the vocabulary of chronology (Key Element 1) and to recall, select and organise historical information, including dates and terms, certainly bears a relationship to positivistic approaches to the subject. However, the focus on historical enquiry through the use of sources (Key Element 4), the examination of others' interpretations of the history (Key Element 3) and the requirement that pupils communicate *their* knowledge in a variety of ways, indicates a strong constructivist element to the Orders. Both positivist and constructivist approaches can also be detected in the Level Descriptions which form a basis for assessment of children's learning. The links between these aspects of the Orders were identified in the National Curriculum Working Group Final Report: 'In the study of history the essential objective must be the acquisition of knowledge as understanding . . . Knowledge as understanding cannot be achieved without a knowledge of historical information' (DfE 1990, p. 3).

This reinforces the idea that the concepts of history need something to link them and those 'nodal' points are historical facts. Conversely, without the conceptual and skill linkage, the facts are impotent in gaining historical understanding.

When we examine the key elements of the National Curriculum we can see how, with some rearrangement, they might fit into an essentially constructivist model.

Figure 10.1 shows that Historical Enquiry (Key Element 4) and Organisation and Communication (Key Element 5) can be seen as 'process' elements which enable the construct to take place and be 'fixed'. The other Key Elements are more concerned with conceptual development (Copeland 1997b, p. 4) and the quality or depth of the construction and the conceptual links between historical facts. The construction takes place as a result of an activity which is focused on one or more of the conceptual Key Elements by questioning, and the more valid

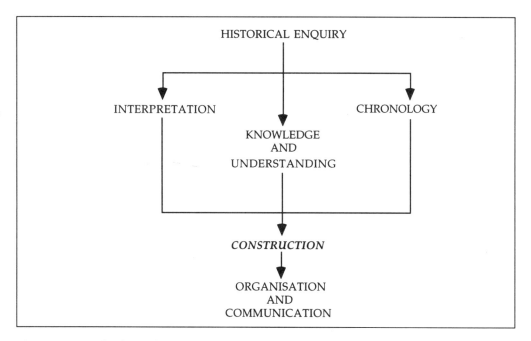

Figure 10.1 The key elements in a constructivist model

constructions will depend on an understanding and use of these concepts. The resulting organisation and communication of the construction enables the teacher to assess the success of the activity and the learning.

A MODEL OF CONSTRUCTIVIST TEACHING IN HISTORY

Stanford (1986) has proposed a schema to suggest how the more significant elements in historical activity come together. In a modified form this schema is used to explain how children construct knowledge in the primary school, and extends the model of the Key Elements given above. Here it is assumed that there are two modes of studying history in the primary school, using primary sources and using secondary sources. Together, these make up an understanding of the past.

Figure 10.2 demonstrates that 'the past' is inaccessible in the present but that we do have access to historical and archaeological evidence, in the form of artefacts, sites, buildings, documents, pictures etc., which can be used to help a child make a construction about life in the past, through asking questions of the visible evidence. A Key Question structures an activity which allows the child to make that construction, although the process of the formation of the construction in the child's mind is not accessible to us. In order for us to ascertain how the child has interpreted the evidence through the construction, he or she must make a communication, a representation, of that construction. This may take the form

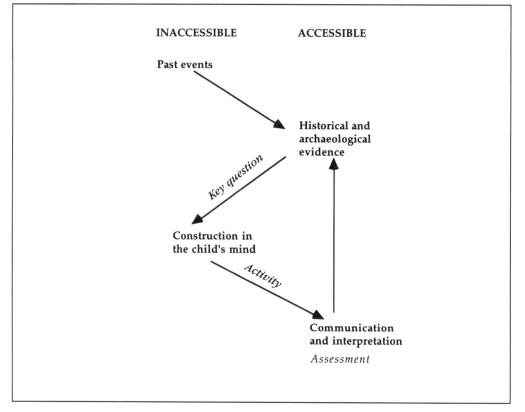

Figure 10.2 Construction using primary sources

of talk, a diagram, role play or a drawing. By examining this representation we are able to assess the validity or fairness of the construction regarding the available visible evidence of the past.

Figure 10.3 shows the construction process when the child is using secondary sources. The initial construction from the primary evidence has already been undertaken by a historian or archaeologist and the results presented in the form of an interpretation, for example in a text book or on activity card. Again, a Key Question is used to structure an activity which will help the child form a construction of the aspect of the past under study. In order for the teacher to have access to the construction formed and to assess it, it will be necessary for there to be a recorded outcome to the activity.

Perhaps the best way of using these models is to see them as a helix which

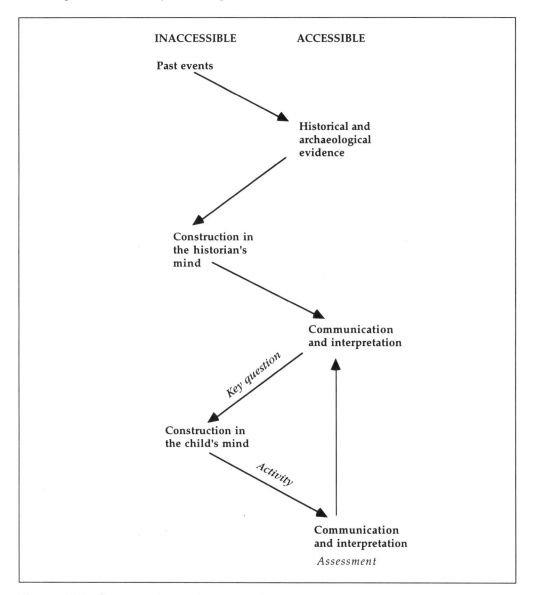

Figure 10.3 Construction using secondary sources

revolves around the evidence, construction and communication aspects:

Past events in the historical field result in historical and archaeological evidence – this enables a construction to be made in the child's mind – and is represented as a historical interpretation and communication which is assessed – this leads to further use of historical and archaeological evidence – this allows a further construction to be made in the child's mind – which results in a more valid or more complex historical interpretation and communication etc.

Actually deciding where a child is in his/her ability to communicate the construction is difficult, largely because of trying to find terms that will describe the state of the construction in the child's mind. A model developed for a mathematics course (Open University 1982) can be adapted to further illustrate the processes. In travelling around the helix the child:

- *Manipulates the concept*: the child links the new evidence to previous experience and current constructs, gained through social and formal learning activities.
- *Gets a sense of*: previous experience is modified by an activity using the historical source and previous ideas are adjusted (accommodation) or new information is added to previous ideas (assimilation). This stage may well take place as a group activity where pupils 'test' their ideas against each other's (Social Constructivism).
- *Articulates*: the child is able to explain the new construction, using reasoning.

It may take several cycles comprising using evidence, undertaking an activity and communicating the results for the child to manipulate, get a sense of and articulate a construction. Often it will be necessary for the pupil to undertake a number of activities in order to begin to manipulate a construction. In this way the helix defines progression in constructing the past from evidence. The identification of the stage at which a child is working is also a valid indicator for the differentiation of activities for the teacher. So at each of these stages a progression of key questions of increasing difficulty and autonomy, activities using an increasing number of sources, and different forms of recording may be appropriate.

AN EXEMPLAR OF CONSTRUCTIVIST TEACHING IN HISTORY

A combination of this model and the constructivist lesson planning sequence adapted from Scott *et al.* (1987) and developed in chapter two can form a template for lesson planning.

Orientation: In many ways the child will have already undertaken a 'circuit' of the spiral before formal teaching takes place, perhaps without asking any key questions and with informal activity, such as reading or watching television. It is important to make links with the child's previous experience of the past through the teacher giving information, or talking about objects or interpretations of the past, preferably in the form of visual stimuli. This is as much to focus the child on what he/she might already know as to raise motivation.

Elicitation: A child will come to a study of the past with different assumptions, interests and experiences. The child will bring this historical interpretation and communication to the teaching and learning episode and it will be important for the teacher to try to ascertain what images and explanations the child has and to use activities based on carefully chosen sources to try to strengthen those images and constructs. (This may take the form of an assessment activity, asking the child 'What do you know for certain about this source? What can you make a good guess at? What would you like to know?') Elicitation is an essential stage in planning activities so that the teacher can provide the necessary interventions to ensure the continuation or alteration of a growing construction about the past.

Intervention: Teacher intervention takes place at a number of points during the process of teaching:

1. Setting the inquiry question: The teacher's main role is in ensuring that the key question is well focused, and able to be handled by the child, so that it will help structure the construction. The choice of question will be intimately linked to the aspect of the past to be constructed in the activity such as chronology, causation, consequence, significance: 'Decide what order' (chronology); 'Why do you think this event happened?' (causation); 'What do you think happened after?' (consequence?); 'What was important to . . . ?' (significance). The difficulty of the question will also be dependent on the child's ability to respond to it, and will be a major determinant in the differentiation of the activity. Progression will not only be seen in the growing demands made on the child by the question, but also in the judgement of the teacher in allowing the child to set their own question.

2. The choice of the historical source to be used: The appropriateness of the source for the inquiry is crucial both for the aspect to be studied and the ability of the child. So one source or several sources may be selected, and these sources may be of similar type (all artefacts) or of a variety (an artefact, a document, a picture). Good examples of sources, matched to the child's ability in number and complexity will allow the opportunity to construct meaning.

3. Setting the activity in terms of defined skills and concepts which allow the child to make a construction; providing 'enabling' information; or asking 'open' questions during the actual activity.

4. Setting the means of communication: The appropriateness of the recording and communication method will also be linked to the concept being used: Venn diagrams to see continuity and change; matrices for sorting information; timelines to focus the chronology of events. The recording method will help the child to 'fix' the construction being made. A vital aspect of enabling the child to form a construction of an aspect of the past will be to structure sympathetically the structures to be used in recording. 'Sympathetically' entails giving appropriate recording structures for the aspect of the past to be studied, that are also within the child's repertoire. Differentiation and progression will be seen in the types of communication the activity demands; talking, drawing, writing.

5. Setting the means of assessment: Often the best way of assessing the child's ability to form a construction will be through the choice of recording and communication method, but the teacher might want to use further methods

such as talk or group discussion.

6. Review: There are two linked aspects to this stage. One is the teacher's review of the child's learning in the form of assessment through the pupil's interpretation and communication (which might be another elicitation point during each cycle). Secondly, it is important for the child to look back on what s/he has learned and how the present construction held is different from that which was held previously. Identifying the difference and the processes that have helped the change are invaluable in understanding the historical process.

7. Looking ahead: As links with previous knowledge were the focus of the earliest stage of this sequence, so it is important to help the child look forward to the next phase of the process of construction by the teacher sharing the focus of the next activity. This will enable the child to place their learning into a continuum.

THE VALUE OF HISTORY IN THE CURRICULUM

In teaching using a constructivist approach there will always be the tension between the teacher determining what is to be learned, which might be almost positivistic in its character, even if based on evidence use, and allowing the child to form their own constructions, the results of which may not conform to accepted historical knowledge. For the historian, this would not be a problem: 'The central problems of a historical methodology or epistemology hinge upon the fact that an objective knowledge of the past can only be obtained through the subjective experience of the scholar' (Holborn 1972, p. 79).

In fact disagreement and perpetual revision of interpretations of the past, far from being symptoms of weakness, are the evidence of historical study, and their presence is a sign of strength.

However, children are not historians, and it may be worrying to teachers that pupils' constructions are 'inaccurate'. Teachers may also have doubts about the ability of their pupils to gain access to an understanding of the past by working with sources and through using their imaginations. It is naive to expect children to act like professional historians; they do not have the skills, concepts, access to a wide range of sources or the life experience needed to use their imaginations historically. This does not mean that history has no value for them: 'Unlike historians, school pupils will not claim to generate 'new' public knowledge from the study of (selected) historical evidence; they will generate new private understandings' (Husbands 1996, p. 26).

Husbands goes onto argue that 'the key is the thinking that the evidence generates' and that the children are thinking in a historical manner, and are getting an insight into how historians work. Lee (1994, p. 47) sees the use of historical processes by children, even if the results are highly simplistic, as necessary to enable them to make more sense of history eventually. While Dickinson *et al.* (1978, p. 14) state: 'It may be a necessary prerequisite of learning history that certain activities in certain respects conflicting with the strict canons of professional practice occur in schools'.

However, the validity of children's constructions of the past will largely depend on the types of evidence that they are dealing with and the conceptual understanding demanded of them in the tasks they undertake. To appreciate history you have to have some experience of the world of men and women. For children this experience will be limited to the social aspects which they have experienced through their own short lives. Much of the political and economic aspects will be beyond their knowledge and it makes sense that the evidence they are dealing with, and we present to them, is from these social aspects. If political and economic aspects are being studied it is an important role of the teacher to provide 'enabling' information. The role of such information is often crucial to the success of children making acceptable constructions outside their own experience.

It would be an understandable reaction to reject the presence of history in the curriculum if it cannot be seen as being 'true' and is subject to different constructions: 'History is bunk' as Henry Ford famously commented. However, from a historian's point of view this view is unrealistic. If the 'real past' is unobtainable, then the whole aim of history is to form a historical past whose authenticity is shared by historians. That historians are largely agreed about the form of the human past demonstrates that this aim is being achieved successfully.

However, there are other aspects to the study of history that are significant for the individual. Primarily, history takes place in the present, even though it is ostensibly about the past. It is not just a description of the past or even a partial description of the past. Since we know the past as something present to us (the evidence exists in the present) and we use our own experiences, interests and assumptions, our constructions of the past are a very 'present' activity and are likely to tell others and ourselves as much about the interpreter as the events. Besides getting an insight into what may have happened in the past, history is valuable because it unveils the process of construction, develops pupils' thinking skills, and through this process enables them to come to terms with their place in the world. This is not the same as transmitting their 'heritage', if 'heritage' is seen as a presented, unquestioning view of the past: 'The transmission of the notion of heritage to a new generation of school children is a fundamental aim of history' (Bloomfield 1990).

Learning history should present the child with a dynamic and enabling set of skills and concepts which allow him or her to come to terms with the nature of the past. History is also valuable in that it helps children understand the nature of the present, since they also construct all of their everyday experiences.

The tendency to simplify the experience of children in studying history to a more positivistic, and more easily testable, process, by presenting them with a curriculum that corresponds with the 'Great Tradition', is a tempting option when the time spent on the subject is being marginalised by the need to raise standards in numeracy and literacy. Any such move to a more positivistic curriculum for studying the past through history would deny not only the essential constructivist nature of the subject, but also conflict with what we know about the way children learn, and the acquisition of the essential life skills that they will need.

ACKNOWLEDGEMENT

In the writing of this chapter the author has benefited from dialogues with David Coles, Kate Thomson and Beate Zuther.

REFERENCES

Board of Education (1905) *Suggestions for the Consideration of Teachers and Others Concerned in the Work of Public Elementary Schools.* London: HMSO.

Bloomfield, A. (1990) 'Heritage Education and the Arts', *Aspects of Education* **42**(90) 87–101.

Brett, D. (1996) *The Construction of Heritage.* Cork: Cork University Press.

Copeland, T. (1997a) *The Ancient Greeks.* Cambridge: Cambridge University Press.

Copeland, T. (1997b) 'Introduction', in Henson, D. (ed.) *Archaeology and the National Curriculum.* York: English Heritage and Council for British Archaeology.

Department of Education and Science (DES) and the Welsh Office (WO) (1990) *National Curriculum History Working Group: Final Report.* London: DES.

Department for Education (DfE) (1995) *History in the National Curriculum.* London: HMSO.

Dickinson, A. K., Gard, A., Lee, P. J. (1978) 'Evidence in the classroom' in Dickinson, A. K. and Lee, P. J. (eds) *History Teaching and Historical Understanding.* London: Heinemann.

Fowler, P. (1992) *The Past in Contemporary Society: Then, Now.* London: Routledge.

Holborn, H. (1972) *History and the Humanities.* London: Doubleday.

Husbands, C. (1996) *What is History Teaching?* Milton Keynes: Open University Press.

Jenkins, K. (1991) *Re-thinking History.* London: Routledge.

Kundera, M. (1982) *The Book of Laughter and Forgetting.* London: Faber and Faber.

Lee, P. (1994) 'Historical Knowledge and the National Curriculum', in Bourdillon, H. (ed.) *Teaching History.* Milton Keynes: Open University Press.

Lewthwaite, J. (1988) 'Living in interesting times: Archaeology as society's mirror' in Bintliff, J. (ed.) *Extracting Meaning from the Past.* Oxford: Oxbow Books.

Metcalf, D. (1993) *How It Was: The Romans in Britain.* London: Batsford.

Open University (1982) *EM235 Developing Mathematical Thinking.* Milton Keynes: The Open University Press

Rock, P. (1976) 'Some problems in interpretive historiography', *British Journal of Sociology* **27**, 353–69.

Scott, P., Dyson, T., Gater, S. (1987) *A Constructivist View of Learning and Teaching in Science: Children's Learning in Science Project.* Leeds: Centre for Studies in Science and Mathematics Education.

Shanks, M. and Tilley, C. (1992) *Reconstructing Archaeology.* London: Routledge.

Stanford, M. (1986) *The Nature of Historical Knowledge.* Oxford: Blackwell.

Stanford, M. (1994) *A Companion to the Study of History.* Oxford: Blackwell.

Sylvester, D. (1994) 'Change and Continuity in History Teaching' in Bourdillon, H. (ed.) *Teaching History.* Milton Keynes: Open University Press.

CHAPTER 11

Constructive learning in Physical Education

Barbara Brown

This Chapter will demonstrate how constructive learning in physical education (PE) implies attention to the diversity of individuals. In the context of constructive learning, a developmental approach to movement skill calls for focused observation, assessment and evaluation. Before examining this, however, we will look at the National Curriculum ethos and its implications for teaching PE.

PE: RATIONALE

The National Curriculum for PE outlines expectations that are common for all children. It is no longer acceptable to view the rationale, content and approaches of the PE curriculum as being different for different schools and different children. Curricular provision in all schools is now part of the National Curriculum, and so it is a common document to which all children must by law have access. Since the Warnock Report (DES 1978) the notion of difference has been changing from a perspective of dividing children in education to joining them as corporate members of a National Curriculum. Since the introduction of the National Curriculum, which was enshrined in the Education Reform Act of 1988 (DES 1988), all children are equally entitled to participate in a common curriculum. Key Stage 1 establishes a sound introduction for movement skill development in games, gymnastics and dance activities (with swimming and water safety as another possible area of experience). At Key Stage 2 the breadth of movement experiences is increased to also include athletic activities, outdoor and adventurous activities and challenges, swimming and water safety (if it has not already been included at Key Stage 1).

In responding to the requirements of the National Curriculum, teachers can be aware of the ways in which schools and teachers have both supported and failed children in the past. For example, some schools (mainstream and special) have declared a recognition of equal entitlement in their school PE policy and curriculum document. Yet in practice the lack of diversity of opportunities has prevented equal opportunites being achieved for the diverse range of pupils. This has not necessarily just included children identified as having Special Educational Needs or who experience movement learning difficulties. It has also embraced children who have quickly discovered since being at school that they are 'no good' at PE, and yet they are succeeding well in other areas of their learning.

Teachers' perceptions of children since the Warnock Report have been changing to recognise and respect the concepts of individuality and diversity. There has been a shift of understanding of children's learning needs, that is reinforced in the 1988 and 1993 Education Acts and Code of Practice (DFE 1994), which requires teachers to be responsible, accountable and responsive to meeting the diversity of children's learning needs. Teachers are becoming more aware of the importance of a recognition of individual learning needs to inform the provision and practice of their teaching. They are developing a much more resourceful approach, which takes account of the diverse learning needs of the children. This has resulted in an increased realisation of equal opportunities for children (DES 1992, G6, 1.22–1.24).

ENTITLEMENT, OPPORTUNITY AND ACCESS IN PE

The ground rules of equal opportunities were outlined in The National Curriculum Physical Education Working Group Interim Report (DES 1991). It re-stated a fundamental educational principle that 'teachers should treat all children as individuals with their own abilities, difficulties and attitudes'. It also stated that the 'overriding aim should always be to create an environment in which, from the earliest age, young people and their teachers will learn to respect and value each other' (p. 16, 2.36).

The Working Group understood that the individuality and diversity of children can strengthen and enrich the learning experience for the whole class. However, they warned that it 'should never be used as a basis for restricting access to, or opportunity for, any learning experience in physical education' (DES 1991, p. 16, 2.36). This rationale for PE clearly identifies the ethos within which the whole process of curriculum planning, implementation, assessment and evaluation should evolve in each school. It requires schools and teachers to perceive the rights of all children as being a fundamental educational principle in physical education: 'children are more important than the activities in which they are engaged. "The game" is not the thing – the child is' (DES 1991, p. 16, 2.36). Respect and value for each other are recognised as necessary features in an educational context, and particularly in a teaching and learning relationship.

The child's nature and needs are the main consideration and they form the focus in the teaching and learning process. All children should have access across a range of activities to 'skills, knowledge and understanding . . .' (DES 1991, p. 16, 2.37) that underpin participation in PE. The Working Group were conscious when considering the issue of equal opportunities 'that mere access cannot be equated with real opportunity', and that the 'distinction between access and opportunity is crucial'. They also recognised that the 'effects of the attitudes and expectations of teachers, the preconditions for access . . . and the previous experiences and relative ranges and levels of the skills, knowledge and understanding of the children must also be considered' (DES 1991, p. 17, 2.38).

The Working Group recognised that these issues of entitlement and opportunity were common concerns with the other subjects in the National Curriculum. They also identified aspects that schools and teachers should have regard to which are particular to PE. For example, the public nature of success and failure; the competitive nature of many activities; its physical nature; constraints on the choices and achievements of disabled children, and of both girls and boys, and the barriers to young people's involvement caused by the restrictive ways some sports and forms of dance are portrayed and practised (DES

1991, p. 17, 2.39). The Working Group considered that PE showed a potential to recognise and accommodate a diverse range of children 'through nurturing the value of individual contributions in group situations' (DES 1991, p. 17), as well as through a breadth of contexts and experiences.

The Working Group's recommendations showed significant insight and sensitivity towards children's learning and participation in PE. They also understood the role and responsibilities shared by the schools and their teachers for developing a strong and sound ethos and rationale. The context for the teaching process should influence and promote the choice of 'content, delivery and style of physical education programmes . . .' (DES 1991, p. 18, 2.40). They charged teachers to develop their awareness, knowledge and skills concerning these central issues of entitlement, opportunity and access, and to consider carefully the way PE was presented in their schools. They recommended that choices of learning experience should be based on:

- the commitment to confront prevailing attitudes and to change practices where they conflict with the principle of equality of opportunity;
- the willingness to see physical activities as educational vehicles, rather than as ends in themselves; and
- a knowledge of the effects of different kinds of groupings on the learning experience . . . with varied educational needs. (DES 1991, p. 18, 2.40)

The rationale that the Working Group were conveying in their report was clear and simple. The implications for schools, teachers and children were significant in terms of equal entitlement, opportunity and access in PE. They brought these issues to the fore and saw them as central and crucial to the whole process of teaching, and to the access of all children to PE. They stated that:

> PE should be accessible, and perceived as possible and relevant by all children. It is the teacher's job to provide equal access and opportunity; to foster respect for fellow human beings; to question those category-based stereotypes which limit children's behaviour and achievements . . . (DES 1991, p. 18, 2.40)

Teaching practice that is working towards equal opportunities involves a range of strategies and practices that are appropriate for responding to individual and diverse needs and contexts. It will require initial and in-service education to promote positive practice. This will involve rigorous and continuous appraisal that challenges long held beliefs and prejudices underpinning discriminatory practice.

> It should be emphasised that these requirements, shared by the whole school, are the basis not only of commitment to providing equal opportunity, but also of the sensitivity needed for good and effective teaching. (DES 1991, p. 18, 2.40)

A CONSTRUCTIVE APPROACH TO TEACHING AND LEARNING IN PE

A curriculum rationale that explicitly embraces equity, entitlement, opportunity and access to learning requires teachers to critically examine teaching in terms of process and practice. It has implications for the ethos, context and conditions in which the curriculum is planned, implemented, assessed and evaluated. Central to this approach is the development of assessment, recording, reporting in order to generate knowledge, understanding and appropriateness in terms of the children's learning capacities and needs. The development of knowledge, skill and understanding is central to a constructive approach to teaching and learning. The individual nature of this process is recognised as being due to the differences created by opportunity, experience, conditions, capacity and quality in the learner. The learning environment should therefore recognise and respond to these considerations. The development of knowledge is crucial to the development of competence, therefore teachers, through the detail of teaching practice, should seek to ensure understanding by the learner. This will influence the participation, motivation, achievement and progress of the learner. It has implications for the way the curriculum is transacted and quality is sought in terms of appropriateness. For example:

- individual levels of access to learning are recognised;
- individual levels of challenge are recognised;
- individual levels of pace and progression are recognised;
- individual levels of achievement are recognised.

The development of knowledge, skill and understanding is fundamental to participation, achievement and progress in PE. For example, in preparing for the lesson young children initially have to solve movement learning problems related to changing for PE, then in moving as a class to the hall or playground.

Throughout the primary school the children have to develop knowledge, responsibility and autonomy about organisational strategies so that they can become more effective and efficient in handling large and small apparatus in increasingly complex conditions as individuals, with a partner, as part of a group or as a class.

They need to develop knowledge so that they can learn how to manage themselves effectively, efficiently and with a high respect for safety in shared movement tasks and situations. Initially this can be in simple and closed contexts, for example, responding individually to agility tasks in a defined area by using a skipping rope or a small mat to define the space in which the movement response is executed. Gradually these can be developed so that they are complex and open. For example, the children could be required to demonstrate agility by employing a range of movement strategies and skills in order to evade each other in a game of tag involving six children within a five metre grid. That is, the children move from a position of dependence to independence as they become more knowledgeable and they are able to demonstrate responsibility and autonomy in challenging and changing conditions and situations.

They should also develop knowledge about how to share space as an individual, with a partner, in a group or as a class in differing movement contexts and conditions that progress from simple and closed to complex and open.

Children should have the opportunity to develop movement knowledge so that they can understand how to move and how to improve. This requires the teacher and the children to focus on how the body is moving through attention to body parts and body action.

Central to the process of developing movement knowledge is the pupils' and teacher's confidence and capacity to explore, develop and refine movement skill through appropriate tasks and situations. This is a highly interactive process that requires the teacher and pupils to share and exchange movement knowledge, understanding, skill and experiences. This entails an ongoing dialogue comprising listening, speaking, looking/observing, inquiring, questioning, problem solving and moving.

The process of development and refinement is achieved through focused observation, analysis and evaluation of movement outcomes. It focuses on the detail of movement tasks and situations. Providing the children with the opportunity to become informed observers of movement enables them to develop movement knowledge, skill and understanding.

It is necessary to provide opportunities for children to use movement knowledge in a variety of contexts and conditions in order to develop movement understanding and competence. They can then utilise this knowledge to progressively develop and refine their movement competence in increasingly complex tasks and situations. This process promotes the development of knowledge, skill and understanding leading to informed and articulate movers. It cannot be achieved if the learning conditions are not constructed appropriately to be receptive and responsive to the individual movement resources and capacities of the children in the class. It allows the children and teacher to recognise the individual nature of achievement and capacities. For example, the resources of a child with quadraplegic spasticity in a movement situation can be greater than those of a child who effortlessly achieves skilfulness. This can only be transmitted to the class of children if the learning culture is one in which courage, confidence, determination, patience, effort, concentration and skilfulness are recognised by the teacher. It can be inspiring for the whole class when they observe and recognise the resources and achievements of a child where the body is impaired or there are difficulties with learning.

It is the detailed observation of achievement shared by the teacher with the class that enables the children to recognise, respect and value the individuality that underpins learning. The learning environment should seek to be interactive and promote opportunities that encourage a quest for achievement, challenge, quality and competence at every level of experience. This is the essential and distinctive feature of constructive learning in PE, and it is the task of the teacher to cultivate such a learning environment.

This approach requires knowledge and understanding by the teacher and children. It can lead to the teacher and children creating a learning environment that is sensitive to the individuality of the learner in differing movement contexts and conditions. It can also promote an ethos of sharing and support, where capacities and limitations are recognised in every member of the class and where they are also celebrated and supported.

Children should develop efficient strategies in response to movement tasks and situations and this requires knowledge so that they can understand how to respond. The teacher is influential here in being able to order, reduce and simplify the demands so that attention can be focused successfully and incrementally on the appropriate information which can ensure that immediate achievement is enjoyed. In games play children require knowledge in order to know how to read and respond to the changing conditions. For example, initially they have to learn how to read and receive a ball. Knowledge is required about how to recognise the pace at which it is moving in order to time the reception; whether it is spinning (backwards, forwards, sideways) and if it bounces, how will the ball react? They have to know how to receive balls of different sizes and weights moving at different levels, pace, and spin and understand how they will respond.

The capacity of the teacher to understand the individual nature of movement competence and the developmental status of the children is crucial to establishing appropriate entry levels to tasks and situations so that achievement and progress can be enjoyed. Linked to this is the individual nature of the pace of progression so that tasks and situations can be developed through an appropriate use of a range of apparatus, tasks and situation demands. It is all too easy to forget the individual nature of the mover-personal resources of a child, for example, health, fitness, experience, opportunity, understanding, knowledge, competence. Tasks and situations should therefore be able to accommodate a diverse range of movement experience and capacity.

This understanding has implications for the planning and implementation of movement tasks and situations that are inclusive rather than exclusive. This is where the demands and outcomes can enable a class of children to share a common setting with differing and appropriate levels of entry and exit to and from tasks and situations, while still providing challenge and seeking quality. To present tasks where the demands are the same for all the children is unacceptable because it will result in failure for some and a lack of challenge for others. It can also create consequences in the learning environment that will lead to factions, misbehaviour, discontent, frustration and demotivation.

Cooperation is a significant aspect of PE. For example, in sharing space; small and large apparatus; in handling and moving small and large apparatus with a partner; in working as a group to assemble apparatus; in efficiently managing themselves in partner and group work; in observing, analysing and evaluating another pupil's movement outcomes. For young children to progressively develop cooperative skills in moving; performing; observing, analysing and evaluating; handling, assembling and organising apparatus; managing themselves as individuals, pairs, groups or as a whole class requires access to appropriate, common and consistent knowledge and understanding. Partner work, for example, when sending and receiving in games play; counter-balance action phrases in gymnastics; sharing a partner's rhythm in dance, all provide exemplars of cooperative movement activities. The development of cooperative knowledge, skill and understanding is fundamental to developing movement competence and skilled behaviour. This knowledge needs to be progressively developed so that it can be utilised in increasingly more specialised and specific sport situations.

Unfortunately, young children are sometimes required to participate in competitive contexts with little or no understanding or knowledge of how to respond effectively with other players to the demands of the complex movement situation. This quickly leads to frustration and loss of interest for some children. The introduction of fundamental knowledge about invasion, striking and fielding, and net strategy can help the children to understand the nature and purpose of the competitive context. This can then help them to develop spatial strategy and know how to work effectively together in the space to outplay the opposing players. For example, they need to know how to create, deny or invade the space, and the meaning of possession and non-possession strategy. Knowledge about the skills underpinning games play has to be developed in context in order to learn appropriateness in terms of what, when, where and how. For example, the skills of deception, anticipation; when and how to apply spin; how to read the ball, player and space; how to change pace (ball and player); how to vary the height, angle and trajectory of the ball. Children require opportunities for access to a progressively complex body of knowledge if they are to participate in increasingly complex competitive situations in an informed and skilful way.

Knowledge should be progressively developed about the movement contexts, for example athletics, dance, games, gymnastics, outdoor activities and challenges, and swimming and water safety. The development of this contextual knowledge will enable the children to demonstrate competence in increasingly specific and specialised movement contexts.

If children are going to participate in shared movement tasks and situations with responsibility and safety for each other they require knowledge, skill and understanding about maintaining a safe learning environment. They need to know procedures, practices and rules that are essential in movement situations that include at least a class of children in shared and changing conditions. These can include the use of large and small apparatus, where sometimes the conditions are potentially dangerous.

It is essential that procedural knowledge, skill and understanding are appropriately and progressively developed with children in every movement context but particularly in gymnastics, swimming and water safety, and outdoor activities and challenges. It requires children to bring to the movement learning situation a high sense of responsibility to listen, look, learn and respond so that they know how to contribute to the safety of the movement environment. This includes procedures and practices related to:

- management and organisation strategies;
- observation, analysis and evaluation of movement situations;
- movement control and awareness of others in a shared movement setting;
- respect, concern and responsibility towards others.

These are all examples of practice where the development of knowledge is central to promoting safe and progressively challenging situations. The children must develop this sense of awareness, responsibility and autonomy through informed participation in PE.

Standards, requirements and expectations underpinning a movement learning environment should be made explicit by the teacher and shared with the children so that progression can lead to greater achievement, challenge, satisfaction and quality.

The quest of the teacher through the employment of a range of teaching strategies, approaches and resources should be the attainment of movement knowledge, skill and understanding, by the children. Equity and opportunity in learning is dependent upon teachers appropriately constructing knowledge with children in learning conditions that facilitate and support access, meaning and application. This is strengthened if the learning environment conveys an explicit ethos of trust and confidence by the teacher and where an equality of value for all (Ainscow 1991) is conveyed.

PE: KEY STAGES 1 AND 2

A developmental approach to teaching PE (Key Stages 1 and 2) enables the teacher to respond to a child's individuality and diversity that underpins movement skill development. It requires teachers to recognise and respond to the developmental status of young children and provide a learning environment that will promote change in their mover-personal resources. The process of change is generated through a transactional relationship (Keogh and Sugden 1985) between the children's mover-personal resources, the task and the learning environment (see figure 11.1).

Each is equally responsive to the other and this responsiveness enables the three dimensions to achieve a sense of balance. This leads to a match between the children's resource levels and the demands in the task and learning environment, resulting in achievement.

A child's mover-personal resources are qualitative and quantitative in nature. Qualitative resources comprise:

- movement *knowledge*, skill and understanding that a child brings to a movement situation;
- the *experience* that each child brings to a movement learning situation;
- participation experiences reflecting a child's *motivation* and *confidence* in a movement learning situation, which is usually influenced by her/his *previous* and *other* movement learning experiences;
- the *strategies* that a child employs in response to a movement/task situation;
- the level of movement *competence* that each child brings to a movement situation.

The observation grid in Table 11.1 shows an example of a record of the progress of a learner at the end of a scheme of work in games and gymnastics. Detail is recorded in an explicit and concise way which provides a clear overview of the learner.

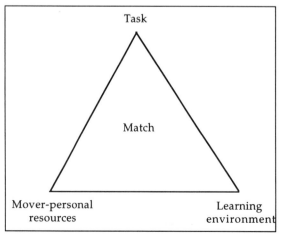

Figure 11.1 A movement situation (Keogh and Sugden 1985)

Pupil	Personal	Social	Home	School	Evaluation
Name: Jane **Age :** 10-11 **Year :** 1996-97 **Class:** VI	the frustrated behaviour has almost disappeared	• she enjoys her class friends • she has learnt to trust her teachers and foster-parents	in a stable foster home	happily settled	
MOVER-PERSONAL RESOURCES Qualitative resources:	Experience	Behaviour	Strategy	Competence	Evaluation
Games activities • net play • striking/fielding • invasion	• having established competence in the fundamental skills she is able to apply them in the development of sport-related skills • she is keen to develop game strategy and apply the appropriate skills	• she has gained confidence as she gained understanding • the fear, anxiety and frustration has been replaced by knowledge, skill and understanding	• she approaches a movement task in an ordered and logical way • she is able to work slowly through the incremental steps to achievement and competence without becoming frustrated	• she has an understanding of how, for example, to apply spin to a ball in net play, and read it in open play • she can read and respond to a semi-open play situation • she is learning to read and respond to cooperative movement situations	she has gained the confidence to participate in games activities because the conditions have allowed her the opportunity to gain a basic mastery
Gymnastic activities • travelling/balance • movement sequences • large apparatus	• a wide movement vocabulary and creative ideas • a sensitive mover who demonstrates the qualitative dimensions	• motivated • confident • committed • involved	• her movement planning results in carefully produced and presented movement ideas and phrases • she is able to observe, analyse and evaluate movement demonstrations • she conveys a capacity to practice and refine her performance	• she performs with understanding and demonstrates good line, degree of stretch and a clarity of body shape • she is always keen to develop her movement skill repertoire	• she has joined a gymnastics club as she enjoys it so much • she has an aptitude for creating and performing movement ideas and phrases • she observes movement situations skilfully and recognises detail that many children do not see

Table 11.1 Pupil observation: mover-personal resources

Quantitative resources are related to the end product of a movement task, and quantify the dimensions of performance in terms of how far, fast, high. This information is not significant for the teacher or child in the movement learning process, although it can be referred to summatively to indicate achievement and progress.

By focusing on a child's qualitative resources in a movement situation the teacher can be responsive to the individuality of change. This understanding enables teachers to appropriately teach all children. It allows children's individuality and diversity to be celebrated in a shared setting. It recognises the individuality in children's learning in terms of their knowledge, skill, understanding and competence. It also understands individual appropriateness related to pace, challenge and progress. It seeks achievement and quality at every level of learning.

The process is about ensuring entitlement to curricular learning and promoting a breadth and depth of opportunities through an appropriate means of access.

Concept of access

In examining the process of access it is necessary to study the children's resources (quantitative and qualitative). The learning environment, and especially the conditions within it, should also be observed. This is in order to gain insight into their influence on the children's learning, and the transactional relationship between the children's resources, the task and the learning environment. An examination of this process allows a teacher to assess the capacity of both to change, resulting in different individuals and different environments over time. This way of examining change will influence the teaching approach as a developmental understanding of the mover-environment interplay presumes that a transactional relationship is central to its meaning (Keogh and Sugden 1985).

In seeking to facilitate children's learning in PE the environment and the conditions within it are understood to be crucial and influential. The environment has significant potential and capacity to be responsive and adaptive.

In order to access children to PE it is considered essential to bring the children to the heart of the planning, and to focus on their developmental status and needs in order to inform the teaching content and approaches.

Access to PE

Access to PE embraces at a macro-level the whole school, where its ethos determines the perceptions, attitudes, standards, expectations, achievements and behaviours of every member of that community. The school policy provides a common framework which helps to generate a whole-school approach. It also creates a common sense of understanding and cohesion to cross-curricular development, progression and delivery. From this sound basis curriculum coordinators and class teachers can bring a high degree of resourcefulness to recognising and meeting a diversity of individual learning needs (DES 1992).

At a micro-level access is about the actual teaching process. This requires teachers to feel a strong sense of responsibility towards the learning environment; for example, its composition, functioning, development, and capacity to be resourceful and responsive. At the centre of the learning environment are the children and the mover-personal resources which they bring to it. This diverse resource determines how the conditions will be cultivated and managed in order to be appropriate and responsive to the children's learning needs. The learning environment should convey a high sense of professional integrity and respect towards the children and this should influence the way each person in the class relates to others.

The planning, implementation, assessment and evaluation process should encompass strategies and approaches that seek to promote positive and responsive learning conditions for all children, including pupils demonstrating special educational needs.

Teaching considerations

In order to respond to the children's learning needs the teacher engages in a process of differentiated practice. This involves:

- the implementation of a range of teaching *approaches*. These allow for flexibility in the development and progression of management, organisation and teaching strategies and approaches and tasks;
- *resourcefulness*, in terms of the teacher's subject and professional knowledge; learning conditions, facilities, resources/apparatus; curriculum interpretation, adaptation, development and presentation;
- the concept of *time* in the learning conditions so that it can accommodate individual pace and time scales for learning.

Table 11.2 demonstrates the potential in the learning conditions to be responsive to a range of movement learning capacities in a shared context.

This *art* of teaching provides a basis upon which the teacher can manipulate the curriculum and teaching variables. This is to ensure that they are appropriate to the individual learning needs of the children. It also enables a match to be achieved between the resource levels of the children, the demands of the task and the learning conditions.

The early recognition of children's capacities can provide the teacher with a starting point. When coupled with a sensitive and perceptive approach the teacher can encourage children into greater participation, as a result of an increase in confidence and motivation, due to incremental achievement.

The conditions in the learning environment are understood to be influential to the progress of children's development. Therefore, children respond differently in differing conditions and environments. Where a match is achieved between the children's resource levels and the environmental conditions, they demonstrate achievement and progress.

Personal and social considerations

Significant influences on change in movement development are the personal and social considerations that 'probably affect involvement in movement activity more than skill development'. The 'participation experiences' of the mover are influenced by her/his perceived level of competence and confidence, and by past and present

CLASS I	DIFFERENTIATED STRATEGY			AUTUMN TERM 1997	
Games activities	Approaches	Resourcefulness	Time	Management	Organisation

ball skills **individual control**
• stationary
• moving
• qualitative dimensions:
  spatial: direction;
  distance; levels
  time: slow/fast
  weight: light/strong
• aiming
• skill sequence
• receiving; catching;
  trapping; stopping;
  sending; striking;;
  kicking
• dribbling; bouncing;
  patting
• body/ball tasks
	• guidance: class/individual
	• focused observation
	• question/answer
	• listen, look, copy
	• task analysis
	• key points
		• size and definition of movement area
		• size/weight of ball, bat etc.
		• variety of small apparatus
		• nature of information
		• amount of information
		• form of guidance
		• frequency of guidance
			• lesson time
			• lesson length
			• pace of lesson
			• on/off task
			• individual guidance
			• understanding
			• competence
				Expectations/standards:
				(Consistency/constancy)
				
				Movement learning:
				• behaviour
				• strategy
				• outcomes
					Procedures/ Practices:
					i) changing
					ii) moving through school
					iii) beginning/end of lesson
					iv) development of efficient strategies for using small apparatus
					v) maintenance of apparatus bases
					vi) during tasks
					vii) between tasks
					viii) sharing movement space

EVALUATION • appropriate tasks • attention to qualitative dimensions essential	EVALUATION • clear, simple guidance essential, that is focused and ordered	EVALUATION • a defined area assists orientation and control • selection of appropriate size and weight assists control • guidance: use the senses separately then jointly • focused and frequent guidance	EVALUATION • time dimension must be responsive to movement learning needs of the children • this aspect influenced the children's capacity to participate • it changed with the children's resources.	EVALUATION • clear, calm and sensitive management promotes change in the children's movement learning behaviour	EVALUATION • ongoing attention to detail in these aspects enables the children to gradually assume responsibility for their role and contribution to the organisation of the lesson.

Table 11.2: Differentiated strategy

movement sensations, experiences and conditions (Keogh and Sugden 1985, p. 378). These personal resources develop within the process of change and they are similarly affected by the conditions, opportunities and experiences that influence learning; participation, achievement and progress. These affective considerations are influential variables and determinants in the process of gaining movement control and competence. The nature and degree of interest, satisfaction, motivation, involvement, expenditure and selection in a movement situation is influenced by the mover's personal resources and the physical and social conditions.

The personal resources of a mover comprise attributes and characteristics such as: personality, temperament, feelings, motivations, attitudes and values. They also include abilities that determine the capacities of the mover to participate, interact and perform to varying degrees of competence in a movement situation. The development of these personal resources is a result of the interplay between the mover's biological and psychological endowment and the conditions within the various environments. Keogh and Sugden (1985) refer to these as being within two different but interactive surrounds, the outer comprising the physical and social environments, and the inner encompassing the biological and psychological environments. Their usage of the term environment means that it is the influence of a variety of environments, rather than of one global one, that affects a mover's resources, and her/his capacities to interact and participate in movement situations.

The mover-personal resources and the influences arising from interacting with the social environment affect participation experiences. Firstly, choice in terms of the nature and extent of involvement, and secondly, the degree of effort expended. A child whose movement experiences are taking place in 'outer surround' environments that provide positive, supportive and appropriate conditions will seek maximum participation in movement situations. The satisfaction derived through achievement will influence the degree of involvement and effort. Conversely, a child who is experiencing negative 'outer surround' conditions will seek to avoid participation. This will result in a decrement in performance and achievement, and a marked loss of involvement and effort (Keogh and Sugden 1985).

When teaching children who experience difficulties in learning it is easy to understand how their perceived level of competence and confidence influences their participation experiences. It should be of central concern to the teacher to effect a change in the children's perceptions through effecting a change in their qualitative resources during the teaching episodes.

Assessment and recording attainment

Schools now have a responsibility to make the curriculum accessible to all pupils, and to monitor its capacity to achieve this purpose, with particular regard for its appropriateness to all pupils.

Assessment is a formative process and is central to teaching (SCAA 1994, OFSTED 1995) as it informs teaching practice. It is a central feature of constructive teaching and learning. It enables teachers to gather ongoing information on the response and progress of children in terms of their knowledge, skill and understanding. It then allows them to develop teaching practice in an informed and appropriate way, relative to the ongoing responses and needs of the children.

The emphasis on assessment being ongoing and continuous within the intervention process is important. It recognises the value of monitoring the children within the range of classroom and home contexts and conditions. Information from these sources contributes to an informed understanding of the children. The class teacher and parent are recognised as being key people in the assessment process, as they are in a privileged position to gather ongoing information. Teachers are viewed as crucial collaborators with parents and other professionals in the assessment and intervention process.

Assessment in PE

The critical aspect to a process oriented approach is that the focus is on developmental changes over time. It uses observational assessment as a valid and reliable way to collect data and compare it within individuals (Gallahue 1989, 1993). It can include total body and segmental observation and assessment, and focus on individuals, a group or class of children. Children experiencing difficulty can be identified and segmental observation can help to pinpoint difficulties by focusing on body parts.

Figure 11.2 illustrates how the skeleton can be used to focus the teacher's observation on a pupil's body parts when performing a fundamental skill. This is particularly helpful if the teacher is concerned to understand the movement difficulties that a child might be experiencing due to developmental delay, dyspraxia, dysfunction, dissociation or a deficit due to a lack of movement understanding. A series of skeletons can be completed reflectively over a unit of work that focus on a range of fundamental skills (locomotor, manipulative and stability). The purpose of segmental analysis is to inform the intervention process.

The process oriented approach to assessment enables teachers to:

- recognise and respond with understanding to the individuality and diversity of the children's mover-personal resources underpinning movement skill development;
- recognise and respond with understanding to the changing resource levels of the children;
- monitor developmental changes;
- identify difficulties (delay; dissociation; deficit; dysfunction);
- provide insight into intervention strategies;
- monitor achievement and progress.

It allows teachers to take a naturalistic-ecological approach in that it adopts a broad perspective by examining performance in the context of relationships between the task, pupil and conditions (Gallahue 1989, 1993). It focuses on the individual characteristics of the children's mover-personal resources in the context of the learning conditions. It also enables the teacher to promote personalised achievement and progress in a developmental PE curriculum. This assessment approach reinforces the concept of individual differences, which is the cornerstone of a developmental approach to PE. It is about observational

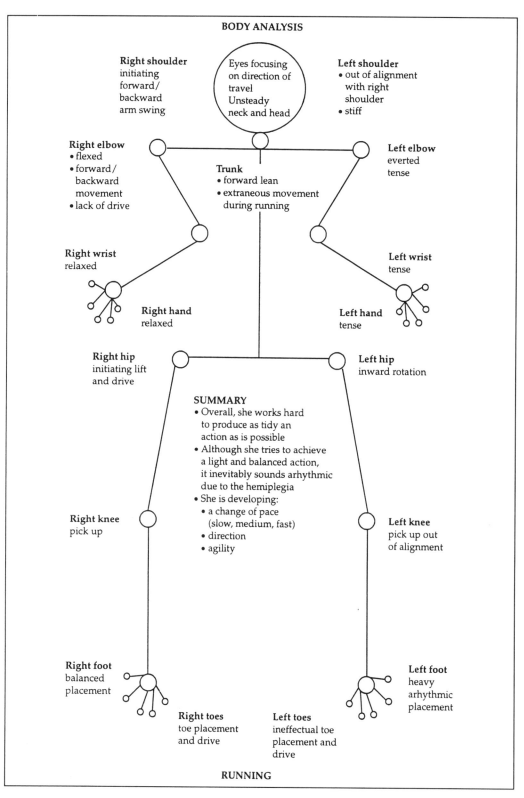

Figure 11.2 Segmental observation and assessment

assessment of process (knowledge, skill and understanding), which is basic to the effective implementation of a developmental approach. It takes account of context, conditions, opportunities, guidance, practice, encouragement and experience, and is not age based.

A product approach can be implemented as a summative assessment process to evaluate achievement and progress in performance. PE has traditionally adopted a product approach to assessing performance, that is, the achievement of the performance, in terms of dimension (distance, height, duration), amplitude and accuracy. This has influenced both the curriculum content and the approaches, which has also focused attention on the achievement of the end product. The performance expectations and activity demands tend to determine the assessment criteria.

Performance can more easily be quantified by people who have minimal movement knowledge. It allows children to be rank ordered and measured against each other and/or a criterion within age-bands. For example, tests can be used to help identify levels and standards of performance against an independently devised criterion. Performance scores are averaged and awarded points and put against a rating scale.

By contrast, qualitative assessment utilises observation as the central tool in the process, with the teacher being required to make judgements based on criteria founded in knowledge, experience and expertise.

A qualitative approach focuses on assessment as a formative and summative process that is central to teaching. The children are assessed within learning conditions that are ecological in nature, and where the approach is developmental. This means that the children are assessed within the context of the conditions and approaches. Their significance and influence are recognised in terms of the children's achievements. The teacher's capacity to promote an ecological environment is dependent on the assessment process to inform the learning conditions. Without an ongoing assessment process the learning conditions cannot be responsive to the developmental needs of the children.

The monitoring process should promote the gathering-reviewing activity that is central to reflective practice. Therefore, it must be clear, concise and systematic, so that detail can be recorded and utilised throughout the teaching scheme. The formative nature of assessment is crucial to maintaining the live dialogue that is implicit in a transactional approach, between the teacher, pupil and learning conditions. The responsive capacity across this triad is crucial to achieving a match. If this is not achieved the children will not experience appropriate and successful learning experiences.

In contrast, a product oriented assessment instrument is not informative in terms of the context, conditions, approaches, and the resource levels and capacities of the children. It is, therefore, appropriate to focus on the qualitative dimensions underpinning the learning conditions and the children's mover-personal resources. This process will inform a developmental approach and transactional context so that the promotion of a match between the teacher, pupil and the learning conditions can be achieved. If a match is to be sought, appropriate information is required relative to the developmental status of the children. It is, therefore, necessary to gather ongoing information on the changing status of the children's movement learning experience, strategies and behaviour (participation experiences), and their movement competence.

A summative process at the end of a school year can then be drawn up so that as the children change classes and schools, current information can inform and support the children's progression within and between schools. The formative and summative process can also inform an Individual Education Programme, Annual Review, as well as Review Meetings and the ongoing dialogue with parents, teachers and professionals. Table 11.3 is an example of a summative profile in PE that can provide an informative picture of a child as s/he moves through and between schools.

The assessment process should not only be able to inform teaching, it should also have the capacity to be shared as teaching is a collaborative process. The information must, therefore, be in a form that can be understood across teacher, parent and professional boundaries.

CONCLUSION

The content and delivery of the primary PE curriculum should take account of the significant changes that occur in children's movement skill development, for example, in terms of their performance in closed and open tasks and situations, due to sensory, perceptual, cognitive, motor development, and biological changes. Primary children solve increasingly complex movement problems, as a result of gaining mastery in fundamental movement skills. They then refine, modify, extend and adapt them in a variety of contexts and conditions (Sugden 1990). Their movement competence (knowledge, skill, understanding) and effectiveness increases as they develop a schema of movement learning experience that allows them to be resourceful in their responses.

A constructive approach to teaching and learning requires an understanding about the potential of the learning environment to be developed in a responsive, flexible and adaptable way so that appropriateness related to the learners' knowledge, skill and understanding can be realised. This responsive way of working between the teacher, learner and the learning environment will promote a change in all the children's mover-personal resources as they progress through the primary years. It requires teachers to develop teaching strategies and approaches that enable them to understand the resources of the learner so that appropriateness in the learning environment can be achieved.

The curriculum should seek to promote opportunities, contexts and conditions that enable these developmental considerations to be propagated and cultivated. Adaptive competence will not be achieved within a curriculum that does not provide the opportunities for the fundamental movement skills to be progressively refined and utilised in a range of increasingly complex closed to open contexts. The children's 'transactional relationships' (Sugden 1990, p. 247) also become complex and sophisticated, in order to cope with the increases in the demands. The curriculum should have the potential to promote these associated psychological, biological, neuromotor and movement changes.

Common practice is developing through the transaction of a common curriculum and common approaches. Qualitative assessment processes are replacing quantitative methods as being more informative and appropriate to a

Year: 1996-1997	MOVEMENT PROFILE	Teacher: BA Brown
NAME AGE	Jane 10–11	
PHYSIQUE HEALTH	Lean, tall Prone to ENT infection (grommets)	
MOTOR IMPAIRMENT	Left hemiplegia	
VISION	No apparent problems	
HEARING	Middle ear infection causing temporary deafness	
BEHAVIOUR (i) Learning (ii) Personal (iii) Social	(i) She demonstrates a capacity to sustain attention and work independently. (ii) She is developing confidence which is enabling her to participate in activities, and share with other children and adults. (iii) Her deep sense of inadequacy and fear of others is difficult to shed, and so she is reliant on others to help her recognise her strengths and values.	
LANGUAGE (i) Receptive (ii) Interpretative (iii) Expressive	(i/ii) A good level of understanding, although she is not able to work in abstract concepts. (iii) Mild articulation difficulties resulting in unclarity, but only when she is nervous and forgets to speak more slowly and clearly.	
PERSONAL/ SOCIAL CONSIDERATIONS	(i) Perceptual difficulties affecting spatial and temporal dimensions of movement processing and production. (ii) Mild autism. (iii) In foster care.	

CURRICULUM EXPERIENCE AND PROGRESS

GAMES ACTIVITIES
She has developed a sound understanding and experience in the fundamental skills. She demonstrates competence in net play, striking and fielding strategy and skill, as she has had the opportunity to develop knowledge, understanding and skill, in the way the games were introduced and developed. In invasion play she can become nervous and apprehensive due to her experiencing temporal and spatial difficulties, unless the conditions are modified to allow her more time to read and respond.

GYMNASTIC ACTIVITIES
She has developed an aptitude and interest. She is keen to develop movement skills on the floor and apparatus, and she understands how to achieve axial, wheeling and inversion skills. She produces good movement sequences, that incorporate a sensitivity to the qualitative dimensions. She demonstrates a good vocabulary of ideas, and a capacity to create and perform. She works sensitively and cooperatively with a partner. She has joined a local gymnastics club with her step-sister.

DANCE ACTIVITIES
She enjoys creating movement phrases that require the involvement of the qualitative dimensions. She demonstrates a capacity to be expressive; creative; sensitive and skilful.

SWIMMING AND WATER SAFETY
She can swim 25m on her front and back; float; engage in water skills and games. She is learning to jump and dive. As yet she is not happy under water. She is gaining confidence, although she is still nervous of the water environment. She is interested in learning about personal survival and water safety.

ATHLETIC ACTIVITIES
Her skill, agility and endurance to engage in run, jump, throw activities is developing with time and experience.

OUTDOOR AND ADVENTUROUS ACTIVITIES
She participates in the tasks with responsibility, and shows a capacity to read, plan and respond to situations.

LINKS

LINKS WITH PARENTS / PROFESSIONALS
Her foster parents are supportive and interested in her progress, and if she did not live so far away her participation in extra-curricular activities would have been more possible.

SUMMARY OF FINDINGS
During her primary school career she has developed a breadth of movement competence in the fundamental skills, which she is now applying in sport-related contexts. She approaches movement situations with strategy and confidence. She has participated successfully in a shared teaching context in gymnastic activities with the neighbouring mainstream primary school, which she enjoyed.

FUTURE GUIDELINES
(i) The opportunities and conditions are crucial for her enjoyment and success. In games activities she requires more time, reduced pace and a slower ball, and then she can enjoy participating with a high degree of success.
(ii) She tends to rush/scramble responses, or avoid them, if the conditions are inappropriate.
(iii) She observes and utilises movement information competently, and in more closed conditions her participation and performance is good.
(iv) She requires sensitive guidance to help her to develop water confidence.
(v) She has shown a good capacity to develop her mover-personal resources, and what was initially a difficult aspect of her development has become her strength.

Figure 11.3 Movement profile

developmental approach in primary PE. The responsibility of the teacher to achieve a match between the children's resource levels and the demands of the task and conditions is becoming part of all primary practice. This is helping to promote an understanding of individuality and diversity as being a more appropriate way to recognise and respond to all children's developmental needs. This is leading towards an inclusive approach to educational provision which is currently informing the transaction of the National Curriculum, and particularly the access to PE by all children.

REFERENCES

Ainscow, M. (ed.) (1991) *Effective Schools for All*. London: David Fulton.

Ainscow, M. and Hart, S. (1992) 'Moving practice forward', *Support for Learning* **7**(3), 115–20.

Ashman, A. F. and Conway, R. N. F. (1989) *Cognitive Strategies for Special Education*. London: Routledge.

Brown, B. A. (1996) *Access to PE by children experiencing learning difficulties*. Unpublished doctoral thesis. The University of Leeds.

Department of Education and Science (DES) (1978) *Special educational needs. Report of the Committee of Enquiry into the Education of Handicapped Children and Young People*. Chairman: Mrs H. M. Warnock. London: HMSO.

DES (1988) *The Education Reform Act*. London: HMSO.

DES (1991) *The National Curriculum PE Working Group Interim Report*. London: HMSO.

DES (1992) *PE in the National Curriculum*. London: HMSO.

Department for Education (DfE) (1988) *Education Reform Act 1988*. London: HMSO.

DFE (1993) *Education Act 1993*. London: HMSO.

DFE (1994) *Code of Practice on the Identification and Assessment of Special Educational Needs. Regulations on Assessments and Statements*. London: DFE Publications Centre.

DfEE (1995) *Key Stages 1 and 2 of the National Curriculum*. London: HMSO.

Gallahue, D. L. (1989) *Understanding Motor Development: Infants, Children, Adolescents,* 2nd edn. Dubuque: Brown and Benchmark Publishers.

Gallahue, D. L. (1993) *Developmental PE for Today's Children*, 2nd edn. Oxford: Brown and Benchmark Publishers.

Keogh, J. F. and Sugden, D. A. (1985) *Movement Skill Development*. London: Collier MacMillan Publishers.

National Curriculum Council (NCC) (1989) *Curriculum Guidance: 2. A Curriculum for All*. York: NCC.

Office for Standards in Education (OFSTED) (1995) *PE: a Review of Inspection Findings 1993/94*. London: HMSO.

Schools Council and Assessment Authority (SCAA) (1994) *PE in the National Curriculum: draft proposals*. London: DFE.

Sugden, D. A. (1990) Developmental PE for all. *British Journal of Physical Education* **21**(1), Spring, 247–9.

Sugden, D. A. and Keogh, J. F. (1990) *Problems in Movement Skill Development*. Columbia, South Carolina: University of South Carolina Press.

Wolfendale, S. (1987) *Special Needs in Ordinary Schools: Primary Schools and Special Needs: Policy, Planning and Provision*. London: Cassell.

CHAPTER 12

Let's look at it another way: a constructivist view of art education

Lynne Hoye

> Art is not a body of knowledge, a skill, a set of rules, a process. The sum of all our visual knowledge is not only what we know, but the way we know it and respond to it . . . Art education is concerned with the development of the senses as our way of 'receiving' our world, and the process that we use to symbolize, externalize, understand, order, express, communicate and solve its problems. (Barrett 1982, pp. 43–5)

The first part of this chapter focuses on a selection of theoretical perspectives which support a constructivist view of the creative process. The second part considers a definition of aesthetics and the child's artistic development. Thirdly, the implications for classroom practice are considered. The work is laced with vignettes to illuminate the relevant points.

A SELECTION OF THEORETICAL PERSPECTIVES WHICH SUPPORT A CONSTRUCTIVIST VIEW OF THE CREATIVE PROCESS

> Looking backwards from end to start point of the creative process we are inclined to say 'Ah yes, it had to be so; the chance had to be taken' . . . But facing forward in time we see only risk and difficulty. (Barron, in Ross 1978, p. 12)

A constructivist view of learning incorporates a creative activity, as the child attempts to 'make sense' of his/her environment in relation to his/her present understandings. This creative activity is a complex interaction of psychological, social, emotional and physical factors, all spurring the child towards activity and the creation of new understandings or constructs. This internal mental activity may be expressed in tangible form through the creation of artworks. This process is not as simplistic as it first appears, for children's artworks may be viewed as the expression of their developing understanding or constructs (individual realities); however they also form part of the child's environment, allowing the child to share experience, to empathise and to learn (social realities). The child can be seen to be influenced by the artwork of others, which in turn influences his/her own artwork. It is through this creative interplay that the child makes sense of the world. Such creative activity is part of the child's inheritance.

Child psychologists have noted the importance of sensory stimulus in early learning. Hunt's work (1971) focused on the child's response to visual stimulus, i.e. pattern. His research showed that, while babies would focus on familiar patterns, such 'recognitive familiarity' soon became 'old hat' or 'boring' and new, more complex patterns were needed to hold the child's attention. Such visual stimulation allowed the child to recognise existing patterns, yet thirst for new, more complex ones. The child then enjoys the recognitive familiarity of old patterns yet demands the novelty of new, more challenging experiences. In relation to learning Hunt (1971) suggests that complexity and incongruity or cognitive dissonance motivate the child to form new understandings or constructs. The classroom should serve the dual function of providing a visually stimulating environment (input) whilst also allowing for creative activity (output) which includes Barron's 'risk and difficulty'.

Elliott (1993) considered the role of the learner as that of a 'practical scientist' who explores and develops new understandings as a result of a reflective and active interaction with the environment. Such reflection may be viewed as a creative response and can be manifest in the scribbles, doodles and artworks produced by the child who reflects upon existing constructs in relation to new stimuli, thus confirming or modifying them. In this sense the practical scientist can also be viewed as a practical artist who creates and constructs new realities.

Much has been written regarding the social construction of reality (Piaget 1955, Sanford 1987). Dubos (1976) noted: 'The various microcosms, or ecosystems, with which man deals are thus his (sic) own mental creations; indeed they derive their size and shape from the characteristics and limitations of his senses and conceptual apparatus' (p. 19). It is not the purpose of this chapter to continue Dubos's debate but rather to focus on his 'mental creations' in relation to the work of Galtung (1990). Galtung suggested that individuals are able to construct a reality 'that is not yet there' (p. 102). Thus each child creates and recreates reality in his/her own terms, extending the boundaries to include new and novel understandings and realizations particular to the child. Through artistic expression the child can develop and express these new realities. The child then can be viewed as a 'practical' scientist or artist (Elliott 1993), exploring the world though sensory experience , perpetually motivated to seek new and novel experiences (Hunt 1971) whilst creating a new reality (Galtung 1990), through both the appreciation and the expression of the creative process.

In order to discuss the role of art education within this process it is necessary to consider both aesthetics and the child's artistic development.

A DEFINITION OF AESTHETICS AND A CONSIDERATION OF THE CHILD'S ARTISTIC DEVELOPMENT

Aesthetics

Elliott's notion of the 'practical scientist' may be viewed not only in relation to the child exploring, investigating and reflecting upon experience but also in relation to the child 'creating' new understandings. This creative process is part of the activity of both the scientist and the artist. However, the extant literature would suggest that 'aesthetics' is implicit in the work of the artist.

A clear definition of aesthetics is elusive, and historically definition has been viewed in relation to a positivist perspective. For the purpose of this work I would extend the original Greek word *aisthetika*, meaning 'things perceptible through the senses', to include an active interpretation of sensory stimuli. Wollheim (1975) in his Preface to *Art and Its Objects* saw this 'active' interpretation as being socially constructed. He stated that aesthetics 'connects both with our understanding of art and with our understanding of society'. Abbs (1989) extends the view of aesthetics as 'artistic activity' and suggests that:

> a formal aesthetic refers to those structural forms which are the poetic grammar of the life of feeling and imagination . . . Our formal aesthetic, then, returns us to life . . . In the arts we could say, in Kantian style, that feeling without form cannot be comprehended, and that form without feeling has in it nothing worth comprehending. (p. 41)

Abbs continues to argue for the establishment of a curriculum which establishes both 'the place of and a place for feeling'. This interpretation of aesthetics allows for a close relationship between the creative process including Abbs's 'feeling and imagination' and the child's construction of both an individual and a social reality. Feeling and imagination are part of the artistic activity evident in most children's early drawings, whether the tadpole figures of the western four year old or the horseshoe figures of the Aboriginal infant. Whilst the child's early representations may be culturally specific they hold the seeds of the child's developing artistic activity and aesthetic awareness. Inherent in the activity is movement between preconscious, unconscious and subconscious states, which gives rise to the unique interpretations of the world constructed by each child. This aesthetic or artistic activity should be viewed as a valid and integral part of the child's education.

Kant (1787) offered a legitimisation of the creative process seeing it as a 'model of cognition which requires understanding'. He stressed the importance of the creative process in allowing the child to develop 'frames of knowing' or ways of constructing an understanding of the world. Gardner (1984) highlighted the complexity of 'knowing' by articulating the notion of multiple intelligences, i.e. logical, musical, linguistic, spatial, and bodily-kinaesthetic. The child's artworks allow the adult insights into the child's world and the child's sensitivity to Gardner's multiple intelligence.

The Gulbenkian Report (1982) did much to legitimise 'creativity' by recognising its cognitive nature and viewing it as a type of intelligence grounded in knowledge. The National Curriculum orders in relation to Art have helped focus the content of the art curriculum on the relevant 'Knowledge and Understanding' and the activities of 'Investigating and Making'. However the range and breadth of the educational potential within the art lesson is rarely explored and many art lessons can be viewed as being rather formulaic. OFSTED (1997, p. 27) commenting on report writing in relation to art note:

> Very few reports comment on key factors such as the development of imagination; creative development or even the creativity in the work itself; the sensitivity of the work; or its energy and dynamism. Very few pick out the nature and quality of the stimulus for work apart from the work of other artists; the contribution of art to the spiritual, moral, social and cultural development of the pupils is rarely mentioned.

Is this criticism because the 'key features' are not being addressed in schools or because the Inspectors are not seeing them? Whatever the cause, 'seeing' such aspects of art education is predicated upon a sound understanding of the rationale for art education, including an understanding of its meta-cognition and of the artistic development of children.

The child's artistic development

Psychologists and art educators have been interested in children's drawings since the eighteenth century when Jean Jacques Rousseau outlined childhood as a distinct stage in human development. Kellogg (1970) identified twenty basic scribbles and suggested that children use these basic scribbles to form diagrams, combines and aggregates. Scribbles can be seen as a development of pictorial representation in the same way as babbles are viewed as precursors to speech; the diagrams, combines and aggregates being analogous to the words, phrases and sentences of language. There has been much criticism of Kellogg's work, notably by Golomb (1981) and Alland (1983) who suggest that representational forms can be created without any previous scribbling stage. However, from a constructivist viewpoint, it can be argued that pictorial representation, whether scribbles, diagrams, combines or aggregates, is visual evidence of the child's ability to create a mark which represents a particular object or feeling which in turn has a particular meaning for the child. Children 'play' with drawing, developing their own unique visual responses to the environment (individual reality), which is refined and modified as they attempt to communicate through their artworks and to create drawings which can be shared with others (social reality).

Children's drawings allow the adult insight into the cognitive and creative processes being developed within the child. Early work by Luquet (1927) while acknowledging a sequence to artistic development also noted a phenomenon which he termed 'fortuitous realism', i.e. the child spontaneously notices a chance resemblance in his/her scribbles to which he/she attributes meaning. Luquet suggests that following this 'fortuitous realism', the child will intentionally create representations which resemble specific objects. Children from an early age are concerned with the visual resemblance between their drawing and the world around them. Goodnow (1977) calls these resemblances a 'search for equilibrium', or as previously discussed in relation to Hunt's work on motivation, a resolution of incongruity or cognitive dissonance. Children pictorially construct their reality and this pictorial construction allows the teacher insights which may not be accessible through language; indeed pictorial representation can transcend language.

The Goodenough 'Draw-a-Man' test is used extensively in schools to offer psychologists insights into the cognitive and emotional functioning of the child. This test, created by Florence Goodenough in 1926 and revised by Dale Harris in 1963, was viewed as a crude measurement of intellectual maturity. Koppitz (1968) designed a 'Draw-a-Person' Test which was scored using thirty developmental items. Both tests can be correlated with the Stanford Binet Intelligence Test and have been used as a guide to the child's intellectual performance. They reinforce the idea of a sequential development to children's artwork.

As early as 1887 Corrado Ricci noted that children's drawings were not attempts towards representation of specific objects but rather expressions of the children's knowledge about the objects. Children between the ages of approximately three and six years draw what they 'know' not what they 'see'. Kerchensteiner (1905) suggested that children included in their drawings features which were dominant to their conception of a particular set of objects. Drawings then can be informed by the child's growing understandings of the world, and, as such, allow the adult access to the way in which the child constructs his/her world. The insightful adult will consider the artwork of the child as a visual map of the ways in which the child constructs his/her developing reality.

While art educators recognise this emergent stage of an aesthetic sensibility which appears to develop intuitively from the child as they interact with their surroundings, they also realise the need to refine and extend the child's ability to communicate visually. Just as the adult extends the opportunities for the child to develop linguistic skills so too must there be opportunities to develop representational skills, interpretative skills and skills to help refine visual and manipulative acuity.

The art teacher needs to be aware of the developmental stages in children's pictorial representations if she/he is to assess the next artistic opportunity to be offered the child, be it a 'reinforcement activity', e.g. to reinforce a particular skill or technique, or an 'enhancement activity', e.g. where the child is developing further insights into a specific element of art, including pattern, texture, colour, line, tone, shape, form, and space. How then can aesthetic or artistic activity, which is part of the creative process, be developed in the primary classroom?

IMPLICATIONS FOR CLASSROOM PRACTICE

How does the work of Hunt (Motivation), Elliott (Practical Scientist/Artist) and Galtung (Creating Reality) help towards creating a perspective upon art teaching which acknowledges the developmental nature of art, recognizes the importance of aesthetic sensibility and reflects a constructivist stance?

Motivation

Intrinsic motivation can be seen as the pivot of learning. It is by definition 'relevant' to the learner. Traditionally teachers endeavoured to 'match' the pre-existing curriculum tasks to individual pupils. However, a constructivist stance would suggest that the pupils 'pitch' the work at their own optimum level, having selected from a field of inquiry initiated by the teacher, e.g. 3D claywork. The children then 'work' or 'play'. I see the words as synonymous, spurred by incongruity or cognitive dissonance, leaving the difficult task of assessing their understandings and skill development to the observant teacher, who responds to their work, enters into a dialogue with the pupils, offers positive feedback and encourages feedback from peers. Curriculum relevance can be interpreted as pupils being intrinsically motivated and working at their appropriate levels. Such a perspective necessitates that the teacher respects and values the pupil's endeavours.

Art lessons hold numerous opportunities for relevance, intrinsic motivation and the nurturing of pupil respect. Problems traditionally associated with the over-emphasis on the regurgitation of 'correct' responses to fulfil preconceived formulaic assessment criteria based on narrow outcomes rather than learning processes may limit individual learning. The National Curriculum Programmes of Study for art (Key Stages One and Two) focus on 'Investigating and Making' and 'Knowledge and Understanding', and are well able to be interpreted using a constructivist framework. The following vignette outlines a first art lesson with a new class of eight year old children, who had previously received questionable 'art' input and many of whom were anxious because, as they stated from the outset, 'I can't draw':

Pupils were given a range of materials (pencils, felt tips, paint, glue, wool, beads etc.) and challenged to 'make a mark' in as many ways as possible. Initially the children were excited by the array of materials but tentative regarding the challenge. After they took the 'risk' and made one mark, usually a straight line with a pencil, and realised that there was not a 'right' or 'wrong' way to make a mark but just 'their' way, they became confident and extended their creative responses. They 'played' with making marks, creating some highly imaginative responses which moved beyond the materials supplied using, for example, dirt, hair and nail clippings! After experimenting with different ways of making a mark some pupils reverted to pencil and began using the pencil in different ways, (etching, shading etc.) One pupil, who had been looking at Henry Moore's drawings of the subway during the war, attempted to imitate Moore's bracelet etching using a variety of different media apart from pencil. Other pupils focused on using just one or two colours and others began to develop pattern.

Throughout the activity pupils were talking about their work, either commenting on their ability to discover 'new' marks or offering each other positive feedback. Each art work was unique and each individual had pitched the work at their own level, free of the constraints of trying to be 'right'. The visual range was extensive, and it offered the teacher insights into the different skills and conceptual levels of each pupil specifically in relation to manual dexterity, tool control, hand–eye co-ordination, plus the elements of creative expression, i.e. flow, fluency, flexibility, novelty and originality. The open-ended activity allowed the children to develop their drawing skills in a stress free manner and altered their attitude to art. The physical movement allowed during the lesson enabled optimum interaction between pupils and ensured that both visual and oral communication took place.

The inter-curriculum links were made as the children discussed the war (history), colour changes (science) and offered descriptions of the work (English). The teacher was able to assess the pupils' ability to use descriptive language (both expressive and technical) as they commented on each other's work. The pupils were intrinsically motivated, pitching the work at their own level and their own pace, while taking 'risks' and making the work relevant to their own understandings. The final products were evidence of a complex process, and allowed the teacher to consider future work in relation to pupil 'need/ability/interest'. All work was 'respected' both verbally and by being incorporated into a display. Pupils who had previously feared being made to draw reported that they had enjoyed the lesson. In fact they had been working on the first stage of drawing without realising it.

Elliott's practical scientist (artist)

Just as the scientist thinks, investigates, explores, hypothesises and models so too does the artist. The vignette on drawing previously discussed included all these elements. Both the artist and the scientist refine their 'frames' or 'ways of viewing the world' in response to incongruity or cognitive dissonance while attempting to reach Piaget's 'equilibrium'. The process involves thinking, problem solving, designing, modifying, evaluating and trialling and it is affected by both the cognitive and affective domains. The following vignette illuminates the importance of visual stimulus in relation to the process skills outlined above:

Each month primary children would visit the city's art gallery for a short time, i.e. thirty minutes. They became fascinated by the Pre-Raphaelite and genre paintings. Each month they would visit their favourite paintings and make up stories surrounding the images. During art sessions some children attempted to replicate the paintings and they also recorded the stories they had made up in their writing books.

In order to 'capture' the children's interest the teacher must cast his/her net wide, so that children with different frames can engage with the challenge. Narrow questions can limit responses, and conceptual fragmentation and confusion may occur if areas are broken down too quickly by the class teacher. Initially a holistic approach to a topic allows multiple entry points, e.g. exploration of colour. Such a global starting point allows all children to engage their thinking at their own level. Subsequent lessons may then develop in a variety of ways dependant upon the teacher's assessment of the children's responses, e.g. they may work on subtle changes in shade, or consider Picasso's use of colour, or try to replicate a particular colour using watercolours. While the scientist works with such global concepts as force, matter etc. the artist works with pattern, texture, colour, line, tone, shape, form and space.

The following vignette illuminates the various 'entry points' of an art challenge set for students undertaking a initial teacher training programme:

Twelve groups of four students were given the challenge of creating presentations for their fellow students in one of the eight visual elements (pattern, texture, colour, line, tone, shape, form and space). Each group worked together over a period of three weeks. Every presentation was very different even when the initial stimulus (e.g. colour) was the same. The activity was open-ended. The students had to investigate the field and present the material in a meaningful way to their peers. Much positive feedback was given and received. Each presentation was video-recorded, allowing the lecturer to review the work. The work allowed tangible evidence upon which the lecturer was able to base future work. It also allowed much student to student debate and the sharing of understanding and the resolution of cognitive dissonance.

Galtung's 'reality that is not yet there'

Each individual constructs his/her own reality. Galtung (1990) comments on the reality that does not yet exist. In relation to art education this may be interpreted as the process of the creative imagination. Aspects of primary art teaching consider the developmental stages of the children's art work, e.g. the human figure, and attempt to encourage the child to draw what they 'see' not what they 'know' as in observational drawing. Art teaching also attempts to develop 2D and 3D artworks using a variety of different media, to enhance visual literacy and knowledge of artists' work and to make critical judgements. All these aspects of art education can be rooted in relevant experiences for the pupils, and can be presented using a constructivist framework. However, the child's 'making sense of the world' moves beyond the reality of everyday experience towards the world of the imagination. The child's artistic activity (aesthetic) is multifaceted, allowing the teacher insights into a) his/her conceptual functioning, b) his/her skill development, c) his/her creative explorations in relation to the flow, fluency, flexibility and originality of his/her imaginings. All these skills are transferable.

The movement from drawing what the child 'knows', to drawing what he/she 'sees', to drawing what he/she 'imagines' is part of each individual's understanding of the world, and the sharing of this understanding, through visual communication, becomes part of the social construction of reality, possibly a reality that did not exist prior to the creation of the artwork.

In terms of problem solving and creative thinking, imagining or 'playing with ideas' to create new and novel interpretations is crucial to human development. Creativity is highly prized in cultural, scientific, technological, psychological and artistic terms, yet in relation to the primary curriculum it is viewed with some suspicion, being seen as a remnant of the post Plowden era, when creativity was viewed as part of the 'progressive' movement. If the curriculum is viewed as a means of transforming rather than transmitting established ideas, then the creative process must be valued and nurtured. The new realities of the twenty-first century are lying dormant, waiting to be released by the novel imaginings of the pupils currently undertaking the programmes of study in today's National Curriculum. A constructivist approach to education in general and art education in particular helps to release such imaginings, and offers a framework for nurturing the 'realities that are not yet there'.

The following vignette considers how such realities may be articulated in an art class:

A class of six and seven year olds had done much work on observational drawing and refining the various techniques of drawing. I wanted to offer new challenge and stimulus and to 'jog' the pupils into a world of imaginings. I wanted to 'see' the children's ability to use their imagination to interpret their worlds in new and novel ways. I posed the open question 'I wonder what we would draw if we could not see?' 'Wonder' is a spur to creativity, and children delight in wondering as it liberates their thinking and allows for frivolous and serendipitous activity. 'Wonderment' is the stuff children's play is made of, it is the basis of inquiry, it allows for enhanced experience and the description of such experience, it forms part of the aesthetic or artistic activity and it extends to include the spiritual dimension of the numinous.

The children were offered a variety of different media (paint, clay, fabrics, assorted papers etc.). The results of this open-ended activity were diverse, and included 2D felt tip drawings of 'space', highly organized Mondrian-like rectangles of colour depicting different 'moods/feelings', and spirals of colour on a black background. The process was enhanced by children sharing their work with each other and talking about their interpretations. Teachers may need this linguistic affirmation of artistic intention if they are to understand the child's changing reality.

The following extracts are a selection of linguistic responses offered by the children in relation to their work.

Space: 'Space, space is all around us, it is everywhere. I have been to space. Space is exciting. Have you been to space?'
Mondrian Rectangles: 'These are the colours I feel during the day. You can't see how I feel but sometimes I'm really red and excited or yellow and quiet. My favourite colour is purple – but I don't feel purple often – and I'm not sure what it really feels like to be purple – I just can't say'.
Spirals: 'The dark, dark is everywhere. When I close my eyes I see nothing – well almost nothing. Nothing at first – then I see all colours, all whirling around, all moving'.

These are the realities of the children. They did not exist in tangible form before the challenge of the lesson. The children used artistic activity to physically construct visual representations of their inner realities. They then shared the art work and talked about it with their peers so that individual realities became social realities.

Such imaginings have obvious application for developing creative thinking. However, it can be suggested that the articulation of 'wonder' or of 'realities that do not yet exist' also has application to enhance mental well being. Much counselling uses symbol and metaphor, or 'wonder', as a way of allowing clients to explore their feelings. The descriptive and emotional language that can be nurtured during art lessons allows the child to articulate such feelings. The positive unconditional regard offered by many Rogerian counsellors equates to the positive feedback given in constructivist classrooms. Both the counsellor and the teacher value the individual and the individual's idiosyncratic or unique perception of reality, and both help the individual to move towards further understanding and learning (Hoye 1987).

HOW CAN WE RECOGNIZE A CLASSROOM BASED ON CONSTRUCTIVIST PRINCIPLES?

A constructivist art class would:

- encourage pupil/pupil interaction, student initiated questions and co-operative learning;
- articulate the relevance of inter-curriculum links;
- encourage pupils to be responsible for their own learning;
- offer supportive feedback while the pupils are working;
- emphasise process rather than product;
- focus on theme/elements, allowing pupils to classify and organise sub-categories for themselves;
- appreciate new and novel ideas/realities and value 'wonderment';
- pose challenging problems which relate to the pupils;
- value each artwork if it is honestly created;
- encourage pupils to see the views/frames of others (empathy);
- encourage open-ended questions and uncertainty;
- value curiosity, exploration, inquiry and 'risk and difficulty';
- appreciate what pupils create, not what they can repeat;
- encourage the adoption of multiple frames or perspectives;
- consider transformation rather than transmission.

The following list suggests some themes for development during art lessons. Each theme is broad enough to allow different entry points, and each theme can be seen in relation to its potential for inter-curriculum links to be made. The work of established artists which could act as visual stimuli in each of the themes is outlined. These suggestions are a personal selection that have been successful in the primary classroom. Teachers will construct and categorize their own themes and resource bases of visual stimuli according to their own preferences.

Suggested themes

Animals

Henri Rousseau [1844–1910]. Naive visions of exotic animals, e.g. 'Jungle with Monkeys Eating Oranges' and 'The Sleeping Gypsy'.

William Blake [1757–1827]. Imaginative symbolism, e.g. 'Midsummer Night's Dream' and 'The Red Dragon'.

Sir Edward Burne-Jones [1833–1898]. English Pre-Raphaelite stained glass work and tapestries, e.g. 'The Pelican'.

Edgar Degas [1834–1917]. Subjects include racecourses and ballet dancers, e.g. 'Before the Start'.

Hieronymus Bosch [1450–1516]. Symbolic absurd and fantastic creatures, e.g. 'Garden of Earthly Delights'.

Buildings

Antoni Gaudi [1852–1926]. Extravagant architecture, e.g. Church of the Sagrada Famila, and the Casa Mila, both in Barcelona.

Frank Lloyd Wright [1869–1959]. Organic architecture echoing the natural environment, e.g. Falling Water House, Pennsylvania.

Le Corbusier (Charles Jeanneret) [1887–1965]. Clear lines of rationalist architecture, e.g. Notre Dame du Haute, Ronchamp.

People

Edvard Munch [1863–1944]. Emotionally charged expressionism, e.g. 'The Scream' and 'Evening on Karl-Johan Strasse'.

Amedeo Modigliani [1884–1920]. Dreamy gentleness of long faces full of sensitivity and pathos, e.g. 'Girl with Black Hair' and 'The Bohemian Girl'.

Henri de Toulouse-Lautrec [1864–1901]. Grotesque realism, e.g. 'Yvette Guilbert' and various posters for the Revue Blanche.

Work which helps to illuminate the eight elements of art education

Pattern

William Morris [1834–1896]. Heavy, complex decorative effects for wallpaper and fabric.
Victor Vasarely [1908–]. Geometric patterns of optical illusion or 'Op' art, e.g. Pal Ket.

Texture

Claude Monet [1840–1926]. Careful adherence to the visual sensation of painting directly in response to real stimuli, e.g. 'The Garden of the Artist at Giverny' and the numerous paintings of Rouen Cathedral created in different lights to show the importance of atmosphere.

Joseph Turner [1775–1851]. Watercolour and oil paintings achieving textural qualities though the use of 'coloured light'.

Vincent Van Gogh [1853–1890]. Heavy forms and expressive textures showing light and emotion.

Colour

Paul Klee [1879–1940]. Free fantasy. The work after his visit to Tunisia reveals a new world of colour.

Paul Gauguin [1848–1903]. Impressionistic simplicity and boldness of primitive colour.

Jackson Pollock [1912–1956]. Action painting to express feelings through the manipulation of colour, specifically the violence of colour and its application.

Line

Albrecht Durer [1471–1528]. Woodcut book illustrations and copper engravings, e.g. 'The Knight, Death and the Devil'.

Wassily Kandinsky [1866–1944]. Linear abstraction and a belief that through colour he could influence the feelings of the viewer, e.g. 'Brief Dream in Red' and 'Sweetened Construction'.

Tone

Peter Paul Rubens [1577–1640]. Warm rounded bodies and realistic landscapes, e.g. 'Holy Family' and 'Evening Landscape'.

Paul Klee [1879–1940]. Tonal variations reflect preconscious and subconscious reflections, e.g. 'Port with Sailing Ships' and 'Caligula'.

Shape

Henri Matisse [1869–1954]. Bold shapes of simplified subjects to evoke clarity, e.g. 'The Egyptian Curtain' and his 'cut outs'.

Jean Arp [1887–1966]. Surrealist experimentation with diverse materials, e.g. 'Fork and Plastron' and 'Terrestrial Form of Forest'.

Form

Antonio Gaudi (see previous examples)
Sculptors, e.g. *Benvenuto Cellini, Michelangelo, Henry Moore* and *Elizabeth Frink*.

Space

Piet Mondrian [1872–1944]. Geometric simplification free of emotional content, e.g. 'Composition in Red'.

Rene Magritte [1898–1967]. Surrealistic and conceptual absurd expressions of space, e.g. 'Evening Dreams'.

The importance of feedback

A critical factor of successful teaching is the teacher's interpretation of the children's developing perceptions as they grope to assimilate and accommodate new understandings. However, often and for a variety of reasons, teachers can 'miss' or incorrectly interpret the work of individuals. The following vignettes exemplify the ease with which teachers can misconstrue children's artistic interpretations:

Alan was a five year old who was involved in an art lesson which focused on observational drawing in the school yard. He had been given a sketch pad, soft pencil and clip board. He had had previous successful experience of observation drawing and had used a cardboard viewer to isolate specific parts of a composition in order to aid his work. The class had been encouraged to 'explore' the yard before deciding upon the area they wished to draw. They had been encouraged to feel surfaces, look for detail and investigate different parts of the yard before commencing the drawing. After twenty minutes the children returned to the class to discuss their work. The teacher was dismayed to see Alan's page void of what she expected to be observations of the yard. When quizzed regarding his response, or perceived lack of response, Alan explained that the three small dots at the bottom of the page were the three small stones he felt through his thin pumps as he stood in the yard.

I took my new kitten into class and explained to the children that I had named him Kandinsky, after the famous artist. We had been previously been looking at the work of Kandinsky and Miro. I thought I had explained myself clearly until I heard children from my class telling their friends at playtime 'our teacher has a new kitten called Kandinsky – and it can paint'!

One aspect of successful teaching lies with the teacher. His/her orchestration of curriculum delivery to include constructivist principles and sensitivity to interpreting the responses of individual children is critical. Feedback, both formative and summative, forms part of the process of the dynamic of constructivism. The teacher, the pupils and the child are all part of this dynamic process. Each time a child decides where to place his/her next brush stroke, he/she is evaluating his/her work and wondering what changes to make. Every time a pupil or teacher offers a child comment on his/her work the child redefines his/her assumptions about the work and about himself/herself. The process integrates Eisner's (1972) contextual, conceptual and productive domains into a reality for the child. The process may also influence the child's self concept and locus of control as well as his/her understanding, thus affecting both the cognitive and affective domains. Feedback may also help both the teacher and the child to articulate their developing meta-cognition of the learning process. Through practical work pupils and teachers can discuss the relevance and appropriateness of the art curriculum. This happens as they talk during art activities, evaluating their developing artwork and critically considering their own work and the work of other artists. Such communication also allows the teacher to understand the conceptual bridges that the children are making with other subject areas. The importance of the dynamic of feedback in the classroom becomes a key factor in the successful implementation of a constructivist orientation.

However, while much emphasis is given to the planning and preparation of art activities, adherence to the Programmes of Study can be done in a formulaic manner. Offering a constructivist orientation to art lessons encourages the teacher to consider the key cognitive and affective areas previously outlined, specifically the areas of imagination, creativity, sensitivity, energy and dynamism which OFSTED (1997) note as being evident in very few reports. The emphasis on formative feedback as pupils manipulate the elements of pattern, texture, colour, line, tone, shape, form and space will enhance the intended learning outcomes for each lesson and the subsequent assessment criteria. Feedback should be:

- non-judgmental;
- based on the activity, not focused on a judgement of innate ability;
- supportive, and encouraging creativity and risk taking;
- given as a stimulus to aid understanding and improvement;
- a model for pupils' self and peer evaluation;
- part of a collaborative discussion of the work, involving the teacher, the child and his/her peers.

Cunliffe warns that concepts used in the art class may be 'used' but not 'owned' by the pupils. He cites the example of making colour wheels:

how many pupils retain knowledge about colour from this activity? . . . how many teachers check to see if pupils have acquired (internalized) this knowledge in a meaningful enough way for it to be transferred and used in both the productive and conceptual domains? (Cunliffe 1990, p. 281).

Teachers must 'check' to evaluate whether internalization has taken place. The quality of teacher 'checking' is predicated upon their own understandings of the purposes and relevance of art education, the insightfulness of the feedback dynamic and their ability to clarify clear and relevant intended learning outcomes both short-term and long-term. The importance of self knowledge and development for both the teacher and the pupil can be viewed as having far reaching effects on the dynamic of the art class, as both teacher and child construct new insights into each other and the socially constructed world in which they are key players.

REFERENCES

Abbs, P. (1989) *A is For Aesthetic.* Lewes: Falmer Press.

Alland, A. (1983) *Playing with Form.* New York: Columbia University Press.

Barrett, M. (1982) *Art Education.* London: Heinemann Educational.

Berger, P (1971) 'Identity as a problem in the sociology of knowledge', in Esland, G. (ed.) *School and Society.* London: Routledge and Kegan Paul.

Cunliffe, L. (1990) 'Tradition, mediation and growth in art education', in *Journal of Art and Design Education* 9(3), 277–88.

Dubos, R. (1976) *A God Within.* London: Abacus.

Eisner, E. (1972) *Educating Artistic Vision.* London: Macmillan.

Elliott, J. (1993) *Reconstructing Teacher Education, Teacher Development.* London: Falmer Press.

Galtung, J. (1990) in Oyen, E. *Comparative Methodology. Theory and Practice in International Social Research.* London: Sage Publications.

Gardner, H. (1984) *Frames of Mind – The Theory of Multiple Intelligences.* London: Heinemann.

Golomb, C. (1981) 'Representation and reality; the origins and determinants of young children's drawings', *Review of Research in Visual Art Education* **14**, 36–48.

Goodnow, J. (1977) *Children's Drawing.* London: Fontana Open Books.

Gulbenkian Foundation (1982) *The Arts in School.* Gulbenkian Foundation.

Hoye, L. (1987) 'Counselling in primary schools', in David, K. and Charlton, T. (eds) *The Caring Role of the Primary School.* Basingstoke: Macmillan Education.

Hunt. J. McV. (1960) 'Experience and the development of motivation: some representations', *Child Development* **31**, 489–504.

Hunt. J. McV. (1971) 'Using intrinsic motivation to teach young children' *Educational Technology,* February, **2**, 78–80.

Kant, I. (1787) *Critique of Pure Reason.* Preface to the 1787 Second Edition. London: Dent and Sons.

Kellogg, R. (1970) *Analyzing Children's Art.* Palo Alto, California: Mayfield.

Kerschensteiner, G. (1905) 'Die Entwicklung Der Zeichnerischen Begabung.' Munich: Carl Gerber, in Cox. M . (1992) *Children's Drawing.* London: Penguin.

Koppitz, E. (1968) *Psychological Evaluation of Children's Human Figure Drawings.* London: Grune and Stratton.

Luquet, G. (1927) 'Le dessin enfantin', in Cox. M . (1992) *Children's Drawing.* London: Penguin.

OFSTED (1997) *Inspection Quality 1996–1997 – A Review of Inspection Report Writing.* London: HMSO.

Piaget, J. (1954) *The Construction of Reality in the Child.* New York: Basic Books.

Ricci, C. (1887) *L'Arte Dei Bambini.* Bologna: N. Zanichelli in Cox. M. (1992) *Children's Drawing.* London: Penguin.

Ross, M. (1978) *The Creative Arts.* London: Heinemann Educational.

Sanford, A. (1987) *The Mind of Man. Models of Human Understanding.* Brighton: Harvester.

Wollheim, R. (1975) *Art and Its Objects.* Harmondsworth, Middlesex: Peregrine.

CHAPTER 13

Teaching composing in the music curriculum

Sarah Hennessey

> Teaching is a developmental process, an unfolding of potential through the reciprocal influence of child and social environment (Gallimore and Tharp 1990, p. 177).

Learning in music is closely identified with learning to perform and, as a consequence, achievement is predominantly measured against technical accomplishments, and teaching becomes associated with an instructional approach. Music education is routinely referred to as 'training' suggesting that achievement is measured by the performance of a given set of observable skills and behaviours rather than by a complex matrix of skills, knowledge and understanding leading to independent, creative practice.

Although teachers have accepted composing as a central component of the music curriculum, it has yet to be fully recognised that different approaches to teaching are the consequence. One of the causes of unease among student teachers (and generalist teachers) is the belief that music teaching requires a style of teaching distinct from that which is employed in other subjects; the music teacher is perceived as a performing musician, a director, an expert instructor and, unless these roles are adopted, nothing useful or meaningful will take place. In this perceived world children acquire performing skills (singing, playing instruments) through practising technical procedures, and come to know a range of repertoire, chosen by the teacher, closely related to their technical abilities. They may also come to appreciate the music they make, to gain knowledge of theory and historical context. Built into this perception is the expectation that many will fail to acquire the precise skills which allow them to play or sing in tune, in time, with good tone etc. These are the 'unmusical' children who will soon realise their shortcomings and drop out or be discouraged from participating.

Even when a more sensitive and imaginative approach to instruction is used, the outcome is still that the children are essentially the performers in the teacher's music. If we are serious about engaging all children in composing we need to a) view composing as a normal part of behaviour which all children will engage in when provided with the right conditions and b) adopt rather different teaching styles which allow children to develop as independent musical thinkers and creators.

COMPOSING AS A FORM OF PLAY

Composing shares many characteristics with play and when one looks at contemporary literature on the role and value of play in learning, the similarities are quite startling. This, of course, should not be a surprise if one considers that the arts reflect and shape a field of human behaviour and activity which is particularly concerned with playfulness: curiosity, exploration, speculation, experimentation, improvisation, and invention. Playfulness and the potential for learning embedded in play are both manifest in the composing process: the stages that every composer travels through in creating a piece, and the way in which composing encompasses past experience, experimentation, and the consolidation of new learning. Free improvisation is the most playful type of composing; in its most elementary form it can be equated with 'doodling'; like play, it is spontaneous and unthreatening. The music which emerges will reflect the composer's skills and understanding that are well-established and familiar. There is a strong match between musical ideas and performance. Many adult musicians fear it because they have unlearned the ability through years of being trained to perform notated music. Among accomplished musicians improvisation becomes a vehicle for more complex and sustained thinking and performing in which there are learned techniques and 'rules', i.e. in jazz, Indian classical, folk and many popular genres. 'It is evident, through watching children play (*compose – my insert*), they constantly apply problem-solving methods and processes in a natural way, unthreatened by outcome restrictions but nevertheless directed towards certain goals' (Moyles 1991, p. 12).

Play is also characterised by a clear sense of ownership: readers may well identify with the oppressive tedium of music practice contrasted with the enjoyable, rewarding experience of mastering a piece chosen independently from the teacher. The same piece could just as well have been prescribed by the teacher but this will often alter our feelings about learning to play it (and here we use 'play' to mean 'perform'). In Hutt's (1982) model three distinct modes of play behaviour are identified:

- *Epistemic play* which involves exploration, problem-solving, acquisition of skills and knowledge;
- *Ludic play* which involves fantasy, role-play, creative thinking, innovation; and
- *Games play* which is rule-based play.

This analysis may be comfortably applied to composing at all levels of musical sophistication. For example: a mixed class of five and six year-olds have explored long and short sounds with their teacher. They first sat in a circle and took turns (singing 'Hot Potato Pass it On') to play long or short sounds on a triangle, a woodblock or a guiro. Each child decides for themselves which kind of sound to play and the 'audience' offer their comments ('*when David made a long sound on the triangle he made lots of short sounds joined together, and then it went long at the end*'). They have learned how to control these instruments, found out what sort of different sounds they make, and found ways to describe what they hear. This exploring is extended as a music corner activity in which pairs of children can play with a variety of instruments and in so doing will discover more about handling and controlling them, and what kinds of sounds they make. These activities might be described as involving epistemic play.

The following week the teacher plans some small group composing where the children create a sequence of movements to accompany a sequence of long and short sounds which they have also invented. The movements give rise to a story devised by the children and finally realised through drama, dance and music. Here there are episodes of ludic play when children improvise, invent and compose. Games play may arise from the teacher 'feeding in' certain musical concepts which offer a structure in which the ideas are contained (e.g. the need for some rhythmic cohesion will mean keeping a steady beat). Alternatively, rules might be invented by the children to give order to a sequence (*'you play first, now it's my turn and then you play again'*).

In many music lessons there is much evidence of 'epistemic' and 'games' playing but often not so much 'ludic' play. This goes back to the problem that teachers (and perhaps, in particular, music specialists) have with 'letting go'. Music seems to be all about learning rules and participating in an existing 'game', especially in school where virtually all music making is collective and recreates an existing repertoire. The playful quality of music-making is not something that should be left behind as we mature and become more skilled. There *are* musical rules to be learned and mastered but our preoccupation with them may lead to creativity being stifled.

Teachers need to consider, thoughtfully, how they encourage the musical imagination through composing. It may be more often that the teacher has 'played' creatively with the ideas in the planning stage of a lesson and that the children merely respond to her creative thinking rather than the other way round. In a conversation about how we recognise creativity in children's composing the teacher described a lesson with his class of ten year olds:

> I provided some photographs of landscapes and abstract paintings and asked the children, in groups, to choose one as the starting point for a piece of music. There has not been much work on graphic scores in the past so I was fairly sure they wouldn't be limited by previous experience.
>
> That seemed to provide them with security without suggesting a structure. I think a lot of the time I'm not even trying to get that creativeness. Sometimes we're practising skills. So we're using composing as a vehicle for developing skills.
>
> I've tried to be a bit freer because I feel that I'm quite structured and that I try to squeeze them too much into a structure which maybe they are not ready for or limits their creativity a bit.

This is a good example of the dilemma: rules or no rules, structured or unstructured. If we return to the notion that composing is a kind of play this dilemma might be resolved by recognising that, in a school setting, all forms of play will need some structure whether they are to do with the bounds of socialised behaviour, physical environment, or the desire to foster particular skills, knowledge and understanding. Moyles (1991, p. 4) writes:

When children play (*or compose – my addition*) they:

- make choices;
- understand what they are doing;
- use their imagination and creativity;
- experiment and explore;
- cooperate and collaborate with their peers;

- develop motor and perceptual skills; and
- develop skills of social interaction.

In the classroom, play activity is planned to offer quite specific learning opportunities. We often hear the argument that music is somehow different from the other arts subjects in how it is taught and learned, particularly in terms of the emphasis on overt technical skills and specialist knowledge. Perhaps the main difference is that children are disadvantaged by lack of early exposure to joining in the 'live' experience of music-making. Children are exposed to vast amounts of music, performed by unseen or untouchable others (radio, recordings, TV); they do not, on the whole, grow up in an environment in which music-making is a 'live', routine, informal activity which happens at home or in social settings. There is, consequently, a greater onus on school to provide such an environment and to offer a rich diet of musical activity throughout the school-life of every child. By viewing composing as a type of play teachers may find it easier to understand not only the composing process but also their own role.

If we adopt a constructivist model of teaching and learning the teacher may regard their role in a composing lesson rather differently: as guide, resource, stimulator of creative thinking and critic, rather than judge and dictator.

In a traditional music teaching setting where the aims of music education are concerned with the transmission of an inherited canon and the acquisition of the skills needed to recreate it the teaching style will be that of master/apprentice. The teacher provides the model and instructs the student in how to accurately copy it; learning will be narrow, specific progress will be fast but short-lived (Tait 1992). There may be all sorts of strategies used to dress this up so that the learning/training experience is more enjoyable, play-like and where goals are achievable but, essentially, this is still a teacher dominated, teleological process. Ends justify the means which cannot be sustained if we want children to become self-regulating, independent and autonomous music thinkers and makers.

TEACHING FOR CREATIVE INDEPENDENCE

In the social-constructivist theory is found a view of children's learning which recognises creativity and independence as hallmarks of development. The model offered by Vygotsky stresses the social, cultural and historical factors involved in teaching, learning and development. It is through interaction and activity with 'more knowledgeable others', be they parents, siblings, teachers or peers, that children acquire the 'tools' for thinking. This process is described succinctly by Wood and Attfield (1996, p. 61) (see figure 13.1).

In the composing process ideas and solutions will arise from a complex mix of previous experience – the application of learned technical skills, musical material and structures absorbed through previous listening, performing and composing, coinciding with new ideas, new circumstances and new demands. In this context 'new' means the focus of attention for the first time in this learning context, not necessarily entirely novel. Children may well have performed and responded to something in the past but not attended to or considered it in a 'knowing' way, in a way that would lead them to recall, reproduce or borrow from it. The skills and understanding which are established as self-regulated and part of the composer's independent practice are applied to a task which involves some new technique, concept, procedure which will need 'other' assistance. Enmeshed with such overt musical activity is the inner world of musical feeling and imagination which is nurtured by all manner of musical experiences both in and out of school. I will illustrate by describing a music lesson using the stages set out in figure 13.1.

Established, self-regulated skills and understanding.
A class of eleven year olds have established skills in keeping a steady beat and performing syncopated rhythms, composing simple melodic phrases on instruments and vocally, and using specialist vocabulary to describe accompaniment, identify instruments and simple structures. Some children are learning instruments and read notation fluently, others have more limited performance skills.

Skilled assistance from the teacher in an enabling environment with appropriate materials, experiences and activities.
The teacher plays the class a recording of a 12-bar blues. The class discuss what they recognise about the style, instruments etc. They practise keeping the beat and respond to the metre (4 beats in a bar). The teacher asks them to focus their listening on the bass-line and to hear when and how it changes. They then invent a step pattern and hand-jive sequence which matches the pattern of the bass-line (i.e. chord sequence).

The whole class sit in a circle and several (randomly selected) children take turns to improvise a melody on a xylophone (using a 'blues' pentatonic scale G Bb C D F G) while the teacher plays the chord sequence on guitar (this could be done on a keyboard with single finger chord setting and slow rock accompaniment). They also try some sung improvisations.

In the following music lesson the children compose their own blues in groups of 3 or 4 combining a bass-line, chord sequence and melody. The teacher supports each group through acting as an 'outside ear', helping to overcome technical or structural difficulties, encouraging children to refine their ideas, leading to: *independent, self regulated practice.*

In the ZPD the novice moves from
other regulation (interpsychological)

with

skilled assistance from
more knowledgeable others (peers and adults)

in

an enabling environment

with

appropriate materials, experiences and activities

combining

social, cultural and historical influences

acquiring

tools for thinking and learning, knowledge, skills, processes, sense-making capacities

leading to

self-regulation (intrapsychological)

Figure 13.1 Vygotsky's theory of the zone of proximal development (ZPD)

The notion of the ZPD focuses on that area of skill, knowledge and understanding which lies ahead of the learner and which can be accessed through assistance or mediation by a knowledgeable other, in this context the teacher or a more able peer. Through observation and talk the teacher identifies the child's level of development and through interaction and assisted performance (questioning, modelling, offering information, collaboration) can draw the child into a 'zone' of operating and understanding which they would not achieve if left to their own devices. In this new zone the learner will first copy the model provided and, through practice and repetition, gain mastery and expertise leading to independent, self-regulated practice.

It needs to be noted that although this theory is concerned with the needs and development of the individual learner it is not inappropriate to apply it to group learning. In classroom composing teachers invariably plan and manage the class in groups, for several reasons, both pragmatic and educational:

- individually not all children will have the ability to realise their musical ideas either because of their own limited playing abilities or lack of ability in the composing process itself;
- a group allows for more satisfying musical sound in terms of textures and dynamics in particular;
- children will feel less exposed when it comes to performing their work if supported by others;
- even very elementary pieces will have addressed, consciously, issues of structure even if it's only in terms of who plays when;
- greater variety of timbre and pitch will be available;
- a group will be learning about keeping in time, listening, texture, ensemble playing, rehearsal, and appraisal through having to share the process with others;
- critical listening and sharing language to describe and explain is fostered;
- it makes it more possible to focus on the achievements of individual children without needing to pick them out for attention;
- there is not enough space to allow each child a place to compose their own piece;
- there is not enough time to hear each composition during or at the end of the process;
- there are not enough instruments to give each child a selection.

The educational rationale for group composing supports and fosters the notion of peer-assistance which can be a marked feature of music in the classroom because of the presence of children who are learning instruments. In music perhaps more than any other subject at primary level a class of children can contain a huge disparity in experience and skill. This is due to the practice of giving some children extra instrumental tuition. No other subject routinely offers this differentiated experience at such an early age, except perhaps for PE, and even then there is a more evident continuum between the two experiences. The only other subject where this disparity might arise is in dance where the child who attends ballet classes may find it difficult to recognise the language and movement content of educational dance experienced in school.

Rather than see such able instrumentalists as a problem in a mixed ability setting they should be exploited for their expertise and knowledge in the context of group work. It is also well-recognised that due to the narrow range of skills and knowledge addressed by instrumental teachers and the instructional teaching style, such children are often less able to improvise and generally experiment with musical ideas than the majority of the class. Encouraging such children to transfer their skills and understanding to a creative context is important; otherwise they can develop as rather 'lop-sided' musicians.

THE ROLE OF THE TEACHER

A class of eight year olds are working on the idea of musical variation: taking a melody and changing different aspects of it while it still remains recognisable. Over several lessons the class have first copied the teacher's examples and then invented their own ways of changing a pitch pattern (they have also looked at patterns in mathematics and art): slowing it down, starting on a different note while keeping the pitch relationships the same, inverting it, adding other parts, decorating it and so on. They listen to a piece of music in which a simple tune is repeated and varied. The children describe what they can hear: *'more instruments join in'* . . . *'it speeds up'* . . . *'it sounds higher'*. The teacher then gives them a composing task: in groups of three or four they are asked to use a familiar tune ('Once a man fell in a well') and compose one or more variations using a mixture of tuned and untuned instruments (including electronic keyboard, recorder and violin) (see figure 13.2).

As the groups work the teacher observes, joins in, offers suggestions and reminds them of what they have learned in previous lessons to help solve problems:

- 'if you sit in a semi-circle you'll be able to see and hear each other better'
- 'that works really well, how about playing it more than once?'
- 'have you thought about how you will start?'
- 'have a think about a contrast for the next variation, remember what we did in the circle game'
- 'that bit sounds very dramatic, who thought of that?'

With each group (and each child) the teacher will judge the level of guidance, challenge, reward or critical comment she gives, based on her knowledge of what the group might be able to deal with, and on what particular music learning she is focused upon. Through this kind of interaction children are more likely to experiment, take risks and be aware of the quality of what they are doing. If left to their own devices a number of things can happen, some of which might have very positive results, others less so.

Figure 13.2 Once a man fell in a well

For instance, they might:

- fall back on reproducing the exemplars from a previous lesson;
- drift off the task and create a very effective piece which has nothing to do with variation ideas;
- find it difficult to develop or explore their ideas;
- become frustrated by technical limitations;
- be unable to maintain their focus on the activity because of group dynamics;
- produce a rather minimal set of ideas which do not exploit what they were able to do when directed, or supported by the whole class.

This way of working demands a very different approach to teaching, one in which the teacher shifts from being a constant 'centre-stage' model/expert/ instructor, to one of moving fluently between several roles. Where ways of working and outcomes are dependent on the child's own ideas, their development and the performance of them, the teacher must become a facilitator, mediator, assistant and partner during the composing process. If this does not happen composing will be merely an exercise in which the child carries out the creative ideas of the teacher. The most important aspect of a composing task is the child's ability to 'make evident' their own musical thinking: 'when students compose they are *showing* what they know even if they are not literally telling us' (Swanwick 1988, p. 131). The teacher must, therefore, provide the means by which children can acquire the skills (or tools) to express their ideas. Teaching composing is not about lighting the touch paper and standing back, there needs to be a supportive and critical guide during the process, and a responsive audience to what emerges.

Gallimore and Tharp (1990) identify six means of assisting performance (in the general rather than the musical sense!): modelling, contingency management, feedback, instructing, questioning and cognitive structuring. It is worth looking at these more closely in the context of a composing activity.

Modelling

When embarking on a composing task it is important that the children have a good understanding of the framework in which they are creating but also an experience of the process and, sometimes, some idea of possible outcomes. This last will depend on how much freedom is built into the task design. The modelling can come from taking the whole class through a version of the task, in which children contribute ideas to the whole and the teacher acts as mediator, clarifier, and musical director.

Contingency management

Whole class and group composing need to be carefully managed and thought given to fostering confident, self-disciplined participation. Children will need guidance in how to contribute to and participate in a composing process: listening, taking turns, talking through ideas, negotiating, becoming critical. The teacher must establish 'ground rules' for behaviour which is appropriate to practical music activity. The most important of these being the control of sound and the valuing of silence.

Feedback

Children need to hear their own work and have opportunities to reflect on its quality and what they have learned and achieved. It is unwise to leave groups to 'get on with it' for long periods of time; a series of short (5–10 minutes) episodes of independent work which are shared and briefly discussed may be more productive, especially with inexperienced composers. Composing music for others to perform, composing at the computer, and tape recording pieces will provide valuable ways of separating performing from composing so that the musical ideas can be appraised more clearly.

Instructing

Although I might have suggested earlier that instructing is inappropriate when teaching composing it is of fundamental importance in developing specialist 'tools' for thinking and making. Composing techniques and the musical understanding which is expressed in a composition arise first through some form of instruction whether direct (taught) or indirect (caught). The music that children perform (songs and instrumental pieces), listen to and talk about are the 'food' which nourishes their thinking.

Questioning

This is probably the most underdeveloped feature of the teacher's repertoire in composition lessons. Gallimore and Tharp stress the need to distinguish between questions which *assist* and those that *assess*. They suggest that teachers are much more likely to ask assessment questions. 'The assistance question inquires in order to produce a mental question that the pupil cannot or would not produce alone' (1990, p. 184).

In discussions with music teachers this problem is often raised: what kind of questions should we ask during the composing process which will not suggest criticism, or override the children's ideas, but will help them to develop and/or refine their ideas? What questions should we ask after the finished piece has been shared? It is important also to avoid suggesting that there is a right answer; there might be a more or less appropriate 'answer' but this has to be considered in the light of the composer's intentions.

Questions during the composing process might be something like these:

- 'I wonder what would happen if . . . ?' (an experiment);
- 'How can we make this tune go on for longer?' (need to encourage the concept of repetition and development);
- 'May I hear how your part sounds on its own?' (encourage attention to detail and how individual ideas relate to the whole);
- 'Have you thought about an ending?' (endings are often neglected or fizzle out);
- 'What could you do to make the beginning more dramatic?' (draw attention to mood and atmosphere);
- 'How can you keep this drone going all the way through?' (solving a technical problem);
- 'Why not think of a contrasting middle bit and then have this section again?' (extending structure and range of ideas).

Questions after the presentation may be like these:

- 'What did you like about your piece?'
- 'How did you come up with that scary sound? Who found it?'
- 'What was the hardest bit?'
- 'What did you particularly like about their piece?'
- 'Did you notice when . . . ?'
- 'How did they create that really quiet passage . . . ?'

These kinds of questions do, of course, have an element of assessment in them but they should also elicit some critical and evaluative responses which will articulate something of what has been attended to and learned. This concern connects with the final category which is cognitive structuring.

Cognitive structuring

It is here that the teacher helps to organise and give structure to the thinking and doing which take place in the lesson. This might be to draw children's attention to the way in which they will (or have) organise(d) their musical ideas. Each composing experience will draw on previous learning and the teacher can make intentions and connections overt. Children will gain independence and confidence through becoming aware of the learning process: knowing what they know.

Our understanding of teaching and learning in music composing is still at an early stage of development. To some extent the educational argument for its status in the music curriculum has been won. However, teachers of music in school need to use the experience and knowledge which resides in other curriculum areas and other fields of educational research to discover and nurture children's creative potential in music. By viewing composing as a form of play and recognising the need for playfulness teachers may reconsider their role in the process. The theoretical model offered by social constructivism should underpin and clarify the relationship between learner and teacher.

REFERENCES

Gallimore, R. and Tharp, R. (1990) 'Teaching mind in society: teaching, schooling, and literate discourse', in Moll, L. (ed.) *Vygotsky and Education. Instructional Implications and Applications of Sociohistorical Psychology*. Cambridge: Cambridge University Press.

Hutt, C. (1982) 'Exploration and play in children', in Herron, R. E. and Sutton-Smith, B. (eds) *Child's Play*. London: John Wiley.

Moyles, J. (1991) *Play as a Learning Process in Your Classroom*. Cheltenham: Mary Glasgow.

Swanwick, K. (1988) *Music, Mind and Education*. London: Routledge.

Tait, M. (1992) 'Teaching strategies and styles' in Colwell R. (ed.) *The Handbook of Research on Music Teaching and Learning*. New York: MENC, Schirmer.

Wood, E. and Attfield, J. (1996) *Play, Learning and Early Childhood*. London: Paul Chapman.

The examples of activities are taken from video material in *Children's Music: The Music Project Part Two*, published by the Education Department of Devon County Council.

CHAPTER 14

Experiential Religious Education and the constructivist paradigm

Melissa Raphael

Since 1990, when the Children's Spirituality Project at Nottingham University produced the foundational *New Methods in RE Teaching*, there has been continuous debate over the practice of experiential religious education (RE). In 1996 a new journal, *The International Journal of Children's Spirituality*, was established to support the discourse. Although not always well received in the more conservative religious education circles, experiential RE is increasingly popular in schools and is having a clear influence on the developmental objectives of curriculum planning for primary RE (Musty 1992, pp. 84–5). Supported by current educational legislation, it is now widely recognised that RE is not solely or even primarily a cognitive project. While experiential RE is not a substitute for more cognitive approaches to religious education, many accept that RE is meaningful only when the meta-cognitive, affective element of religion and of children's learning about religion is taken seriously.

The 1988 Education Reform Act (ERA) (DES 1988) requires the school curriculum to promote the spiritual, moral, cultural, mental and physical development of pupils and of society as a whole. That the State can legislate for the spiritual development of children has been questioned, especially by educators, especially those who are not familiar with the study or practice of religion, and who often find the term 'spirituality' confusing and obscure. Post ERA definitions of children's spirituality abound (see e.g. Hay and Nye 1996, pp. 7–8.) One thing, however, is clear. Most educators no longer narrowly define spirituality as the ascetic discipline by which one attains union with the divine or as the mystical dissolution of the self into the whole. The common (some would say secularist) thread running through most contemporary educators' use of the term 'spirituality' is the belief that spiritual maturity may be attained without any specific or formal religious affiliation. To be spiritually developed is not necessarily to be religious in any denominational sense of the word. 'Spiritual development' refers more to a child's understanding of what it means to be human in an inclusive, rather than exclusive or culturally divisive, manner.

Children are considered to have developed a good way towards spiritual maturity when they have a capacity to reflect on the significance of human life, to feel awe and wonder at its mystery and beauty and to empathise with others. Educationalists concur with the legal view that RE is particularly well placed to promote spiritual development, but not exclusively so; the personal growth of the child is the responsibility of the whole school curriculum, and the capacity of a given school to foster such growth through its pastoral structures and educational methods and style is held to be assessable by OFSTED inspectors.

Nonetheless, the 1988 ERA gives with one hand and takes with the other. On the one hand, its promotion of spirituality encourages an undetermined inclusive approach to teaching and learning. And on the other hand, the ERA requires that the school curriculum must reflect that religious traditions in Britain are, in the main, Christian, while taking into account other religions represented in Britain. Worship too must be of a 'wholly or mainly' Christian character. By doing so, the ERA places limitations on the extent to which any RE syllabus can be truly constructivist. For it implies that whatever the child's perspective and context, RE curricula and daily acts of worship should normally privilege the Christian tradition in an objectivist manner more typical of the religious instruction (RI) before about 1970.

Although this law is subject to varying interpretations, this more confessional counter-trend has contributed towards over-determined, content-laden syllabi that suggest the opposite of open enquiry into religion. Cognisant of RE's lack of a National Curriculum subject status and wishing to maintain RE's serious academic profile, some LEAs have adopted the prescribed style, content and method of National Curriculum subject syllabi. Syllabi such as the 1995 Gloucestershire RE Cube are admirable in many respects. The Cube fully acknowledges the importance of teaching styles and learning experiences that are sensitive to children's spiritual development. And yet it sets end of key stage statements and non-statutory guidance for Key Stages (KS) 1 and 2 in which experiential RE is almost conspicuous by its absence. Despite the stated importance of the 'style' dimension (Gloucestershire County Council 1995, p. 4), the methods suggested are almost exclusively those of explicit, objectivist, descriptive RE. The attainment targets set out in the syllabus prescribe that children should know about the beliefs, practices and lifestyles of two (KS1) or three (KS2) world religions, though principally of the Christian religion (Gloucestershire County Council 1995, pp. 10, 18).

THE CONTEXT OF EXPERIENTIAL RE

Experiential RE has come to the fore during the 1990s but its origins lie in nineteenth-century science of religion and in the 'secular' theologies of the 1960s and 1970s. The contemporary distinction between spirituality and religiousness owes much to the late nineteenth-century scientific study of religious experience when scholars of religion attempted to identify a spiritual impulse common to all human beings regardless of their religious affiliation. By the early twentieth century, Rudolf Otto's conviction that all human beings had a spiritual capacity to sense and respond to the numinous or non-rational basis of all religion (Otto 1958) sustained the view that there was such a thing as a primary or essential religious experience which was distinct from and transcendent of religio-social constructions of the holy – what William James called 'over-beliefs'.

By the 1960s, this kind of epistemological project informed Alister Hardy's biological research into spirituality. Hardy suggested that spiritual awareness was a natural property of human beings which had evolved through natural selection because of its value to the survival of the individual. At this time, the theological avant garde was concerned to show that secularisation need not entail the end of religion; in some ways secularity could liberate 'original' religious experience from its tired institutions and traditions. The old distinction between the sacred and the profane was rejected (Raphael 1997, pp. 177–185). Ordinary experience, whether that of children or adults, could be as potentially religious as that to be had within the sacred traditions themselves.

In ways typical of the period, religious discourse was being democratised and among liberal religious educators of the late 1960s and 1970s, the confessional religious instruction or RI of the 1950s and early 1960s was beginning to look like a relic of pre-Enlightenment Christian hegemony. Among religious educators, the work of Harold Loukes (1965) and Michael Grimmitt (1973) was influential in the development of 'implicit' RE. These implicit approaches to RE assumed that reflection on the child's own secular (but proto-religious) experiences would prepare them for the 'explicit' religious concepts that Ronald Goldman (under the influence of Piaget) had claimed only children from the age of about eleven could grasp (see Goldman 1964 and 1965). Goldman's denial that children could think abstractly led to both implicit (that is, indirect) RE and its parallel, concrete or material approaches to RE which focus heavily on what religious people do, but not why they do it. Ninian Smart's account of religion, as defined by its seven dimensions: ritual, experiential, narrative, doctrinal, ethical, social and material, has commonly informed this latter phenomenological approach to RE, with the doctrinal, ethical and social dimensions coming into play during secondary education and concrete phenomena such as festivals, rites of passage and religious buildings being seen as more suitable for primary school children. (See further, Smart 1969, 1989, Bastide 1992, pp. 185–203, Bates 1992, pp. 109–110.)

However, as Dennis Bates points out in his invaluable survey of developmental theory in primary RE, by the 1980s Goldman's Piagetian developmentalism was coming under question and religious educators were beginning to regard Goldman's case as overstated. It was now argued that young children could, in fact, understand explicit religious discourse and could have a limited grasp of abstract ideas (Bates, 1992, p. 108). This was a shift in developmental perspective that would contribute to the production of RE syllabi in the National Curriculum style.

Experiential RE spans developments in liberal RE over the last three decades. While being committed to the implicit approach to RE, and clearly believing that the private affective dimension of religion is more essential than its public dimension (Hammond *et al.* 1990, p. 10), experiential RE also refuses to underestimate children's capacity to think – even philosophise – about directly religious issues and values. More generally, experiential RE is the logical product of about a century's history of religious studies and remains strongly dependent on the Ottonian legacy of scholars who have asserted that the non-rational feeling of the numinous or sacred is the primary and definitive religious emotion. At the same time, experiential RE is a peculiarly late modern phenomenon. It is secular in being post-institutional and post-traditional, yet at the same time it is passionately religious – arguably it is more intentionally spiritual than those approaches to RE which, previous to the late nineteenth century, have taken the political and cultural power of (Christian) religion for granted.

Experientialists (as the proponents of experiential RE are sometimes known) have objected to the wholesale reification of religion and any reduction of religion to the sum of its parts. It is undoubtedly important that primary school children understand something of the main constitutive elements of the world religions selected for study. But a descriptive, quasi-sociological approach that appears methodologically committed to bracketing out the interiority of religious phenomena and children's evaluation of religious phenomena may give children a sense that lessons do not require an engaged or affective response and that religious intentionality is not of significance. The experientialist emphasis on the intentionality and affectivity of religion stops RE degenerating into a mere accumulation of data or into anthropology (Hammond *et al.* 1990, p. 11, Hayward 1990, p. 17. See also Grimmitt 1987).

An exclusively cognitive approach, and one which is too theologically particular, forecloses children's spiritual and religious possibilities and dampens the affective spark which, in the experientialists' view, ignites the impulse for religious observance and the construction of religious meaning in the first place. Predominantly cognitive approaches also miss the essential point that 'religious language is not primarily informational but inspirational'. Religion's sense of mystery does not require us to, factually, 'wonder *why*' but to 'wonder *at*' (Watson 1993, p. 55). As Rebecca Nye and David Hay write:

> The self-confidence of cognitive psychology no doubt lies behind the dominant influence of cognitive developmental theory in the field of religious education, particularly through the work of Ronald Goldman and his successors James Fowler and Fritz Oser. In our opinion they have encouraged, if not themselves fallen into, an ontological error which has misled religious education for the last thirty years. The 'knowing' out of which religion grows is different from knowledge *about* religion, in that it is much more akin to sensory or affective awareness. Whilst not divisible from cognition, it is logically prior to it (1996, p. 144).

In fact, the more intuitive uses of phenomenological methods by some historians of religion are not superficially cognitive and an attempt is made to penetrate empathetically to the affective heart of a religious phenomenon. However, debased uses of phenomenological methods can indeed impoverish children's study and experience of religion in the classroom. Olivera Petrovich's doctoral research at Oxford University into three and four year old children's concepts of God suggests that these children's concepts of the divine can be more sophisticated and less anthropomorphic than those of older children who have absorbed their theological naiveté from adults (cited in Watson 1993, p. 58). Experiential RE believes that the decline in sensitivity and awareness that has usually set in by the middle years of the junior school may have been accelerated by over-simplified, simplistic, concretised, rationalised accounts of religious belief and of the divine which latter are likely to be couched in crudely anthropomorphic terms. As Brenda Watson points out:

> The picture of an old man in the sky is not taught by any of the great religions

– yet this may come as a surprise to many people today. Many adults have grown up in an environment in which they have picked up extremely infantile notions – notions which . . . cause religion itself to be rejected as people become more sophisticated in other departments of life and other areas of knowledge (1993, p. 58).

But for many experientialists, all is not necessarily lost. Empirical research conducted in Britain (and especially by the Alister Hardy Research Centre) during and since the 1980s has confirmed that spiritual experience is by no means disappearing in a secular age which (despite recent evangelical and fundamentalist revivals) has seen a general decline in routine, traditional religious observance. Contrary to the expectations of many sociologists of religion during the 1960s and 1970s, modernity has not eradicated spiritual experience; children, as much as or more than adults, are capable of responding to basic religious stimuli such as candlelight, peace, and natural beauty. And further research suggests that 'about two thirds of the adult population are aware of a spiritual dimension to their lives' (Hay and Nye 1996, pp. 6–9).

Also, rightly or wrongly, experiential RE has developed from a specific (neo-romantic) ontology of childhood. That is, by virtue of his or her very being, the young child is held to possess an 'original vision': a pristine vision and a capacity for wonder and integrated response that is gradually eroded by our culture and our pedagogic methods (Robinson 1983, Best 1996). Since modern positivism is unsympathetic to the spiritual dimension of life, and education tends to give the impression that any mystery can be solved or explained by science, it is to be expected that young children's 'natural' spirituality will diminish in direct ratio to their socialisation. Kalevi Tamminen's (1991) finding that out of 3000 children and young children there was a marked decline in reported spiritual experience after the age of about twelve supports the development of the experientialist project and its contention that children have 'an innate spiritual capacity', though one which 'may focus in particular ways and take different and changing forms as children's other capacities develop' (Nye and Hay 1996, p. 145).

While it seems evident to many that children from the age of about three to eight have an unselfconscious freshness of vision, a formal theory of innate and originally (literally) unadulterated spirituality is difficult to prove. The value of such a thesis may be more religio-political in character: namely, it may constitute a rhetorical claim on children's 'natural' capacity for wholeness that is incorruptible and retrievable despite overlays of oppressive or otherwise alienating religious and political indoctrination. It is a view that children can survive 'bad' religious and moral education and that, in any case, spirituality can only be developed, not inculcated in any mechanical manner by those in religious or educational authority. Moreover, for those who are religious but do not confess a positive faith, a thesis of essential, global, human spirituality can redeem the purposes and meaning of RE in spite of a secular materialist culture where children might never be exposed to the humanising influences of authentic spirituality and where the once-authoritative supernatural religious truth claims have largely lost plausibility (see further Hay and Nye 1996, p. 7).

THE CONSTRUCTIVIST PRINCIPLES OF EXPERIENTIAL RE

Religion is itself a human construction or response to the conditions humanity finds itself in. Religion does not offer irrefutable answers to existential questions. Its object – the divine – is 'wholly other' and is only knowable in so far as it is revealed in history or to the transcendental understanding of faith. Religious language is analogical rather than literal; its symbols are polysemic or supportive of a plurality of meanings. So too, experiential RE is almost paradigmatically constructivist since its outcome is not a single, defined cognitive product but that of having initiated a process whereby the child is orientated towards a deeper, but nonetheless *his or her own*, awareness of self and world. The style is one of encouraging children to trust their instincts and, as feminist theologians might put it, 'to hear themselves and each other to speech'. The aim is not to give children a religious experience in the classroom, but to 'alert them to the kind of consciousness which characteristically accompanies such experience' (Nye and Hay 1996, p. 146).

Moreover, the methods used by experiential RE cannot be other than wholly non-didactic. It is assumed that children's sensitivity can be developed and extended by methods of elicitation, but cannot strictly be taught. Spirituality is 'a dynamic and creative area which cannot be measured and dissected; it can only be enjoyed and wondered at' (Beesley 1990, pp. 3–4). Experiential RE and the cross-curricular connections it feeds, cannot, therefore, be timetabled as a separate subject in itself. The activities are designed to initiate a fluid, non-testable process in which a child sharpens her focus on the world; it is the environment in which teaching and learning takes place. Experiential RE involves not the development of a specific faith but an orientation of care, attentiveness and curiosity that extends across and beyond the curriculum, to become part of the child's world view, regardless of his faith or the lack of it. It is not *what* you believe, but *how* you believe that is significant. That is, a child's coming to hold a specific faith position is secondary to his or her feeling free to explore given religions and values in an empathetic manner.

The primary school teacher can use the aesthetic sense of awe, wonder and mystery generated by experiential RE not only to approach explicitly religious phenomena, but also to help children engage with story, science and environmental education, art, drama and movement. But in so far as experiential RE is non-quantitative and non-quantifiable, it cannot be mechanically assessed. Its lack of substantive, factual content and right or wrong answers mean that children can only be assessed on the expressiveness, sensitivity and truthfulness with which they have participated in an activity or discussion. Experiential RE is constructivist in the way that it respects children as the subjects of their own experience. There is no higher textual or institutional authority to which children's interpretation of their own experience must defer.

FACTORS AFFECTING SPIRITUAL DEVELOPMENT

Constructivist approaches to RE would accept that experience is mediated and conditioned by gender, ethnicity, class, historical period and so forth and that people must find their own way within (and perhaps in spite of) the varying parameters of these and other factors. In a plural society where children in a class may well come from diverse religious or non- or anti-religious standpoints, constructivist approaches to RE are particularly significant. The diversity of religious positions within a classroom might also be growing. For instance, since the late 1970s there has been a rise in alternative religious practice in Britain and increasingly a small minority of children will come from families where feminist and alternative spiritualities are practised. It is estimated that there are between 20,000 and 50,000 Pagans in Britain today (Cush 1997, pp. 85, 87) and that the numbers are growing. A Pagan background will influence the way a child learns in RE and environmental education particularly. Although Paganism is not usually practised by those under the age of eighteen, an older child from a Pagan family will probably understand and experience environmental education from a different standpoint to, say, a Jewish or Muslim child for whom nature is not, in and of itself, revelatory of the divine.

Other factors need to be taken into consideration when planning a constructivist approach to RE. For instance, for an infant school child the distinction between the mysterious and the familiar may not be a meaningful one (Nye and Hay 1996, pp. 148–9). Clearly, for primary school children, especially those in the infants, much of life is inexplicable, intimidating or mysterious. The spirituality of infant school children will be different, and perhaps less self-conscious than that of late juniors and adolescents for whom modern (as opposed to postmodern) science education has 'cured' them of religious or 'superstitious' accounts of the origins and ends of creation. And by the junior years, many children will inhabit a materialist culture of learned cynicism and acquisition.

As Crawford and Rossiter (1996) have pointed out, young people, even in primary education, may not regard religious institutions as relevant or authoritative and may prefer to address their ethical and spiritual concerns eclectically with the help of the mass media, especially television and popular music. Such factors influence a child's response to the educator's efforts to develop their spirituality. As Crawford and Rossiter rightly note:

> If religious education acknowledges the ways youth perceive religion and meaning, then it will be more likely to make constructive connections with the spiritual processes that are most prominent for them at that stage of their lives. This is just as important for those who will not have any association with organised religion as it is for those who will. (p. 133)

There must be 'compelling links' between RE and what the children themselves consider to be important issues for them. It may be that children will not insist on the relevance of other subjects to the same degree as RE; but if RE 'where the content is personal and value laden' appears irrelevant then studying religion may 'appear to be a contradiction in terms' (Crawford and Rossiter 1996, p. 134).

EXPERIENTIAL RE AND THE INDIVIDUAL'S CONSTRUCTION OF MEANING

That individuals construct their own meaning is the assumption upon which experiential RE rests. As recognised by postmodern religious theory, the subject negotiates with the tradition; religious texts have no one final meaning or message determined by their most powerful readers. Although there is no reason why a teacher should not, for example, make an informed attempt to interpret what the biblical authors were trying to say about the nature of God in a given passage, if the Bible is to be genuinely transformative (and that cannot be a pre-determined outcome) children should be encouraged to interpret biblical stories in the light of their own experience. All knowledge is interpretative and children are intelligent in so far as they can interpret rather than merely remember the representations of reality set before them by the curriculum.

Constructivism regards the construction of meaning as a continuous and active process. Many children, especially those from backgrounds which encourage reflective conversation, begin to ask urgent metaphysical or 'big' questions from the age of about three years old (see e.g. Fay 1994, pp. 6–8). A relative or pet's illness or death or the birth of a new sibling may well prompt such questions. And as Nye and Hay put it, 'The possibility arises that some of the children's own, apparently soluble, questions must be considered as arising from as profound an experience as those of the religious contemplative or theologian' (Nye and Hay 1996, p. 153). It is to be hoped that children's existential curiosity will not decline as they become acclimatised to a materialist culture.

Experiential RE emphasises that imagination must be stimulated and developed by education if the child is to enter actively into a work of literature, historical period, or religious world view. Living religious traditions can be said to be themselves collective, continuous, imaginative constructions driven by changing readings of their symbols, metaphors and stories. So too, experiential RE encourages each child's ownership of her or his own life story by imagining that life as a journey or narrative of which the child is main protagonist and author. (For activities, see Hammond *et al.* 1990, pp. 95–6)[1]

Constructivist educational methods work to give each child the ability to reconfigure knowledge or adapt it to a new paradigm, concept or experience that is essential to critical intelligence. Experiential RE assumes that personality is not a static given and its activities are therefore designed to meet children where they are situated. This is particularly apparent in those exercises suggested by the authors of *New Methods in RE Teaching* where children are invited to explore 'The Real Me' in a variety of ways. These include the use of a Russian doll as a visual aid to convey the difference between the public and private self, and the popular game 'If I Was [a fruit, an animal, a drink etc.] I Would Be . . .' (Hammond *et al.* 1990, pp. 99, 105–112).

There is, of course, a danger that such activities could suggest that 'The Real Me' is some sort of unmediated, timeless essence. But when these exercises are repeated it is precisely to show how children's concepts of themselves (and handled extremely carefully, how others see them) are constantly subject to change. This activity can be undertaken, say, two or three times a year and each

---

[1] It should also be borne in mind that spiritual development may not be linear. The linearity of the common experientialist journey metaphor may suggest, ironically, a progressivist, modern view of human development that is not true to the organic multi-directionality of people's life-stories where an emergent order or coherence can be born of seemingly random events.

time, by comparing results, children may come to see that their identity can develop or change according to age, mood, and circumstance. The realisation that image and identity are not fixed for all time can be particularly significant for an inadequately loved, difficult or less able child with a poor self-image. Such activities can help to raise self-esteem by allowing children to 'name' their identity in positive terms and affirm their own value and the processes of their development and change. Or if children are bullying, activities such as 'Who Sees The Real Me?', where the self is imaged encircled by a series of concentric rings representing groups of people from friends to strangers within a child's ambit (Hammond *et al.* 1990, pp. 92–3), can help these children (without direct teacher counselling) to understand how they might be perceived and experienced by others. Here, the child who is failing in these relationships is helped to realise that the self is not indentical to its perception by others; that the self is multi-dimensional and that this is not all he or she is or or has the potential to be.

The constructivist view that learners have the final responsibility for their own learning is enshrined in experiential RE. The limits of a teacher's power in this type of learning are readily apparent in the open-ended nature of activities such as guided fantasies whose intended function is to be a 'tool in the search for meaning'. Although there has been (mainly right-wing Christian) criticism of the potentially indoctrinatory nature of guided fantasy (e.g. Osborn 1992) experientialists are well aware of this pitfall and warn against it themselves (Hammond *et al.* 1990, p. 219).

Rather than convey content, guided fantasy 'allows us to approach areas of our personality which lie beyond the immediate conscious mind and so has the potential to deepen our knowledge and understanding of who we are' (Hammond *et al.* 1990, p. 153. See also Hall *et al.* 1990, p. 88). Although the teacher stimulates and guides the fantasy, the child must be free to reflect on where the fantasy has taken them; the teacher should never attempt to interpret the fantasy experience (Hammond *et al.* 1990, p. 154). Although experiential RE builds trust and openness in the classroom, the teacher should not force any child to disclose private feelings or views or make them feel that such is expected of them. The primary classroom is not the place for counselling or the 'sharing' of intimate or disturbing experience. The teacher does not adopt the powerful role of therapist (though experiential RE can be, loosely speaking, therapeutic).

The teacher should also exemplify or demonstrate the values she or he asserts. Making the classroom a flexible, plant- and art-filled, occasionally candle-lit or fragrant space where children feel safe is of obvious help. Chaotically noisy (or absolutely silent) classrooms that are ordered by fear of the teacher and/or of bullies are not conducive to experiential RE. But no environment need preclude experiential RE; in fact, reflexive and 'stilling' activities can ameliorate poor discipline or hostilities between pupils, by calming the class and helping children to be more centred, self-aware and attentive to and trusting of others (see Beesley 1990).

Aimless reflection and discussion is not the correct way to go about experiential RE which should provide carefully planned and structured activities. Even so, it is rarely necessary or desirable for experiential RE to be taught spatially or metaphorically from the front. Having children form whole-class circles, group clusters, or lying on gym mats disprivileges the teacher as a dispenser of knowledge. At the same time, the relaxed posture of the activities helps children to think in non-linear ways. The circle, by virtue of its form is most especially a model of connected, non-hierarchical learning and helps children to experience and review the profound commonality of basic feelings such as fear, joy, sadness and mystery.

THE PROBLEM OF RELATIVISM IN EXPERIENTIAL RE

Not even the most conservative of religious educators would object absolutely to a measure of affectivity or spirituality in RE lessons and a reflective approach to the whole curriculum. But experientialist constructivism as such is in many (but not all) respects a deeply liberal project and, where it claims more power and significance than an optional extra, it has not gone unchallenged by conservative religious educators. For the constructivist nature of experiential RE is such that it de-centres or displaces the dominant voice of tradition. It 'deindoctrinates' by offering a plurality of religious perspectives to the pupils, implying that any or none of these perspectives may be appropriate to their (changing) spiritual needs.

It is not at all easy to steer a satisfactory path between confessionalist and relativistic tendencies in RE. Christian teachers (mainly those of the evangelical right) object to the 'procedural neutrality' of experiential RE, just as they do, in different ways, to the procedural neutrality of the phenomenological approach to world religions (including Christianity). The restricted time available to RE seems to some to be better, and more reliably, deployed in pursuit of knowledge and understanding of the positive world religions and of Christianity in particular. Christians are concerned that experiential RE encourages spiritual eclecticism or that it veers towards a Buddhist or Hindu world view, neglecting those of the Western traditions, and especially Christianity. Fred Hughes has (justifiably) questioned whether 'general notions of spirituality are linked to particular beliefs without being explicit about what they are' (Hughes 1992, p. 29). Hughes goes on, 'It could well be alleged that to heighten spiritual awareness and activity without offering a means of discernment or reconciliation with God is irresponsible and cruel, because it expands an appetite for what appears to be only elusive' (p. 32). More strongly, Hughes discourages RE teachers from subscribing to the (literally) demonic possibilities of conducting spiritual development exercises outside the parameters of faith in Christ and without giving children any way of distinguishing good from evil (Thompson 1991, p. 136, Hughes 1992, pp. 29–30, 31; cf. Osborn 1992, p. 18, Marfleet 1992).

Certainly a *radical* constructivism would indeed lead to a relativism that ill fits most religious people's world views. A radical constructivism which allowed the private construction of truth such that 'truth is what you make it' can undoubtedly lead, as Thatcher points out (1991, p. 25), to permitting the validity of private prejudice. If, to use Adrian Thatcher's example, a child expresses racist or sexist beliefs, the (extreme radical constructivist) teacher would have no grounds on which to claim that the child is absolutely wrong. But it must be stressed that this kind of relativism is not what is being prescribed by the kind of social constructivism which we find in experiential RE. This approach to RE balances private feeling with shared knowledge and experience. In any case, such 'feelings' would be prejudices which destroy connection and therefore represent a capacity for evil that is the opposite of spiritual development.

Some experientialists (like John Hammond) may be more relativist than others (Mott-Thornton 1996). But the social constructivism proposed by the present volume and by experientialists does not want to suggest that there are as many truths as there are children in a class. As Kevin Mott-Thornton sensibly observes, experiential RE is not necessarily relativist. It 'might rather be said to amount to no more than a procedural recognition that each person's perspective will be different; it will reflect their particular life experience and level of spiritual development' (p. 160). Hay and Hammond are right that just as in particle physics where the observer's model of reality can shape the perceived result of an experiment, so too, the student of religion's world view will impact upon or even construct the truth and nature of the religion studied:

> The perspective of the subject cannot be discounted and for an individual to have space to undertake this exploration there has to be room to move, a certain openness to other possibilities in life, a tolerance of many points of view. This is not to disparage truth; far from it, it is to undertake the difficult project of finding truth through open dialogue, undamaged by the rigidities produced by the social sedimentation of a single point of view. (1992, p. 146)

So the conservative view that experiential RE prescribes a wholesale and ultimately nihilistic relativism is unfounded. In fact Hay and Nye (1996, p. 8) explicitly reject the 'relativising wilderness of postmodernism'. What is, however, postmodern about this approach is its refusal of a single, authoritative, revealed, or otherwise normative, source of religious knowledge and its celebration of each child's difference.

While values are relative to the extent that they are not formally bounded by a single, exclusive, normative tradition, experiential RE is not value neutral. To recognise certain foundational values and to seek for the wholeness of those within the school community and beyond it, as experiential RE does, is to participate in a type of confessional discourse. The ethico-religious implications of experiential RE and its evident belief that each person (and, more contentiously, animals, plants and land) are ends in themselves make it quite apparent that this kind of RE is not relativist but has a specific holistic good in mind. The sense of the preciousness or non-instrumental value of persons and natural objects and that the world signifies more than the sum of its parts is, it seems to me, the precondition of good moral development and for understanding why people follow religions. As Nathan Söderblom, Rudolf Otto and, later, Joachim Wach's early twentieth-century studies of religion insisted, religious is the person for whom something is not merely good but holy. What appears as relativist indifference to religions' competing truth claims is in fact a procedural or methodological concern that experiential RE can fertilise the ground that is the child's potential sense of the sacred, but by virtue of the non-rational nature of the sacred, the integrity of the child, and a thirty year tradition of liberal RE, that must be the limit of a curriculum's intervention in the child's spiritual development.

Experientialists are also aware that 'parroted' abstract moral precepts are easily forgotten because they are learnt without being felt. Experiential RE enables the child to experience the beginnings of obligation from within and as integral to her very experience and knowledge of self and *only to that extent* is morality relative. At Key Stage 1 and 2 a child's reasoning might go as follows: If I can have feelings of hope, sadness and joy and if there is only one person in the world like me, then I am irreplaceable and I matter. If the children sitting on either side of me are also capable of such feelings and are also unique then they matter too. The relational nature of spirituality fosters a sense of connectedness such that the harm done to others or the well-being of others cannot be detached from the well-being of the self.

The child's experience of love or lack of it will affect his or her capacity to empathise with and care for others. But when the child ceases to make rigid, hostile or exploitative distinctions between self and other, alienation from and oppression of others can begin to wither from the root. The empowered self becomes a self that has power for and with others, instead of power over others. Experiential RE has a central social function in encouraging social cohesion in ways that coercive, authoritarian forms of moral education based less on solidarity and connectedness than on obedience have largely failed to achieve. It is clear that spiritual development implies moral development. But experientialists resist more conservative educators' attempts to use opportunities for spiritual development to moralise; to merely *tell* children the difference between right and wrong without engaging their feelings. Rather, although, for children, the ethical implications and application of their feelings may not be immediately apparent and may need to be spelled out, they can only begin to do (for example) 'deep' moral education and 'deep' environmental education when their care for the social and natural other is both affectively *and* rationally grounded.

EXPERIENTIAL RE AND THE COMMONALITY OF TRADITION

Experientialism has been criticised for encouraging the privatisation of experience. Adrian Thatcher has mounted a well-known critique of experiential RE, attacking its apparent liberal individualism, its misidentification of spirituality as inwardness and hence its apparent neglect of the 'embodied, material word as the medium and context of the love of God' (Thatcher 1991, p. 23). Thatcher argues that 'emphasis on the 'Real Me' as pure, private interiority damages the sociality of the human person. It is a distraction which impedes an understanding of 'persons-in-relation' (Thatcher 1991, p. 23). But that is a misreading of the 'inwardness' evoked by Hammond and others in *New Methods in RE Teaching* and Thatcher's arguments were quickly rebutted by, among others, David Hay and John Hammond (1992). David Hay has recently noted that 'though we overlooked it originally' that 'blindness' to relationality arose 'at least in part from our socialisation within a highly individualistic culture' (Hay and Nye 1996, p. 12). Inwardness signifies not a soul imprisoned within the flesh, but 'depth' (Hay and Hammond, 1992, p. 145). And in this sense, depth or inwardness is also to be read as 'other' to a depthless mass culture. A contemporary non-dualistic understanding of spirituality is by nature, as recent green and feminist theologians, as well as experientialists, have persuasively argued, embodied and relational. That is, spiritual energy or divine presence is not owned by a priestly (sometimes ascetic) elite, but generated in the dynamic, sacramental connections between all living things. (See also pp. 146–7)

Constructivist approaches to education, then, are not trying to simply privatise reality, but work on the assumption that perceptions of reality are contextual and local to individuals. While the teacher should be aware that pupils have their own constructions of reality conditioned by the particularities of their own context, these constructions do not appear ex nihilo and they are not entirely private. The pupil lives in community and must use common language and concepts to understand and to be understood.

In this way, experiential RE complements and informs the phenomenological study of religion so that the child can construct his or her own meaning inside or against the given tradition. Although experientialism tends to state or imply that private spirituality has some sort of priority over positive practice and the tradition, constructivism epistemologically questions the possibility of any universal defining essence of spiritual experience and detects clear causal connections between conceptual and social religious structures and actual spiritual experience (Katz 1978). So that for children, as for adults, there will be a reciprocal relation between beliefs and experience, with the former conditioning and mediating the experience.

This means that, contrary to the apparently essentialist, a-historical (non-constructivist) experientialist tendency to refer to a real inner Self, the child probably cannot enter an unmediated world of pure inner reality or discover who they 'really' are as if 'The Real Me' were detachable from some sort of husk of behavioural convention. Experiential RE cannot redeem a pristine self from the accretions of tradition. We cannot expect children to invent their views on religion from unconditioned religious feeling, but to situate themselves within, outside or on the boundaries of tradition. The social constructivist recognition that knowledge is communal as well as born of individual experience must be reflected in experiential RE where inner experience is only comprehensible to the self and others in so far as it is articulated, known and recognised as such in publicly available language.

Dennis Bates argues that understanding of religious concepts does not derive from experience, but rather the other way round: children bring religious concepts to their experience and make sense of their experiences in that way. For Bates, there is no inevitable transition from naturalistic experiences of awe and wonder to, say, Otto's sense of the numinous which is qualitatively other and decidedly non-natural. Bates regards the view that wonder at the beauty of nature will generate an idea of God as 'simplistic and romantic' (1992, pp. 124–5). Instead, according to Bates, primary RE should introduce children to 'religious' concepts, language, buildings, worship and people, rather than have 'doubtful "religious" experiences contrived for them in the classroom' (Bates 1992, p.120).

Social constructivist approaches to education, however, advocate a balance in which the child is given a central role in the construction of understanding through its open, affective and non-didactic methods. Spiritual experience is at once private and public, affective and cognitive. The dual nature of the experience cannot be set into a temporal sequence; the cognitive and affective are wholly interwoven. However, if the child is to be said to be religiously educated she must know something of how others, the not-her, perceive the divine without that substantive knowledge becoming inert and standing over and against her.

An ability to read, as opposed to merely receive, tradition is a prerequisite to the teaching, study (and practice) of religion. In helping children to interpret religious phenomena, constructivism goes some way to resolving the moral problem that teachers so often face when presenting aspects of religion that seem ethically and politically unacceptable to them. For to an appropriate degree, RE teachers and children should both be aware of the ambivalence of religion: that the world religions are not necessarily morally perfect; that as well as preaching a prophetic and profoundly liberative love of creation, by law and custom world religions routinely marginalise women, dominate nature and, more generally, sacralize bigotry and oppressive modes of authority. Children should learn about and learn from tradition, but the constructivist approach also frees them to begin to negotiate with and test its truth claims against their own experience. (It is no coincidence that this is also the method of contemporary emancipatory theology.)

Little wonder, then, that there is conservative distrust of constructivism in RE. Even if unintentionally, such approaches to the religious traditions can permit a (subversive) dissonance between the child's perception of the divine and the divinity of the self and that offered by tradition where, for example, women are not named in its concepts of God.[2] Even in the most basic ways, teachers should develop the primary school child's capacity to question religious claims to authority by virtue of their own experience and by virtue of their own moral principles of care.

There is no reason why the principles informing the RE training of primary teachers should lag behind intellectual and political developments in theology within tertiary education. Many religious and non-religious critics have wanted to say that biblical theologies (and therefore some types of RE which are grounded in them) are not, in fact, common, but are the gendered product of an almost exclusively white, elite, masculine world view. And women's distinct experiences will condition the way they construct the meaning of those theologies (Raphael 1994). As Christian and Jewish women begin to do theology that is based on women's experience its content and meaning will change (see e.g. Slee 1989, Trevett 1989, Blair 1992). A responsible religious education should not give the impression that religious discourse is monolithic, fixed and non-negotiable. Junior school children (not just girls) might be encouraged, for example, to challenge received views of the (exclusive) fatherhood God and develop alternative images of God on the basis of their experience of their mothers' pregnancies and their giving birth and care to new life.

---

[2] Useful introductory accounts of the basic feminist theological position include Isherwood and McEwan (1993, 1996).

SUMMARY

It seems probable that children's consciousness is not a tabula rasa of unconditioned, pristine spiritual awareness upon which positive spiritual values can be straightforwardly inscribed. Most contemporary epistemologists reject or regard as unlikely the possibility of unmediated and unconditioned religious awareness. Children inhabit a cultural environment that will condition their responses from the moment of birth and this will inform but not exhaust their spiritual experience. Therefore there must be a balance between content and feeling in RE. The role of experiential RE is not to supplant all purely and necessarily cognitive approaches nor to provide access to the pure interior pre-linguistic essence of children. Rather, it seems to me that its primary purpose is to convey to children that their deepest feelings and convictions are of relevance and value; that morality and religion are grounded in such feelings; that intentions are as important as results and that one's actions have consequences for the whole web of life.

There is some justification in claims that the holistic spirituality that informs experiential RE renders it a differently or newly confessional form of RE and that it is not, therefore, as liberal or, indeed, constructivist, as it might understand itself to be. Experiential RE seems to want children to be a certain kind of caring (green, left-of-centre) children and hopes that they will have certain kinds of positive feelings. But postmodern or, as I prefer, late modern, education is properly aware that the aspiration to be wholly value neutral is futile and dishonest. Although education must be wary of overt indoctrination it would be perverse to argue that the values of sensitivity, care, empathy and self-awareness should not be openly encouraged and supported in the classroom. It is a central part of good religious and moral education to support such values (as, in some ways, it always has done). Although social constructivist RE has shared goods and does not entail a relativistic liberalism, its contention that religious meaning is contextual and subject to historical shift will remain the subject of interesting debate on several philosophical, educational, religious and political fronts for some time to come.

REFERENCES

Bastide, D. (1992) 'Attainment in RE: an exploration', in Bastide, D. (ed.) *Good Practice in Primary Religious Education 4–11*. London: Falmer Press.

Bates, D. (1992) 'Developing RE in topic-based approaches to learning', in Bastide, D. (ed.) *Good Practice in Primary Religious Education 4–11*. London: Falmer Press.

Beesley, M. (1990) *Stilling: A Pathway for Spiritual Learning in the National Curriculum*. Salisbury: Salisbury Diocese.

Best, R. (ed.) (1996) *Education, Spirituality and the Whole Child*. London: Cassell.

Blair, C. E. (1992) 'Women's spirituality empowered by biblical story', *Religious Education* **87**(4), 532–44.

Crawford, M. and Rossiter, G. (1996) 'The secular spirituality of youth: implications for religious education', *British Journal of Religious Education* **18**(3), 133–43.

Cush, D. (1997) 'Paganism in the classroom', *British Journal of Religious Education* **19**(2), 83–94.

DES (1988) *Education Reform Act*. London: HMSO.

Fay, M. (1994) *Children and Religion: Making Choices in a Secular Age*. New York: Simon and Schuster.

Gloucestershire County Council (1995) *The Gloucestershire Agreed Syllabus for Religious Education*.

Hucclecote: The Professional Development Consultancy.

Goldman, R. (1964) *Religious Thinking from Childhood to Adolescence.* London: Routledge and Kegan Paul.

Goldman, R. (1965) *Readiness for Religion.* London: Routledge and Kegan Paul.

Grimmit, M. (1973) *What Can I Do in RE?* Great Wakering: Mayhew McCrimmon.

Grimmitt, M. (1987) *Religious Education and Human Development: The Relationship Between Studying Religions and Personal, Social and Moral Education.* Great Wakering: McCrimmon.

Hall, E., Hall, C., Leech, A. (1990) *Scripted Fantasy in the Classroom.* London: Routledge.

Hammond, J., Hay, D., Moxon, J., Netto, B., Raban, K., Straugheir, G., Williams, C. (1990) *New Methods in RE Teaching: An Experiential Approach.* Harlow: Oliver and Boyd.

Hay, D. and Hammond, J. (1992) 'When you pray go to your private room: a critical reply to Adrian Thatcher', *British Journal of Religious Education* **14**(3), 145–50.

Hay, D. and Nye, R. (1996) 'Investigating children's spirituality: the need for a fruitful hypothesis', *The International Journal of Children's Spirituality* **1**(1), 6–16.

Hayward, M. (1990) Planning Religious Education', in Jackson, R. and Starkings D., (eds) *The Junior RE Handbook.* Cheltenham: Stanley Thornes.

Hughes, F. (1992) 'Is there a biblical view of spirituality?', *Spectrum* **24**(1), 29–34.

Isherwood, L. and McEwan, D. (1993) *Introducing Feminist Theology.* Sheffield: Sheffield Academic Press.

Isherwood, L. and McEwan, D. (1996) *An A to Z of Feminist Theology.* Sheffield: Sheffield Academic Press.

Katz, S. (1978) 'Language, Epistemology and Mysticism', in S. Katz (ed.) *Mysticism and Philosophical Analysis.* London: Sheldon Press.

Loukes, H. (1965) *New Ground in Christian Education.* London: SCM Press.

Marfleet, A. (1992) 'Whose spirituality?', *Spectrum* **24**(1), 21–7.

Mott-Thornton, K. (1996) 'Language, dualism and experiential religious education: a critical appraisal of the debate between Adrian Thatcher and the authors of *New Methods in RE Teaching*', *British Journal of Religious Education* **18**(3), 155–65.

Musty, E. (1992) 'Making RE special in the primary school', in Bastide, D. (ed.) *Good Practice in Primary Religious Education 4–11.* London: Falmer Press.

Nye, R. and Hay, D. (1996) 'Identifying children's spirituality: how do you start without a starting point?', *British Journal of Religious Education* **18**(3), 144–54.

Osborn, L. (1992) 'Magic in the classroom?: educational uses and misuses of guided fantasy', *Spectrum* **24**(1), 9–19.

Otto, R. (1958) *The Idea of the Holy: An Inquiry into the non-rational factor in the idea of the divine and its relation to the rational.* New York: Oxford University Press.

Raphael, M. (1994) 'Feminism, constructivism and numinous experience', *Religious Studies* **30**(4), 511–26.

Raphael, M. (1997) *Rudolf Otto and the Concept of Holiness.* Oxford: Clarendon Press.

Robinson, E. (1983) *The Original Vision.* New York: Seabury Press.

Slee, N. (1989) 'Women's silence in religious education', *British Journal of Religious Education* **12**(1), 29–37.

Smart, N. (1969) *The Religious Experience of Mankind* (sic). London: Collins.

Smart, N. (1989) *The World's Religions.* Cambridge: Cambridge University Press.

Tamminen, K. (1991) *Religious Development in Childhood and Youth: An Empirical Study.* Helsinki: Suomalainen Tiedeakatemia.

Thatcher, A. (1991) 'A critique of inwardness in religious education', *British Journal of Religious Education* **14**(1), 22–7.

Thompson, P. (1991) 'Spirituality and an experiential approach to RE', *Spectrum* **23**(2), 125–36.

Trevett, C. (1989) 'Patriarchal structures and religious education', *British Journal of Religious Education* **12**(1), 6–10.

Watson, B. (1993) *The Effective Teaching of Religious Education.* London: Longman.

CHAPTER 15

Promoting access across the curriculum

Barbara Brown and Susan Shorrock

This chapter is concerned with pupils who experience difficulties in learning; it seeks to establish principles which might inform policy and planning across the whole curriculum. Much of the recent literature related to 'special education' implicitly reflects constructivist theory (Ashman and Conway 1989, Feiler and Thomas 1989, Gross 1996, Clark *et al.* 1997) and benefit would be derived from adopting a clearer theoretical framework. The use of a constructivist framework which views the learner within a position of power and embraces all dimensions of teaching and learning would allow educators to articulate meaningfully the ways in which they might provide for children's educational rights.

Consideration of special education prior to 1978 and children's difficulties in learning focused upon 'handicap' (medical or psychological), a concept which arose from the view that some pupils fail to cope with the demands of mainstream curricula and schooling. The Warnock Report (DES 1978) represented a significant change in thinking, with an educational, interactive and relative approach to defining special education which attempted to take into account all the factors which might affect educational progress (Roaf and Bines 1989).

Prior to the report, children experiencing learning difficulties had been considered as requiring a modified curriculum: modified in the sense of being different in aims and objectives, limited in content and experience, in terms of depth and breadth, and restricted in teaching and learning resources. As a result of their findings the committee recognised that the learning environment (or context) and the factors which impinge upon it have a crucial influence in promoting successful learning for children, and especially those experiencing difficulties.

A constructivist theory of learning also emphasises the interplay between the individual's 'resources' (his/her prior experiences, knowledge, attitudes and goals etc.) and the environment in which learning takes place (Driver and Bell 1986). Successful learning outcomes depend upon the transactional nature of learning, that is, that the learner's resources, the task and the learning environment are equally responsive to each other in a learning situation. It is imperative, therefore, that a systematic and clear sighted examination of the context for learning is made, in order to understand how difficulties in learning might arise.

Equality of entitlement and opportunity for learning are explicit in the Education Acts of 1988 (DES 1988) and 1993 (DfE 1993) and the National Curriculum is a fundamental right of all children. While most teachers would wholeheartedly endorse the rights of all children to a 'broad and balanced curriculum' (NCC 1989a), translating those rights into classroom practice can be very difficult. However, establishing a meaningful learning environment in which individual children are able to construct their own learning must be at the heart of effective teaching and an inclusive understanding which truly reflects the spirit of current legislation.

THE LEARNING ENVIRONMENT: UNDERSTANDING THE ECOLOGICAL, TEACHING AND CURRICULUM VARIABLES

The learning environment has a crucial influence on children's success in learning. It should convey expectation, motivation, encouragement, curiosity and security for the learner. A learning environment that conveys quality is largely a reflection of a whole-school approach through the formulation of successful policies, plans and practices (NCC 1989b). The following features contribute to a good learning environment:

- a positive atmosphere that conveys encouragement, acceptance, respect and sensitivity;
- the high standard of presentation and organisation of the classroom;
- easy access to resources;
- flexible grouping of pupils;
- effective management of pupil behaviour through a whole-school approach to discipline;
- cooperative learning among pupils;
- effective management of support through clear definition of roles and use of room management;
- real access to specialist advice;
- cooperation between special and mainstream schools;
- appropriate in-service training;
- communication with parents, and mutual parent-teacher support. (NCC 1989b, p.7)

The conditions in the learning environment are understood to influence the progress of children's development. Therefore, children respond differently in differing conditions and environments. Where a match is achieved between the children's resource levels and the environmental conditions, they demonstrate achievement and progress.

It is proposed by Ashman and Conway (1989) and Feiler and Thomas (1989) that the context for learning must be understood in terms of the 'ecological', curriculum and teaching variables.

The 'ecological' variables are concerned with the social context created in the classroom, the quality of life that pervades the classroom setting, the optimum use of classroom space and time in order to ensure that children have the maximum chance to develop their learning skills, the opportunity and degree of participation and interaction by the children in the learning conditions, and the promotion of children as active participants of learning rather than as passive recipients.

The curriculum variables focus on the selection, development, presentation and utilisation of the material and resources, while the teaching variables relate to the way in which information is actually presented to the learner, and the management of the learning behaviour. These variables include the means by which the children's attention and time on-task may be extended, the organisation of input, how they respond to instruction, and the quality and quantity of feedback given.

If classrooms develop conditions that are ecological in nature then teachers can recognise and meet the learning needs of children. Implicit in this approach is that a child's behaviour cannot be separated from the context in which it occurs, and so the learning conditions must be appropriately adapted, managed and organised to promote successful learning experiences.

When the environment for learning is understood and appreciated in terms of the interplay between the ecological, teaching and curriculum variables, this can inform a teaching practice that is adaptive, flexible and responsive to a diversity and individuality of learning needs. For example, an ecological understanding recognises the significance of classroom 'routines' for the learner, and so these are analysed and utilised and where necessary manipulated to promote effective practice. Ideally it allows the teacher and children to understand and interpret the learning context in order to facilitate learning. So if children are to understand the learning environment, it must be well organised and accessible to all. Poor classroom organisation can lead to lack of pupil involvement, wandering about, interruption, lack of interest or poor motivation and poor use of resources (Bennett and Kell 1989). Classroom routines allow children to participate in establishing and maintaining classroom organisation. For example, children must understand how and when movement about the room is appropriate, what to do when they first come into the classroom, and what they should do when they have finished their work. A learning environment which is developed through such an understanding is 'unhindered by processes' and 'unrestrained by factors' (Feiler and Thomas 1989, p. 29), that might obstruct change and prevent children from learning.

Many teachers may support these views in principle. It is clear that practice often fails to reflect this. The importance of group work, for example, is recognised by theorists and educators alike (Johnson and Johnson 1987, in Gross 1996), and is central to a constructivist view of learning. Bruner and Haste (1987) claim that social dialogue with 'more knowledgeable others' is fundamental to human learning and development. Children with learning difficulties require learning environments which encourage collaborative learning, negotiation, oral problem solving and discussion between pupils. In addition, Johnson and Johnson (1987, in Gross 1996) found that effective group work can serve to enhance pupil self-esteem and to increase engagement with the tasks by as much as 20 per cent.

Yet, Croll and Moses (1985) found that children with identified learning difficulties were given less time on work involving cooperating with other pupils than were their classmates. Often such pupils are seen to be unable to work and/or 'behave' appropriately in groups, and so teachers try to avoid potential management problems by giving children individual work. An ecological understanding allows the teacher to examine more closely the knowledge, skills and understandings which a child needs in order to work within groups, and the teacher is then able to scaffold and support the learning context appropriately.

Therefore each of the variables emphasises the importance of the teaching role, for example, the appropriateness of the content and task; the way in which it is presented and developed; the nature and quality of the interactive guidance, and the teacher's influence on the children's capacity to involve themselves in the learning experience (Ashman and Conway 1989). Similarly, the emphasis within the National Curriculum is upon how to adapt tasks, teaching and learning strategies and approaches to enable the shared Programmes of Study to be accessible and meaningful to all the children in a class.

THE TEACHING ROLE: MAKING THE CURRICULUM ACCESSIBLE TO CHILDREN

The notion of access could be considered as central to the whole process of teaching and learning. The concept embraces meanings related to entry, such as reaching, approaching, undertaking and admitting in a context of opportunity and rights. Access suggests a right of way, and, just as on a map, it can vary in terms of complexity and degree of difficulty. The rights of way to the map reader indicate a variety of routes providing differing opportunities, interests and challenges on the way. The map provides a wealth of differing possibilities to the traveller. In order to make sense of the rights of way, the traveller requires the concepts and skills to understand the map and utilise the information meaningfully, to efficiently navigate the rights of way. It usually takes time to become proficient at navigation, but when mastery is achieved the rights of way are endless, resulting in almost open access.

The process of teaching should enable children to gain entry to new and increasingly challenging learning situations. This is in order that they can become proficient and successful travellers (learners) in their education through life. Access suggests that there are usually differing entry and exit points, and although they are different, they are equally 'rights of way'. What might be suitable for one traveller may not be suitable for another. After all, it is not uncommon for two people of a similar age to demonstrate differing capacities in terms of travelling. One walker may be able to enjoy the demands of a winter day's hike in the fells, where the arduous conditions have to be tolerated, along with the mileage and degree of ascent. Whereas, another might enjoy a half-day's sheltered valley walk. Their differing capacities have determined their differing routes and rights of way, but they have both achieved similar aims. The rights of way sometimes require significant others to reopen them because they have ceased to function through disuse and neglect. At other times there is a need to charter a new right of way in order to ensure access. It is also logical that access should assume a hierarchical pattern of entry in terms of degree of complexity, challenge and difficulty. Access should be appropriate to the person's level of functioning, capacity and experience. As their resources develop, and they progressively achieve mastery of access, so they can travel further and explore the pleasures of inquiry and discovery through the process of learning.

Access should provoke inquiry, initially perhaps to just view and satiate the curiosity. The right of way becomes accessible if it is perceived as being open and charitable to everyone and without prejudice. The route should be clearly defined and sign-posted, with plenty of guidance along the way for those requiring it, and frequent resting places for those who need to pause. (Learning can be a tiring activity, especially if the traveller is not experienced.) Routes should convey to the inexperienced traveller at the start/entry point that they can journey with trust and confidence. If the support and guidance along the way ensures an enjoyable, safe and successful passage it will serve to encourage the traveller to participate. In time, as their confidence grows, they might seek further, perhaps more challenging routes.

Surely teaching is about enabling access to learning. Access should, therefore, take into account the capacities, needs, experiences and functioning of the learner. That children have changing and diverse needs throughout their school career is an inevitability. This should be recognised, respected and responded to through the ways in which we ensure access to learning. Set routes are counter-productive to the notion of access as they lead to exclusion for some children. For others the route might be inappropriate for their level of experience, and so be insufficiently demanding. This can also result in a non-learning situation. The teacher should be able to construct a variety of routes that clearly convey to the learner that the rights of way on each route are accessible and navigable with and without guidance. The length of the journeys should vary to accommodate the varying appetites for inquiry and levels of learning fitness.

Access embraces within its meaning a sense of accommodation of diversity and differentiated modes and means of access. Access can be conceived as a multifaceted and multidimensional concept in terms of its entry/exit points and rights of way.

The right of access to the National Curriculum is common to all children, and the 'intervention process' is the means of achieving this for all children. The process seeks to achieve a match between the resources of the child and the learning conditions. Schools now have a responsibility to identify learning conditions that promote an open access to the curriculum.

INTERVENTION STRATEGIES: RESPONDING TO INDIVIDUAL AND DIVERSE LEARNING NEEDS

Discussions of children's difficulties in learning invariably include 'differentiation' (e.g. Gross 1996, NCC 1989a). Differentiation is about adapting tasks, teaching and learning to make the curriculum accessible to all pupils. It could be argued that in practice not only does this place the pupil in a passive rather than active position within the learning process, but also research has shown that primary teachers find differentiation very difficult to implement (Bennett *et al.* 1984).

The concept of intervention 'in children's learning is usually perceived to be the provision of something over, above, and additional to the curriculum, and as epitomised by programmes, kits, and packages that have come to be associated with remedial approaches to the slow learner' (Wolfendale 1987, p. 12). However, Wolfendale perceives it as 'identifying the requisites for optimal learning by all children and organising the learning environment accordingly'. In this conception the distinction between remedial and non-remedial 'is blurred if not abolished, as intervention becomes education for all children' (p. 12). This perspective is being developed through the recognition of individual learning needs and differentiated teaching approaches in the planning, delivery and implementation of the National Curriculum. This is resulting in teachers positively engineering and organising the curriculum and the learning environment so as to enable all children to achieve an optimal level of learning (Wolfendale 1987).

The central role of assessment within an intervention strategy

Intervention is concerned with establishing a match between the resource levels of the children and the conditions in the learning environment: curriculum, teaching strategies and approaches, resources, classroom organisation and management. Learning conditions that promote access to the curriculum are managed and organised so that they can recognise, respond to and support the individual and diverse needs of primary children. It means that access requires a resourceful approach to curriculum delivery, so that modifications and adaptations can enable children to participate in a common curriculum with integrity and satisfaction.

The emphasis on assessment being ongoing and continuous within the intervention process is important. It recognises the value of monitoring the children within the range of classroom and home processes, practices, contexts and conditions. Information from these sources contributes to an informed understanding of the nature of the learning difficulties. The class teacher and parent are recognised as being key people in the assessment process, as they are in a privileged position to gather ongoing information. Teachers are viewed as crucial collaborators with parents and other professionals in the assessment and intervention process. The assessment process is central to effective teaching practice as it enables the teacher to become informed about the learner in the context of the learning situation, that is, the learner's resources, the task and the learning environment. Assessment seeks to understand the learning situation in order to promote change as a result of the transaction across these three variables. The assessment process must engage the teacher in recognising and responding to detail in the learning environment and the potential for change in the learner's resources, task, and learning.

Assessment is a formative process and is central to teaching, as it informs practice. It enables teachers to gather ongoing information on the response and progress of children in terms of their understanding, knowledge and skills. It then allows them to develop teaching practice in an informed and appropriate way, relative to the ongoing responses and needs of the children.

The School Curriculum and Assessment Authority (SCAA) recognise that assessment has been central to the teaching process for teachers concerned with children experiencing difficulties in learning. SCAA view the continuous assessment carried out by the teacher as part of the teaching process, and central to the delivery of the National Curriculum. They consider that the assessment process informs the teaching, and enables teachers to present the curriculum so that it is accessible to all pupils, as far as possible. It is also 'so that pupils can be assured equality of access to assessment opportunities as well as to the Programmes of Study' (NCC 1989b, p12).

The National Curriculum Council (1989b) suggest that teachers will have to accommodate the pupils' level of functioning in the way they approach and structure the teaching and assessment process, for example, in terms of being flexible with aspects of time allowed for the completion of a task, and by enabling the pupil's participation to be differentiated relative to their learning difficulties and disabilities.

Intervention as a whole-school strategy

The intervention process recognises and responds to individuality and diversity across the whole school community through a whole-school approach to curriculum policy, provision and practice.

The process of intervention is central to the access of *all* children to learning. Inquiry in schools, particularly since 1988, has centred on the development of appropriate intervention strategies as a means for promoting access, within a whole-school approach to curriculum delivery.

The significance of a recognition and provision of learning effectiveness and breakdown (Ainscow 1991) in the functioning of a school is central to intervention strategy, as it influences the detail of daily school practice. The intervention process needs to develop within a school and learning environment that promotes opportunity and access for all children. It is informed by an assessment process that is central to effective teaching and learning.

The concept of special educational needs has come to be viewed as a relative and interactive term in the context of degree of difficulty, the child's resource levels and the positive/negative conditions in the learning environment. The considerations underpinning the process of intervention are common to *all* children.

The recognition and meeting of individual learning needs is central to the working of the whole school, and not just remedial/special needs teachers and departments. It affects everyone in the school community and influences how they live, work and recreate together. It must permeate every school policy. It is about 'attitude and action' (Wolfendale 1987, p. 1). Schools that convey tolerance and understanding of disability, deviance and differing backgrounds in their policy making 'will eventually inform and influence a wider public' (Wolfendale 1987, p. 2). Fortunately, the 1988 and 1993 Education Acts and the Code of Practice and Regulations (DfE 1994) are explicit in identifying the responsibilities that schools have in formulating open communities that promote equality of entitlement, opportunity and access to education and the National Curriculum.

The outcomes of the findings by Booth and Potts (1983), Galloway (1985), Wolfendale (1987), NCC (1989a, 1989b), Ainscow and Florek (1989), Brown (1996), Clark *et al.* (1997) all convey a central message that children who are experiencing difficulties with learning can and do achieve success in their life and work at home and school. Success occurs for the children when schools adopt an ethos that recognises and respects equality of entitlement, opportunity and access to a common curriculum as being a fundamental right for all children. Policies should be developed that enable this ethos, through the generation of a context where the teaching and curriculum variables demonstrate a capacity to be resourceful and flexible. This will enable teachers to appropriately meet the individual learning needs of all the children.

REFERENCES

Ainscow, M. and Florek, A. (1989) *Special Educational Needs: towards a Whole School Approach.* London: David Fulton/National Council for Special Education.

Ainscow, M. (1991) 'Effective schools for all: an alternative approach to special needs in education', in Ainscow, M. (ed.) *Effective Schools For All.* London: David Fulton.

Ashman, A. and Conway, R. (1989) *An Introduction to Cognitive Education. Theory and Applications.* London: Routledge.

Bennett, N., Desforges, C., Cockburn, A., Wilkinson, B. (1984) *The Quality of Pupil Learning Experiences.* London: Lawrence Erlbaum.

Bennett, N. and Kell, J. (1989) *A Good Start? Four Year Olds in School.* Oxford: Blackwell.

Booth, T. and Potts, P. (1983) *Integrating Special Education.* Oxford: Blackwell.

Brown B. A. (1996) 'Access to physical education by children experiencing learning difficulties.' Unpublished doctoral thesis. University of Leeds.

Bruner, J. and Haste, H. (eds) (1987) *Making Sense: The Child's Construction of the World.* London: Methuen.

Clark, C., Dyson, A., Millward, A., Skidmore D. (1997) *New Directions in Special Needs: Innovations in Mainstream Schools.* London: Cassell.

Croll, P. and Moses, D. (1985) *One in Five.* London: Routledge

Department of Education and Science (DES) (1978) *Special Educational Needs. Report of the Committee of Enquiry into the Education of Handicapped Children and Young People.* London: HMSO.

DES (1988) *Education Reform Act.* London: HMSO.

Department for Education (DfE) (1993) *Education Act.* Part III. Chapter 35. London: HMSO.

DfE (1994) *Code of Practice on the Identification and Assessment of Special Educational Needs.* London: HMSO.

Driver R. and Bell, B. (1986) 'Students' thinking and the learning of science: a constructivist view', *School Science Review* **67**, pp. 443–56.

Feiler, A. and Thomas, G. (1989) 'Special needs: past, present and future', in Thomas, G. and Feiler, A. (eds), *Planning for special needs: a whole school approach.* Oxford: Blackwell.

Galloway, D. (1985) *Schools, Pupils and Special Educational Needs.* Beckenham: Croom Helm.

Gross, J. (1996) *Special Educational Needs in the Primary School. A Practical Guide.* Milton Keynes: Open University Press.

National Curriculum Council (NCC) (1989a) *Implementing the National Curriculum – Participation by Pupils with Special Educational Needs.* (Curriculum Guidance Five). York: NCC

NCC (1989b) *A Curriculum for All.* (Curriculum Guidance Two). York: NCC.

Roaf, C. and Bines, H. (eds) (1989) *Needs, Rights and Opportunities.* London: Falmer Press.

Wolfendale, S. (1987) *Primary Schools and Special Needs: Policy Planning and Provision.* London: Cassell.

Index